FAMOUS SINGLE POEMS

Famous Single Poems

And the Controversies Which Have Raged Around Them

By

Burton Stevenson

Essay Index Reprint Series

 BOOKS FOR LIBRARIES PRESS
FREEPORT, NEW YORK

PS
303
.S75
1971
c. 2

First Published 1935
Reprinted 1971

INTERNATIONAL STANDARD BOOK NUMBER:
0-8369-2078-3

LIBRARY OF CONGRESS CATALOG CARD NUMBER:
70-142703

PRINTED IN THE UNITED STATES OF AMERICA

One lyric is enough. . . . It will carry
your name down to posterity like the ring
of Thothmes, like the coin of Alexander.
OLIVER WENDELL HOLMES, *The Poet
at the Breakfast-Table*, p. 129.

CONTENTS

FAMOUS SINGLE POEMS

ONE-POEM MEN

ONE swallow may not make a summer, but one poem makes a poet. Immortality may be—and often has been—won with a single song. Nothing is known of Louisa Crawford except that she wrote "Kathleen Mavourneen"; William Douglas would have been forgotten many decades since save for "Annie Laurie"; William Shenstone's name is kept alive only by his careless lines written at an inn at Henley. These are not, it will be observed, in any sense great poems; but they have one quality in common, that vein of pensive sentiment which, as W. P. Trent puts it, "finds an echo in the universal human heart"—an echo which Time seems powerless to diminish.

Not infrequently, out of a lifetime of metrical composition, out of thousands of lines produced with fearful labor, only a dozen or so survive. (To survive, be it understood, is to keep on living; and no poem can be said to live unless it is read and loved and quoted.) Blanco White's sonnet, "To Night," was considered by Coleridge the finest in the language,—and it represents the sum of White's poetic achievement. Francis William Bourdillon has covered many reams of paper during the course of a long

3

life, but a single sheet, the one on which he wrote the eight lines beginning, "The night has a thousand eyes," is worth all the rest. "The Burial of Sir John Moore" lives on, but everything else which Charles Wolfe wrote has long since lapsed into obscurity. Two lovely quatrains, "A Death-Bed," worthy to rank with the immortal two in which Landor laments Rose Aylmer, are all that survive from the pen of James Aldrich.

From the citation of such examples, which might be prolonged indefinitely, one is tempted to proceed to a consideration of how infrequently even the greatest poets write great poetry, or to an enumeration of the poets who wrote none at all—this last to console certain one-poem men who bitterly resent being called such. But this, however instructive and amusing, would be to wander outside the purpose of these papers and must be left to another time.

Robert Graves, in his little book, *On English Poetry*, evolves an ingenious theory about one-poem men. He believes that true poetry is the result of a sort of brain-storm, in which the poet, in a state of self-hypnosis, produces something quite beyond the capacities of his normal waking state—a diamond in the rough, as it were, with a heart of flame, but full of surface faults which require the patient craftsmanship

4

of his waking state to remove. The professional poet, by long practice and quick recognition of the preliminary symptoms, grows adept in inducing in himself this trance-like condition, and learns how to invite it and how to yield himself to it—how, in a word, to "go under." Also long practice has given him the skill needed to cut and polish the diamond thus produced.

But one-poem men are either born poets tortured by a life-long mental conflict to which only once in their whole lives are they able completely to yield themselves, or they are not naturally poets at all, but men who, just once, are driven by some force beyond themselves to express in verse a sudden intolerable clamor in the brain. And of course since they are not skilled craftsmen, their diamonds usually show many flaws.

This theory is well enough as applied to those rare flashes of genius which are recognized as great poetry, but it fails to explain one-poem men, because very few of them ever wrote great poetry. It is not altogether astonishing that a masterpiece should live; but, by some curious quirk, a mere jingle which possesses no possible claim to inspiration, often proves more immortal than an epic. "Bo-Peep" outlives "Paradise Regained," and grave and scholarly men, after a lifetime of labor in their chosen fields, have been astounded and chagrined to find that their sole claim to public remembrance rested upon a bit of careless rhyme written in a moment of relaxation. William Allan Butler was a distinguished lawyer, but to-day he is remembered only by some lines of society verse. Clement Clarke Moore was a learned professor of Oriental literature and the compiler of a Hebrew lexicon, but his name has been kept alive by a nursery jingle.

Poets have always been the special sport of Fortune, which delights to play with them, to whirl them aloft and to cast them down, to torment them with fleeting glimpses of happiness in the midst of long nightmares of despair, and especially to condemn their favorite children to swift oblivion and to raise up some despised and rejected outcast for the admiration of mankind. Nobody—poets least of all!—has yet discovered the formula which will assure immortality to a poem. Mere size will not do it—the most ambitious edifices are usually the first to crumble. Neither polished diction nor lofty thought will do it—most deathless songs are written in words of one syllable on the simplest of themes. Indeed, it would almost seem that the surest way is to waste no time in laboring and sweating over the fabrication of a masterpiece, but to wander idly along the pleasant places of the world, seeking love and laughter, writing a song

when the spirit moves, and tossing it into the air
for the wind to blow where it listeth!

Whether the song survives is largely a matter
of chance. Many people cherish the comfortable belief that a great work of art never perishes,
that it holds within itself, in some mysterious
way, the seed of deathlessness. But this is nonsense. The dust we tread is compounded of
great works of art, and many lovely songs have
passed into darkness along with the lovely women
who inspired them. That some few live on is
due largely to the "Reliques" and "Pastorals"
and "Garlands" put together by the loving hand
of the anthologist, who, industrious and undiscouraged, is continually assaying huge masses of
very low-grade ore in the hope of discovering
a grain of gold. Needless to say, many such
grains escape him, and are carried down to
oblivion by the sheer weight of the uninspired
mass in which they are embedded. Sometimes,
in turning over the old material, one of them
is found, but many have been lost forever.

The poems dealt with in the following pages
have no claim to greatness. They are, for the
most part, curiosities, literary orphans which
have flitted through the columns of the press,
their parentage uncertain. They have been
mutilated by brutal scissors, debased by stupid
compositors and marred by careless proof-

readers, into mere pitiful shadows of their proper selves. To rescue them, to cleanse their wounds and heal their bruises, and finally to trace their parentage, is all that is attempted here.

It is the fate of almost every fugitive poem, as soon as it gains a certain celebrity, to be claimed by many people, with the most amusing and astonishing results. The question of authorship is one (among many) which the anthologist must decide, and the material upon which these articles are based was accumulated during the compilation of *The Home Book of Verse*. It has seemed worth while to gather it together in the hope that it will settle certain historic and more or less heated controversies once for all.

THERE IS NO DEATH

THERE IS NO DEATH

There is no death! The stars go down
To rise upon some other shore,
And bright in heaven's jeweled crown
They shine for evermore.

There is no death! The dust we tread
Shall change beneath the summer showers
To golden grain or mellow fruit
Or rainbow-tinted flowers.

The granite rocks disorganize
To feed the hungry moss they bear;
The forest leaves drink daily life
From out the viewless air.

There is no death! The leaves may fall,
The flowers may fade and pass away—
They only wait, through wintry hours,
The coming of the May.

There is no death! An angel form
Walks o'er the earth with silent tread;
He bears our best-loved things away,
And then we call them "dead."

11

He leaves our hearts all desolate—
  He plucks our fairest, sweetest flowers·
Transplanted into bliss, they now
  Adorn immortal bowers.

The bird-like voice, whose joyous tones
  Made glad this scene of sin and strife,
Sings now an everlasting song
  Amid the tree of life.

Where'er He sees a smile too bright,
  Or soul too pure for taint of vice,
He bears it to that world of light,
  To dwell in Paradise.

Born unto that undying life,
  They leave us but to come again;
With joy we welcome them—the same
  Except in sin and pain.

And ever near us, though unseen,
  The dear immortal spirits tread;
For all the boundless universe
  Is Life—there are no dead!

                              John Luckey McCreery

THERE IS NO DEATH

In Glenwood Cemetery, at Washington, D. C., there is a modest monument marking the last resting place of one John Luckey McCreery, and on it, under the dates of birth and death, appear the following lines:

> There is no death! The stars go down
> To rise upon some other shore,
> And bright in heaven's jeweled crown
> They shine for evermore.

No doubt other tombstones scattered up and down the land bear these same lines, for they were once unbelievably popular, but the one at Washington stands above the grave of the man who claimed to be their author, who fought to establish that claim for more than forty years, and who finally died sick at heart, knowing that he had failed. There have been other men who have written one famous poem; but McCreery stands unique, for his poem brought him nothing but ridicule and disillusion. And no more striking proof ever existed of how difficult it is for truth to overtake error, once error gets a **start.**

13

Famous Single Poems

For the lines which are cut on his gravestone form the first stanza of a poem called "There Is No Death"—a poem which has been reprinted in newspapers all over the English-speaking world, in hymn books and song books and school readers, in countless collections of verse, in legislative reports, and even in the *Congressional Record*—credited almost everywhere to Edward Robert Lytton Bulwer, first Earl of Lytton, otherwise Owen Meredith!

Now at first thought it may seem to be of no great moment who wrote "There Is No Death." If Bulwer wrote it, it belongs to English literature; if McCreery wrote it, it belongs to American literature; but it may be pointed out with perfect justice that it enriches neither very much. Its importance, however, lies not in its poetic content, but in its wide popularity, for it is one of those semi-religious, semi-didactic, quasi-mystical, pensively sentimental poems which find their way straight to unsophisticated hearts; the sort of poem which orators on the Chautauqua circuit love to spout, and literary societies of Gopher Prairie to recite, and obituary writers of the country press to quote. It is, in short, one of those poems which are familiar to a far wider public than anything by Browning or by Keats. And, after all, however the judicious may grieve and the clever may sneer, that is fame!

14

There Is No Death

It is too easy to sneer; let us do it justice. There is no poem in the language which has been spoken so often above an open grave, none which has brought so much consolation to stricken hearts. There is about it a calm certainty of faith, a serene courage, infinitely inspiriting. The persistent repetition of the phrase, "There is no death!" is in itself reassuring. It is, in fact, a very concrete application of the Coué method of autosuggestion. Its simple and homely lines are intelligible to every one and echo a thought and a hope which are all but universal. It is a defiance and a challenge. Surely any man might well be proud to have written such a poem!

So perhaps the question of its authorship is not so unimportant after all. At any rate, it forms one of those curiosities of literature which are always interesting; and the whole story is here told, so far as the present writer knows, for the first time.

Three or four decades ago, Bulwer was one of the most popular of poets. His verses combined in an unusual degree the universally appealing qualities listed above, with the added zest of a certain spiciness. No drawing-room table was complete without "Lucille," usually gilt-edged and in padded leather; indeed, it is still to be bought in that form. Maidens and matrons were enraptured with the sad romance

15

of "Aux Italiens," which had also a pleasant foreign flavor: the grand monde, Paris, the opera, the Emperor looking grave (or perhaps only bored), Eugénie with a tear in her eye, while the tenor sang, *"Non ti scordar di me!"* Editors of *Queries and Answers* were kept busy explaining the meaning of that phrase, and many editions found it expedient to carry a translation in a footnote. Jasmine (or what passed for it) became a favorite perfume.

Then there was "The Portrait," with its cheap dramatics, for all the world like a novel by Hall Caine or Marie Corelli; with its confrontation across the body of the dead woman, and the priest's face in the locket at her throat. Even Madame la Duchesse de Chevreuse, it will be remembered, found a certain piquancy in the thought of damning an abbé; how irresistible, then, must this situation have been to the simple hearts of the 'eighties and 'nineties! So when a sadly sentimental poem called "There Is No Death," credited to Bulwer, began going the rounds of the poetry columns, everybody accepted it as his without question, and it gradually found its way over his name into the most serious collections.

To be sure, it could not have been found in any volume of Bulwer's poems, had any one thought to look, and it lacks completely Bulwer's sophisticated manner. Also a fellow named

16

McCreery was vociferating as loudly as the press would permit that he and not Bulwer was the author. But nobody had ever heard of McCreery, who was only an obscure government clerk, and everybody had heard of Bulwer, so McCreery was usually set down as a crank possessed by a harmless mania and dismissed with a pitying smile. It was just another instance of the old truth that to him that hath shall be given, while from him that hath not, even that shall be taken away!

There were a few who stopped to listen to McCreery's story, but he injured his case by setting forth at various times three versions of how he came to write the poem and what he did with it after he wrote it—versions which differed in important details. And if he was not sure in his own mind about it, how could he expect anybody else to be?

Before considering these versions, it may be well to give the facts of McCreery's life, so far as they are known.

John Luckey McCreery was the son of Joseph and Jane Luckey McCreery, and was born at Sweden, Monroe County, New York, on December 21 (or 31), 1835. Joseph McCreery was a Methodist minister, and the boy was destined to the same profession, but, as he himself puts it, he "became skeptical of many points of dogma regarded as essential by orthodox churches," and one suspects from the internal evidence of his poems that later on Darwin got him. At any rate, he gravitated to a printing office and into newspaper work, and in 1857 started west to seek his fortune, stopping finally at Delhi, Iowa, where he bought a weekly paper, *The Delaware County Journal,* giving a mortgage to cover most of the purchase price.

He was publishing this paper in 1859, and he continued to publish it during the Civil War, but he failed to make a success of it, and shortly after the war moved to Dubuque, where he worked in some sort of editorial capacity on both the *Times* and the *Herald* for twelve or fourteen years. At the end of that time, he managed in some way to secure the patronage of Senator Allison, who got him a long-desired appointment as stenographer to the Committee on Indian Affairs at Washington, and McCreery spent the remainder of his life at Washington in minor governmental positions. He died on September 6, 1906 (at Duluth, Minn., as it happened, after an operation for appendicitis), leaving a wife and two daughters.

He seems to have had a thoroughly unpractical character, and was quite unable to get along in the world or to lift himself out of the groove of governmental routine. Like many such men, he harbored various vague and grandiose schemes for the betterment of mankind, for he says in

18

the characteristic "last message," which he wrote the day of the operation, "My only regret is that all the great work I have always contemplated doing for humanity remains undone. The bread-and-butter necessities of life have prevented my getting to it."

The controversy over the authorship of "There Is No Death" began in 1869 and lasted the remainder of his life. He had apparently claimed the poem as his before that date, for in February, 1869, the Dubuque *Times* published a caustic article ridiculing the claim. McCreery was at that time working on the rival paper, the *Herald,* and he replied in the issue of March 1, 1869, and there gave his first version of how he came to write the poem.

He stated that he had written "There Is No Death" in 1859, and published it in his own paper, *The Delaware County Journal;* that some time later one Eugene Bulmer copied the poem, signed his own name to it, and sent it to the *Independence Offering* at Chicago, where it was printed with Bulmer's name attached; that the scissors editor of the *Farmer's Advocate,* published in Wisconsin, saw the poem, cut it out and used it, but, concluding that Bulmer was a misprint, changed the name to E. Bulwer—*et voila!*

The second account was printed as a preface to a collection of his verse called *Songs of Toil and Triumph,* which he published at Washington in 1883, "There Is No Death" being the first poem. Here he says it was written late in the fall of 1862, and the next spring was sent to *Arthur's Home Magazine* of Philadelphia, appearing in the issue for July, 1863. "One E. Bulmer, of Illinois, copied it, signed his own name to it, and sent it (as his own) to the *Farmer's Advocate,* Chicago. The editor of some Wisconsin paper clipped it"—and changed Bulmer to Bulwer as aforesaid.

The third version appeared in the *Annals of Iowa* (New Series, Vol I, page 196) for October, 1893. It is much more elaborate than either of the others—and also probably much more imaginative. He reviews at length the mental processes which, during a long drive behind a slow horse, led up to the idea of the poem, the first four lines of which, he says, came to him "in their completeness." He labored at the poem during the following days, and finally evolved ten stanzas. This, he states, was in February or March, 1863. He sent the poem to *Arthur's Home Magazine,* which published it in the issue for July, 1863, and he gives volume and page (Vol 22, page 41). He copied it in his own paper, *The Delaware County Journal,* and sent a marked copy to a friend of his, John H. Moore, of Dixon, Illinois, who worked on a paper called the *Telegraph,* and who reprinted the poem there. It was in the *Telegraph* that the mysterious Eugene Bulmer saw it. McCreery says that Bulmer lived "somewhere south of Dixon," but he did not know whether the name was a real one or a pseudonym. Anyway, according to McCreery, Bulmer wrote a column-and-a-half article on "Immortality" for the *Farmer's Advocate* of Chicago, concluding with the poem and signing his name beneath it. Another paper copied it and signed it E. Bulmer, then a third changed the *m* to *w*, and the deed was done.

Now it is strange that McCreery should have thought in 1869 that he wrote the poem in 1859 and first published it in his own paper; while twenty-five or thirty years later he decided that he wrote it in 1862 or 1863 and that it first appeared in *Arthur's Home Magazine*. One may question whether, in 1893, after the lapse of more than three decades, he could really remember so clearly all that he thought about during that long drive. Also there is a certain insubstantiality about Eugene Bulmer; he does not, somehow, impress one as a real person.

But in spite of all this, there can be no reasonable doubt that McCreery wrote the poem— which was destined to be the Frankenstein of his life. In the first place, nobody else has ever claimed it. Whether Bulwer ever specifically repudiated it may be questioned—one would think that McCreery might have secured a letter from him which would have settled the matter once for all—but it *is* certain that it appears nowhere among Bulwer's works. Eight or nine years ago, the present writer had an exhaustive search made, because he himself, in the first edition of *The Home Book of Verse,* had attributed it to Bulwer. McCreery once offered to pay a thousand dollars to any one who could find it anywhere prior to its appearance in *Arthur's Home Journal.*

Investigation discloses the fact that the poem *did* appear in *Arthur's Home Journal,* as McCreery alleged. The set preserved in the library of Drexel Institute at Philadelphia has been examined, and the poem found, as McCreery said it would be, in the issue for July, 1863. It is in ten stanzas, identical, except for two or three unimportant words, with the version which accompanies this article. It is stated to be "by J. L. M'Creery," and, at the end, is dated from Delhi, Iowa.

It is worth noting, also, that McCreery *did* write other verses, and while none of them approaches "There Is No Death" in poetic merit (such as it is), they do bear a certain family resemblance to it. *Songs of Toil and Triumph* contains one hundred and forty-three pages and the character of its contents may be judged by a few titles—"The World Is Waiting," "The

Child's Prayer," "Usefulness Better than Fame," "Voices of the Soul," "The Voice of Duty," "Lazarus and Dives," "Hearth and Home." There is a portrait of the author at the front of the book, showing a dogmatic and contentious face, typically Scotch-Irish. How it happened that he was a Methodist and not a Presbyterian is a mystery.

Occasionally during his long years of controversy he succeeded in convincing other people of the justice of his claim. His first triumph came in 1875. In 1870, Harper & Brothers issued a series of school readers, using "There Is No Death," and crediting it to Lord Lytton. McCreery took the matter up with the Harper firm, and after five years of effort, succeeded in having the poem credited to himself. In 1889, *Lippincott's Magazine* ran a series of "One Hundred Questions" concerning various literary matters, and question number eighty was about the authorship of "There Is No Death." After considering the evidence, the editor decided in McCreery's favor. But these were mere evanescent gleams in the darkness, and to the day of his death McCreery continued to see his poem attributed to Bulwer Lytton.

Besides involving him in endless strife and, as he says, killing in him all ambition to write any more poetry "for the public," "There Is No Death" interfered with his life in another

Famous Single Poems

way. In the fall of 1868 some friends of his at Galena, Ill., called upon General Grant, then newly elected to the presidency, to urge him to appoint McCreery as his official stenographer. All was apparently going well until one of the party was so ill-advised as to take a copy of "There Is No Death" from his pocket and read it to the old war-horse. Grant listened with a lowering face and at the end remarked that it might be good poetry—of that he was no judge —but when he became president he would need about him men who understood public business and whose minds would be on that business, while so far as his experience and observation went, a man who was good at making poetry was not good for anything else, and he would therefore have to decline to appoint Mr. McCreery. So the poet had to wait a dozen years longer before he was able to land a government job.

Once settled in this longed-for haven, which he was never again to leave, and freed to some extent from those "bread and butter necessities of life" about which he complained in his "Last Message," he turned with new vigor to poetastry, and in 1883 published his collected verse, *Songs of Toil and Triumph*. His family thought it worth while to issue a second edition in 1907, the year after his death. It is a book of 143 pages—a dreary waste from end to end.

There Is No Death

"There Is No Death" is the first poem, and the only one which possesses the faintest spark of life.

"None of the following poems," says McCreery in his preface, "were originally written for the general public. Most of them, especially the longer ones, were meant only for my own family and a circle of intimate personal friends; whence it results that many of them refer to a greater extent than would otherwise be the case, to myself, my personal experiences, hopes, beliefs, doubts, and feelings . . . Just how much of what seems personal herein is fact, and how much of it is fancy, it will be time enough to tell when I come to write my autobiography."

But that was another task which—like his "great work for humanity"—he never found time for. Instead he seems to have preferred to spend his spare moments tinkering with his one famous poem and trying to expand it, no doubt under the impression that if he could produce some additional verses it would prove that he had also written the original ones. He succeeded in adding six stanzas, which are reproduced in *Songs of Toil and Triumph*, but they are vastly inferior to the first ones, and his other revisions are all for the worse. What he evidently labored to do was to make the poem more "elegant," and he nearly ruined it in the proc-

ess. He was not the only poet to do that—
Coates Kinney did the same thing with his
"Rain on the Roof"—and, in spite of all his
mistakes and inconsistencies and contradictions,
there is no reason to doubt that at some time
(whether in 1859 or 1862 or 1863 does not
matter), John Luckey McCreery *did* sit him
down and pen the ten stanzas of "There Is
No Death" as herewith given. So let it be recorded in future anthologies, that his poor,
troubled spirit may rest in peace!

KAISER & CO.

KAISER & CO.

Der Kaiser auf der Vaterland
Und Gott on high, all dings gommand,
Ve two, ach, don'd you understandt?
    Meinself—und Gott.

He reigns in heafen, und always shall,
Und mein own embire don'd vas small;
Ein noble bair, I dink you call
    Meinself—und Gott.

While some mens sing der power divine,
Mein soldiers sing der "Wacht am Rhein,"
Und drink der healt in Rhenish wein
    Auf me—und Gott.

Dere's France dot swaggers all aroundt,
She ausgespieldt—she's no aggoundt,
To mooch ve dinks she don'd amoundt,
    Meinself—und Gott.

She vill not dare to fight again,
But if she should, I'll show her blain,
Dot Elsass und (in French) Lorraine
    Are mein—und Gott's.

Von Bismarck vas a man of might,
Und dought he vas glean oud auf sight,
But, ach! he vas nicht goot to fight
    Mit me—und Gott.

Ve knock him like ein man auf straw,
Ve let him know whose vill vas law,
Und dot ve don'd vould standt his jaw,
    Meinself—und Gott.

Ve send him oudt in big disgrace,
Ve giff him insuldt to his face,
Und put Caprivi in his place,
    Meinself—und Gott.

Und ven Caprivi get svelled headt,
Ve very bromptly on him set,
Und toldt him to get up und get—
    Meinself—und Gott.

Dere's grandma dinks she's nicht shmall beer,
Mit Boers und dings she interfere;
She'll learn none runs dis hemisphere
    But me—und Gott.

She dinks, goot frau, some ships she's got,
Und soldiers mit der sgarlet coat,
Ach! we could knock dem—pouf! like dot,
    Meinself—und Gott.

Kaiser & Co.

Dey say dat badly fooled I vas
At Betersburg by Nicholas,
Und dat I act shust like ein ass,
    Und dupe, Herr Gott!

Vell, maybe yah und maybe nein,
Und maybe czar mit France gombine,
To take dem lands about der Rhein
    From me—und Gott.

But dey may try dat leedle game,
Und make der breaks; but all der same,
Dey only vill ingrease der fame
    Auf me—und Gott.

In dimes auf peace, brebared for wars,
I bear der helm und spear auf Mars,
Und care nicht for den dousandt czars,
    Meinself—und Gott.

In short, I humor efery whim,
Mit aspect dark und visage grim,
Gott pulls mit me und I mit him—
    Meinself—und Gott.

Alexander Macgregor Rose

31

KAISER & CO.

THE war which recently shook this planet and in whose backwash we are still struggling is habitually alluded to as the greatest in all history, but, so far as this country is concerned, the war with Spain, comparatively insignificant as it was, surpassed it in at least two respects: the World War inspired no poetry to equal William Vaughan Moody's "An Ode in Time of Hesitation," nor has it (to date) produced any sensation comparable with that which burst upon these United States on the night of April 21, 1899, when Captain Joseph Bullock Coghlan, of the cruiser *Raleigh*, rose at a banquet given in his honor at the Union League Club in New York, and recited "Hoch! der Kaiser."

The mists of the intervening years have dimmed the memory of that incident, and probably few of the younger generation ever heard of it; but it held column after column of front-page space for days and days, rocked the country with mighty laughter, nearly involved us in a serious international complication, and brought forth frenzied frothings in the German-American press.

Kaiser & Co.

This last circumstance might have given thoughtful men to pause but for the comfortable theory every one had in those days that we were all loyal Americans, brothers living together in this land of plenty, ready to defend it against aggression from any quarter and to die for it if need be. Also there was another comfortable theory quite generally held that the Germans were a peaceful and home-loving race, thoroughly good-hearted and inoffensive, and that they were as much amused with their saber-rattling, shining-armored Kaiser as we were. Most of us looked upon the Kaiser as a joke; certainly few of us suspected that his people really regarded him as a demigod, and that many thousands of those people were even then living in the United States, under the protection of its laws and its flag.

The cruiser *Raleigh*, with Captain Coghlan in command, had belonged to Admiral Dewey's squadron which steamed into Manila Bay on the first of May, 1898, and sank the Spanish fleet. It had fired the first shot of the battle, and it was the first ship of that squadron to be sent home. A mighty welcome greeted it when it entered New York harbor, and on the evening of April 21, the Union League Club gave a banquet to its officers, headed by Captain Coghlan. It was an elaborate affair, with Elihu Root as toastmaster and Chauncey Depew as one of

33

the speakers. There were many courses, a great popping of corks, and every one was very happy.

Mr. Root made the first speech and then called upon Captain Coghlan. That gallant officer at first demurred on the ground that he had never made a speech and didn't know how, but at last he was prevailed upon to rise and tell the story of the battle. That story, of course, his hearers already knew, but what they did not know (since Admiral Dewey had kept it out of the dispatches) and heard for the first time was the story of the insolent behavior of the German squadron in Manila harbor, and its interference with Admiral Dewey's blockade orders. The climax of the tale, as reported in the papers next day, ran something like this:

The German squadron was in command of Admiral von Deiderick, and one night one of his staff officers, approaching the *Olympia* in a launch and refusing to stop when challenged, was fired upon and very nearly sunk. He climbed the *Olympia's* ladder in a state of excitement thoroughly Teutonic.

"How dare you fire upon us?" he demanded. "We fly the German flag!"

"Those flags can be bought anywhere for a dollar and a half a yard," retorted Dewey. "Go back and tell your admiral that the slightest infraction of any rule will mean but one thing —war! If your people are really ready for war with the United States, they can have it right now!"

"After that," Captain Coghlan added, "the Germans didn't breathe more than three times consecutively without asking permission."

Now, of course, this was after-dinner history rather than the sober article; it had a foundation in fact, but it was dressed up to suit the occasion—with the reference to the wholesale price of black, white and red bunting, for example. But it brought that audience to its feet with a wild roar of approval; there were three cheers for Captain Coghlan, and then everybody joined with acclamations in the toast to Admiral Dewey which Captain Coghlan proposed. Then the other officers gave short talks and then somebody at the speakers' table called upon Captain Coghlan to recite "Hoch! der Kaiser."

Again he demurred, saying it might give offense to some of the guests, but when everybody clapped and cheered and yelled for him to go ahead, he rose again and started on the soon-to-be-famous lines:

> Der Kaiser auf der Vaterland
> Und Gott on high, all dings gommand,
> Ve two, ach, don'd you understandt?
> Meinself—und Gott.

They were not famous then—very few of Captain Coghlan's audience had ever heard them before; and while they evoked roars of laughter, it was not until the poem appeared in the papers next day that its rare satirical quality was really appreciated. It was so unfamiliar that there was considerable confusion about it. Some of the papers said it was a song and that the captain had sung it—an aspersion which he indignantly denied. Nobody knew where it had come from. The *Staats-Zeitung*, in a boiling article, asserted that it "was composed by a Bowery bard as he lay before Manila," and gave this account of the incident:

"After Captain Coghlan, Dewey's nephew, Lieutenant Winder spoke, but he was interrupted by some Jewish persons who asked Captain Coghlan to sing the mocking song, 'Hoch! der Kaiser.' Captain Coghlan, he of the eyeglasses, who could not see a German warship a thousand yards, sang the stupid, jeering song— in the Union League Club, amid loud applause." And the *Staats-Zeitung* went on to denounce the captain as impudent and his stories as absurd and brutal. He had been disrespectful to the Kaiser!

It is worth noting that Captain Coghlan never retracted a word of his story, merely explaining that he had told it in order that justice might be done to Admiral Dewey, and that half the truth about the battle of Manila was not yet known to the American people. He added that he knew nothing about the poem, except that he had heard it in the East, where it had been very popular among the men of his ship. He was kept busy for a while explaining other things to the Navy Department, and the Navy Department was also busy explaining, and the country at large (with the Germanophile exceptions aforesaid) was very happy over the affair.

The day after the banquet, the German Ambassador, Dr. von Holleben, called on Secretary Hay at the State Department. What transpired was never disclosed, but the avowed attitude of the German Government was that it could not overlook so gross and public an affront to the Emperor. Two days later, a cablegram from Berlin stated that Secretary Hay had expressed to Dr. von Holleben his strong disapproval of Captain Coghlan's conduct. On April 27, Dr. von Holleben was received by President McKinley, who informed him that the Navy Department had administered a reprimand to Captain Coghlan, and Von Holleben expressed himself as satisfied. The German press was also satisfied, but ventured the hope that there would never be another such incident to jeopardize the kindly feelings of Germany toward the United States. The last reference to Captain Coghlan is in the papers of October 1, which tell of a second reception given in his honor at the Union League Club, at which he was warmly received.

The above facts have been gleaned from the public press. A letter to the Navy Department, asking for some information about the incident, brought the following remarkable response:

"A thorough search has been made of the official files of the department, including Admiral Coghlan's personal jacket, and no record whatever can be found of the incident of which you speak. I should have answered you before this, but we have been diligently trying to trace down some dim recollections of the incident as reported by some of the older persons in the Navy Department. I am sorry to say we have been able to find nothing, however."

Sic transit! Or perhaps Captain Coghlan was not reprimanded, after all!

But neither Wilhelm II, nor the German Ambassador, nor Secretary Hay, nor the Navy Department, nor all of them combined could suppress "Hoch! der Kaiser." That masterpiece had been lifted suddenly into immortality. It had found a fit interpreter at a supremely fit moment, and its fame was secure. Yet nobody knew the name of its author, or where it had first appeared. It was just one of those fugitive poems, those nameless orphans, which drift through the columns of the press, their origin shrouded in mystery, and which gradually fade from sight unless preserved for posterity by some such accident as had befallen this one.

Kaiser & Co.

Rodney Blake, which was a pseudonym used by William Montgomery Clemens, included it in a collection of *After-dinner Verse,* and for a while he was credited with being its author. Then somebody claimed that it had been written by a wandering newspaperman named A. M. R. Gordon; but presently it was discovered that that, too, was a pseudonym. But it was the pseudonym of the real author, Alexander Macgregor Rose, and the whole story at last came out of Montreal, Canada, where Rose had written the poem during the last year of his life, and where he had died.

It is an everlasting pity that "Hoch! der Kaiser" does not belong to American literature, but it was written by a Scotchman, and first appeared in the columns of the Montreal *Daily Herald.*

Alexander Macgregor Rose was born in the village of Tomantoul, South Banffshire, Scotland, on August 7, 1846. After attending the village school, he went to the grammar school at Aberdeen, where in 1863 he gained the Macpherson bursary of twenty pounds. He entered the University of Aberdeen the same year, and finished his arts course in the spring of 1867. During the next three years he was classical master at boarding schools in different parts of England, and in 1870 was appointed master of the Free Church school at Gairlock, Rosshire.

Soon afterwards he began the study of divinity, and in 1875 was licensed as a minister. His reputation seems to have been excellent, for almost immediately, on September 9, 1875, he was ordained as minister of the Free Church of Evie and Randall, at Orkney.

Up to this point his life reads like a chapter out of the biography of any eminent Scotsman: an orderly progress, through school and college, to the natural and inevitable haven of the church; studious and laborious years leading to the ministry at the age of twenty-nine—a good age, neither so young as to be foolish, nor so old as to feel oneself slipping behind in the battle of life; a position respected and influential, assuring a comfortable livelihood, and thoroughly congenial to one of scholarly tastes. So the future of the Reverend Alexander Macgregor Rose seemed to stretch fair and straight before him, along a predestined and thoroughly Presbyterian path.

But four years later he cast all this aside, changed his name to Gordon, forswore the ministry, and became a wanderer upon the face of the earth.

No one knew why—at least no one in America. In Orkney, of course, the affair created an immense sensation, as any scandal connected with the church was certain to do; but Rose never referred to it, and the friends whom

40

he made over here had to content themselves with guesses. All of them, naturally, were tinged with romance. It was variously suggested that a woman had betrayed him, that doubt had assailed him, that his wife had deserted him. It was evident enough that, whatever the tragedy, it had shaken him to the depths, for he fled not only from his home, but from his profession and from all the old, ordered habits of his life. During the twenty years that remained to him, he was never once to find safe harbor and be at rest.

The reality had no romance about it. Dr. Oliver Dryer, the present pastor of the United Free Church of Evie, Orkney, tells the story quite simply:

"I have only been about three and a half years minister of Evie," he writes, "so that I can give no personal evidence. But the memory of Mr. Rose is quite fresh to many of my congregation. They speak very highly of him. He had great gifts, literary and poetic, and was a powerful and energetic preacher, but he had one serious fault—he was a victim of intemperance —and that to such an extent that on several occasions he suffered from delirium tremens. For this cause he was sent to America, and I know nothing further concerning him."

It is not quite fair to say that he changed his name. What he actually did was to add Gordon to his own name. Thereafter he was known as A. M. R. Gordon, but it would have required a master mind indeed to identify the wandering newspaperman of that name with Alexander Macgregor Rose, erstwhile minister of the Free Kirk of Evie and Randall!

It was for America that Rose sailed when he turned his back on Scotland. He reached these shores in June, 1879, and at once began the series of wanderings which was to last until his death. He found a natural haven in newspaper work, which was not then the extremely serious profession it has since become. Newspapermen were rather expected to be eccentric and bohemian, and many of them, especially in the smaller cities, drank to excess. The history of American journalism in those days is filled with escapades which would not be tolerated now, any more than a drunkard, however gifted, would be tolerated on the staff.

Moreover there were hundreds and hundreds of such men who had no fixed abode, but wandered from place to place as fancy moved, holding a job as long as they liked it, or until they were fired, and then moving on to hunt for another one. Usually they had no difficulty in finding it, for the paper across the street or at least in the next town had almost certainly just lost a man in the same way. Walt Mason has

42

told the story in some recently published reminiscences of his own early years.

A most interesting bit of newspaper history
could be written about these men, and about the
all-pervasive genus of tramp-printer which in-
fested the land at the same epoch. Rarely was
the country newspaper office without one or two
tramp printers, drooping their pendulous noses
above the cases as they threw in the type which
the foreman had permitted to accumulate
against their arrival. There was always some
work for them to do; but the linotype killed the
tramp printer, just as the realization that drink
and genius do not necessarily go together gradually killed off these vagrant knights of the
pencil.

It was a journalist of this sort that Rose
became, wandering up and down across America
for more than twenty years, never staying long
in any place. Only a vague record of this
period has survived. For a couple of years he
edited three papers in what was then Washington Territory, and for eight months he was a
reporter in Victoria, B. C. He drifted down
to San Francisco, the natural haven of the derelict, and found the town so attractive that he
remained four years, most of the time as sporting editor of one of the papers. His thorough
and unusual education must have stood him in

good stead, giving him a vast advantage over the ordinary run of reporters, and he probably had no difficulty in holding a job as long as he really wanted to.

In a letter to a friend dated November 9, 1896, Rose refers to his roving life, and adds: "I simply could not remain in one place, and I have wandered all over the North American continent, from Quebec to Vancouver, and from Mexico to Alaska."

Finally he started to walk across the continent from the Pacific coast, stopping to work whenever he ran out of money, and then starting on again. The year 1895 found him in Toronto, Canada, and there he had a severe attack of typhoid fever. His convalescence was slow, but as soon as he was able to take the road he started on again, and got as far as Montreal on what proved to be his last journey. At Montreal he was given a position on the staff of the *Gazette*, but after a few months moved over to the *Herald*.

During the years of his wanderings Rose had cultivated the knack of writing humorous and topical verses—a feature which most papers welcomed and which probably enabled him to escape the more arduous side of a reporter's duties. Legend has it that many such poems from his pencil went the rounds of the press, but if any have survived they are among those waifs and strays usually grouped together at the back of anthologies and marked "Unidentified." The Reverend Dr. Dryer speaks of his high poetic gifts. Perhaps in Scotland there still may be some poems associated with his name; in America there is only one.

The city editor of the *Herald* turned to Rose one day in 1897, after one of the characteristic outbursts of the German Emperor, and said, "Gordon, give us some verses about the Kaiser." An hour later Rose turned in a set of sixteen stanzas entitled "Kaiser & Co." They were published the same day, but through some mistake on the part of the make-up man, only half of them appeared in the first edition of the paper. Rose noticed the mistake and in the later editions the complete poem appeared, but it was the first edition which got into the mails, and so, when the poem was copied by other papers, it was only eight stanzas long. The version which accompanies this article is the complete poem, as Rose wrote it.

While copied here and there, laughed over a little, and eventually re-christened "Hoch! der Kaiser," the poem created no great sensation and might even have dropped out of sight, as so many other fugitive poems have done, but for the sudden shove into the limelight which Captain Coghlan gave it two years after it was written.

Famous Single Poems

One day in the early part of May, 1898, the body of an unknown man was picked up on the streets of Montreal and taken to Notre Dame hospital. There he was found to be suffering from something which was diagnosed as paralysis of the brain. Nothing could be done for him, and he died on the tenth of May without regaining consciousness. There was no clue to his identity, no inquiry had been made for him, and, as was usual in such cases, the body was set aside for dissection.

Meanwhile one of Rose's friends, a merchant at whose shop Rose had been in the habit of stopping almost every day, had been searching for him. The search led finally to the hospital, where the body was discovered, rescued and given burial. Among his papers was found a memorandum directing that, in case of his death, a lawyer by the name of Rose, living in Aberdeen, Scotland, be notified. This was done, and the Scotch lawyer proved to be Rose's son. He came to Montreal at once, reimbursed Rose's friend for the expenses of the funeral, and told the story of his father's life, much as it has been set down here.

So Alexander Macgregor Rose never knew that his name was to survive as the author of one famous poem. Perhaps he would have preferred that it die with him!

A VISIT FROM ST. NICHOLAS

A VISIT FROM ST. NICHOLAS

'Twas the night before Christmas, when all
    through the house
Not a creature was stirring, not even a mouse;
The stockings were hung by the chimney with
    care,
In hopes that St. Nicholas soon would be there;
The children were nestled all snug in their beds,
While visions of sugar-plums danced in their
    heads;
And Mama in her 'kerchief, and I in my cap,
Had just settled our brains for a long winter's
    nap;
When out on the lawn there arose such a clatter,
I sprang from the bed to see what was the
    matter.
Away to the window I flew like a flash,
Tore open the shutters and threw up the sash.
The moon on the breast of the new-fallen snow
Gave the luster of mid-day to objects below,
When, what to my wondering sight should
    appear
But a miniature sleigh, and eight tiny reindeer,
With a little old driver, so lively and quick,
I knew in a moment it must be St. Nick.

More rapid than eagles his coursers they came,
And he whistled, and shouted, and called them
    by name:
"Now, *Dasher!* now, *Dancer!* now, *Prancer*
    and *Vixen!*
On, *Comet!* on, *Cupid!* on, *Donder* and
    Blitzen!
To the top of the porch! to the top of the wall!
Now dash away! dash away! dash away all!"
As dry leaves that before the wild hurricane fly,
When they meet with an obstacle, mount to the
    sky,
So up to the house-top the coursers they flew,
With the sleigh full of toys, and St. Nicholas
    too.
And then, in a twinkling, I heard on the roof
The prancing and pawing of each little hoof—
As I drew in my head and was turning around,
Down the chimney St. Nicholas came with a
    bound.
He was dressed all in fur from his head to his
    foot,
And his clothes were all tarnished with ashes
    and soot;
A bundle of toys he had flung on his back,
And he looked like a peddler just opening his
    pack.
His eyes—how they twinkled! his dimples how
    merry!
His cheeks were like roses, his nose like a cherry!

A Visit from St. Nicholas

His droll little mouth was drawn up like a bow,
And the beard of his chin was as white as the
snow;
The stump of a pipe he held tight in his teeth,
And the smoke it encircled his head like a
wreath;
He had a broad face and a little round belly,
That shook when he laughed, like a bowlful of
jelly.
He was chubby and plump, a right jolly old elf,
And I laughed when I saw him, in spite of
myself;
A wink of his eye and a twist of his head
Soon gave me to know I had nothing to dread;
He spoke not a word, but went straight to his
work,
And filled all the stockings; then turned with
a jerk,
And laying his finger aside of his nose,
And giving a nod, up the chimney he rose;
He sprang to his sleigh, to his team gave a
whistle,
And away they all flew like the down of a
thistle.
But I heard him exclaim, ere he drove out of
sight,
"Happy Christmas to all, and to all a good
night."

Clement Clarke Moore

A VISIT FROM ST. NICHOLAS

NOTHING is harder to kill than a nursery rhyme.
Once let it become part of the patter of childhood and its immortality is assured.   Jack Sprat,
King Cole, Miss Muffet and Boy Blue are
known and loved by thousands upon thousands
who have never heard, nor cared to hear, of
Endymion or Prometheus or Childe Harold.
Mother Goose will probably be the last work
of English literature to perish.

It is astonishing how a mere jingle will sometimes win a tremendous vogue.   When Julia
Fletcher Carney wrote

> Little drops of water,
> Little grains of sand,
> Make the mighty ocean
> And the pleasant land,

as a lesson in ethics for her Boston Sunday school
class, she had no idea that she was winning everlasting fame; and when Henry Wadsworth
Longfellow tried to soothe his second daughter
by chanting

> There was a little girl
> Who had a little curl

52

A Visit from St. Nicholas

Right in the middle of her forehead,
When she was good
She was very, very good,
But when she was bad she was horrid,

as he walked up and down the garden carrying her in his arms, he would have been aghast had he suspected that these lines were to become more widely known than "Evangeline" or "Hiawatha."

Similarly, when a learned professor of Oriental and Greek literature in the General Theological Seminary of New York City, the editor of a monumental Hebrew lexicon, and a thoroughly grave and learned man, so far unbent as to write some merry Christmas verses for his two little daughters, he would have been indeed disillusioned and impressed with the vanity of human attainments had he foreseen that of all his works this jingle alone was destined to survive. Yet such was the strange fate which befell Clement Clarke Moore.

Stranger still, it has recently been alleged that Dr. Moore did not write the poem, but had it forced on him, as it were, by a curious series of circumstances, and was finally impelled to the moral turpitude of claiming it as his own.

The poem in question is that nursery classic, "A Visit from St. Nicholas," which has probably given pleasure to more children than any other

53

poem ever written, and which seems destined to live as long as Christmas itself.

Its first appearance in print was in the Troy (N. Y.) *Sentinel,* on December 23, 1823. It was called "An Account of a Visit from St. Nicholas," occupied nearly a column of the paper, and was unsigned. The editor of the paper, Orville Holley, prefaced it with an appreciative note, of which this is the first paragraph:

We know not to whom we are indebted for the following description of that unwearied patron of music—that homely and delightful personage of parental kindness, Santa Claus, his costume and his equipage, as he goes about visiting the firesides of this happy land, laden with Christmas bounties; but from whomsoever it may come, we give thanks for it. There is, to our apprehension, a spirit of cordial goodness in it, a playfulness of fancy and a benevolent alacrity to enter into the feelings and promote the simple pleasures of children which are altogether charming.

From which it is evident that Mr. Holley was one of those rare personages who know a masterpiece when they see it! He was not mistaken in thinking the poem would have a wide appeal. It standardized Santa Claus. It visualized the appearance of the old saint so clearly that no artist since has dared to depart from the specifications there set down. Clarence Cook well called it "a true piece of Dutch painting in verse." No homely detail is overlooked, and each is drawn with rare precision. St. Nicholas is painted for all time as a jolly, fun-loving, rotund old elf, whose ruddy skin and bright eyes belie his snow-white beard, who dimples with merriment and makes one laugh just to look at him. Clad in furs, his sack of toys slung across his back, he skims over the housetops in his little sleigh, whistling and shouting to his reindeer. That sleigh drawn by reindeer was pure inspiration!

For two or three years following, the *Sentinel* used the poem in its Christmas number, and then issued it as a broadside to be distributed by its carriers on their Christmas round. In this form, it was embellished by a clever woodcut engraved by Myron King, of Troy, showing the old saint flying in his sleigh above the housetops on his merry errand.

During all this time, there had been no disclosure of its authorship, but on January 1, 1829, the New York *Courier* published the poem with an inquiry as to who wrote it, and on January 20, Mr. Holley, who was still editor of the *Sentinel*, gave the following hint:

A few days since, the editors of the New York *Courier*, at the request of a lady, inserted some lines

descriptive of one of the visits of that good old
Dutch Saint, St. Nicholas, and at the same time
applied to our Albany neighbors for information as
to the author. That information, we apprehend, the
Albany editors cannot give. The lines were *first*
published in this paper. They came to us from a
manuscript in possession of a lady of this city. We
have been given to understand that the author of
them belongs, by birth and residence, to the city of
New York, and that he is a gentleman of *more* merit
as a scholar and a writer than many more of more
noisy pretensions.

No doubt, during the years which had intervened since the first appearance of the poem,
Mr. Holley had been investigating the question
of its authorship for himself; he had discovered the person who had originally sent the poem
to him, had learned from her who the author
was, and by this play upon words was endeavoring to indicate a name which he did not feel
wholly at liberty to reveal.

The poem continued to be widely quoted during the next few years, always unsigned, but in
1837 a collection of verse called *The New
York Book of Poetry* was published by George
Dearborn. "A Visit from St. Nicholas" was
one of the poems included, and the name of
Clement C. Moore appears beneath its title as
its author.

In 1844, Dr. Clement Clarke Moore, of

A Visit from St. Nicholas

New York City, published his collected poems, and one of them was "A Visit from St. Nicholas."

This apparently settled the question, and from that time forward the poem has always been ascribed to him. Griswold in his *Poets and Poetry of America*, published in 1849, is said to have so credited it (though the poem has been replaced by another one by Dr. Moore, possibly at his own suggestion, in the 1852 edition of that work owned by the present writer); it is so credited in Duyckinck's *Cyclopedia of American Literature*, published in 1855; and there has been no question concerning its authorship in the mind of any subsequent anthologist. Indeed such a question would have seemed preposterous.

Accompanying the verses in Duyckinck is a very complimentary note about Dr. Moore, from which the following is taken:

Professor Moore has lightened his learned labors in the seminary by the composition of numerous poems from time to time, chiefly expressions of home thoughts and affections, with a turn for humor as well as sentiment, the reflections of a genial, amiable nature. They were collected by the author in a volume in 1844, which he dedicated to his children. Though occasional compositions, they are polished in style, the author declaring in his preface that he does not pay his readers "so ill a compliment as to offer the contents of this volume to their view as the mere amusements of my idle hours; effusions thrown off without care or meditation, as though the refuse of my thoughts were good enough for them. On the contrary, some of the pieces have cost me much time and thought; and I have composed them all as carefully and correctly as I could." The longest of these poems is entitled "A Trip to Saratoga," a pleasant narrative and sentimental account of a family journey. Others are very agreeable *vers de société*, commonly associated with some amusing theme. One, a sketch of an old Dutch legend greatly cherished in all genuine New York families, has become a general favorite wherever it is known. It is "A Visit from St. Nicholas."

The lesson of the amiable life and character of this accomplished Christian gentleman is happily expressed in one of the resolutions passed by the faculty of the General Theological Seminary, which he had served as a professor for nearly thirty years, and endowed with a magnificent grant of land. "We recognize in him," is its language, "one whom God has blessed with selecter gifts; warm-hearted in friendship, genial in society, kindly and considerate to all; possessed of fine literary tastes, poetic instincts and expressiveness, and of cheerful humor withal; at the same time well accomplished in severer studies and resolute for more laborious undertakings, as his learned works in Hebrew grammar and lexicography distinctly testify."

Dr. Moore's life seems to have been an exceptionally full and happy one. He was the

only child of the Right Reverend Benjamin
Moore, president of Columbia College and
Bishop of the Protestant Episcopal Church in
New York, one of the most prominent men of
his time, who had, among other things, assisted
at the inauguration of George Washington as
first president of the United States and administered the last communion to Alexander Ham-
ilton as he lay dying after his duel with Aaron
Burr. His wife had inherited from her father
a tract of land extending from the present
Nineteenth street to Twenty-fourth street, and
from what is now Eighth avenue to the Hudson River. Here the family mansion, known
as "Chelsea Farm," stood on a knoll, looking
down upon the Hudson, and here on July 15,
1779, Clement Clarke Moore was born.

He graduated from Columbia in 1798 and
prepared for the ministry, but never took orders. Instead, continuing to live in his father's
house, he devoted himself to oriental and classical studies and to the occasional writing of
verse. The first fruit of his studies was a Hebrew and English lexicon, in two volumes, published in 1809. It was a decidedly important
work for those days, the first of its kind published in America. Though long since super-
seded, it was undoubtedly, as its compiler hoped
it would be, "of some service to his young
countrymen in breaking down the impediments

59

which present themselves at the entrance of the study of Hebrew."

In 1818, Dr. Moore presented to the newly organized General Theological Seminary of the Episcopal Church the tract of land between Ninth and Tenth avenues and Twentieth and Twenty-first streets, with the water-right on the Hudson belonging to it, on the sole condition that the seminary buildings be erected there —a truly magnificent gift which few millionaires could duplicate to-day. In 1821, he accepted the appointment of "Professor of Biblical Learning" in the seminary, a designation which was afterwards altered to that of "Oriental and Greek Literature." He resigned this position in 1850, was appointed Professor Emeritus, and passed the remainder of his life placidly either at Chelsea Farm or at a summer place at Newport, where he died July 10, 1863.

He was buried in the Trinity Church cemetery at One hundred and fifty-third street and Amsterdam avenue, and around his grave on every Christmas eve the children from the Chapel of the Intercession near by gather to sing hymns and to recite the poem which has made St. Nicholas a real person for so many generations of young folks.

Dr. Moore's book of poems (*Poems* by Clement C. Moore, LL.D., New York, Bartlett & Welford, 1844), begins with a preface explaining why and in what manner the collection was made. It is important because it is self-revealing, and is in part as follows:

My Dear Children:

In compliance with your wishes, I here present you with a volume of verses, written by me at different periods of my life.

I have not made a selection from among my verses of such as are of any particular cast; but have given you the melancholy and the lively; the serious, the sportive, and even the trifling; such as relate solely to our own domestic circle, and those of which the subjects take a wider range. Were I to offer you nothing but what is gay and lively, you well know that the deepest and keenest feelings of your father's heart would not be portrayed. If, on the other hand, nothing but what is serious or sad had been presented to your view, an equally imperfect character of his mind would have been exhibited. For you are all aware that he is far from following the school of Chesterfield with regard to harmless mirth and merriment; and that, in spite of all the cares and sorrows of this life, he thinks we are so constituted that a good honest hearty laugh, which conceals no malice, and is excited by nothing corrupt, however ungenteel it may be, is healthful to both body and mind. Another reason why the mere trifles in this volume have not been withheld is that such things have been often found by me to afford greater pleasure than what was by myself esteemed of more worth.

61

Which would indicate that Dr. Moore was very far from being the dry, humorless pedant he is sometimes pictured. It shows, too, that he was very fond of his children—indeed he wrote more than one set of verses for them, though, it must be confessed, more often to instruct than to amuse!

He seems never to have suspected that his authorship of any of these poems would be questioned, and so made no effort to authenticate it. Nor, so far as known, was the original manuscript of any of them preserved. The only record of any direct statement by him as to the circumstances of the composition of "A Visit from St. Nicholas" is contained in a letter written in 1862, the year before his death.

In that year, the librarian of the New York Historical Society, wishing to secure an autograph copy of the poem to be preserved in the society's archives, received the following response to his request:

> 73 East 12th Street,
> New York, March 15, 1862.

George H. Moore, Esq.,
   Librarian of the New York Historical Society.
DEAR SIR:—

I have the pleasure to inform you that Dr. Clement C. Moore has been so kind as to comply with my request (made at your suggestion) to furnish for the Archives of our Society an autograph copy of his

A Visit from St. Nicholas

justly celebrated "Visit from St. Nicholas." I enclose it to you.

I hardly need call your attention to the distinctness and beauty of his handwriting—very remarkable considering his advanced age (he completed his 82d year in July last), and his much impaired eyesight.

These lines were composed for his two daughters as a Christmas present, about forty years ago. They were copied by a relative of Dr. Moore's in her Album, from which a copy was made by a friend of hers, from Troy, and, much to the surprise of the Author, were published (for the first time) in a newspaper of that city.

In an interview which I had yesterday with Dr. Moore, he told me that a portly, rubicund Dutchman, living in the neighborhood of his country seat, Chelsea, suggested to him the idea of making St. Nicholas the hero of this Christmas piece for his children.

I remain, very resp'y,
Your o'b't S't,
T. W. C. MOORE.

This is the nearest approach, so far as known, to a statement as to the authorship of the poem made directly by Dr. Moore. But it is surely explicit enough and the autograph copy of the verses which accompanied it is signed by Dr. Moore as follows:

Clement C. Moore
1862, March 13th.
Originally written many years ago.

Objection has been made that in 1822 Dr. Moore had three daughters, Margaret, born in 1815, Charity, born in 1816, and Mary, born in 1819, and that consequently if it was written for two daughters, it must have been written before September, 1819. But this is mere trifling. What Dr. Moore undoubtedly meant was that the poem was written for his two elder daughters, who, in 1822, were aged seven and six respectively—just the ages to enjoy such a bit of jollity.

It was not until 1897 that any story appeared in print which explained fully how the poem came to be published in the Troy *Sentinel*. In that year, Mr. William S. Pelletreau, of New York City, published a little volume entitled *The Visit of St. Nicholas*,[1] in which the story is told substantially as follows:

The poem was written by Dr. Moore in 1822 as a Christmas present for his children, and with no thought that it would ever be published. Up to the end of his life, indeed, he seems to have regarded it as merely a nursery jingle without any serious merit. Among the many friends of Dr. Moore's family was the family of the Rev. Dr. David Butler, then rector of St. Paul's

---

[1] *The Visit of Saint Nicholas,* by Clement C. Moore, LL.D. Facsimile of the original manuscript, with life of the author. By William S. Pelletreau, A.M. New York: G. W. Dillingham Co., Publishers. MDCCCXCVII.

A Visit from St. Nicholas

church in the city of Troy, N. Y., and Dr. Butler's eldest daughter Harriet happened to be visiting the Moore children and to be present when Dr. Moore read the verses. She liked them so much that she copied them in her "album"—an essential property of all young ladies of that epoch—and carried them home with her to read to the children at the rectory.

When the following Christmas season rolled around, she bethought her of the verses which she had found so delightful, and could not resist the inclination to make them public. Accordingly she made a copy of them and sent it to Mr. Holley, the editor of the Troy *Sentinel*, without other communication of any sort or any indication of the authorship, and Mr. Holley used the poem, as has been stated, in his issue of December 23, 1823.

This is a reasonable and straightforward narrative, but it has been objected that it was written by Mr. Pelletreau more than thirty years after Dr. Moore's death, and that he nowhere indicates his sources of information. However, it is only fair to infer that he got the story from the Moore family, where it must have been well known. At least it agrees in essence with such details as Dr. Moore himself gave in the letter of 1862.

It is said that Dr. Moore was considerably chagrined by the publication of his verses—as

well he might be. Any author would be chagrined to have one of his poems copied by a
guest and published without his consent! And
it should be pointed out that it is only on the
theory that he was really the author that such
chagrin is understandable. If he was not the
author, there was no reason why he should feel
any concern as to the fate of the poem or care
how often it was published. But if he was
really the author, its unauthorized publication
in this manner must have seemed to him very
much like a betrayal of confidence.

No public and formal challenge of Dr.
Moore's authorship of "A Visit from St. Nicholas" has ever been made; nevertheless, for
more than a hundred years, the belief has persisted among the descendants of Henry Livingston that he and not Dr. Moore wrote it, and
a great-grandson of Mr. Livingston, Dr. William S. Thomas of New York City, has for
many years been assembling the evidence in the
case. This evidence Dr. Thomas has been kind
enough to place at the disposition of the present
writer.

Henry Livingston was born on October 13,
1748, in his father's home, the old Livingston
mansion, on the bank of the Hudson about a
mile south of Poughkeepsie, and passed most of
his life on an estate of 250 acres near by,
known as "Locust Grove," given him by his

66

father at the time of his marriage. He served as a major in General Montgomery's expedition to Canada, but was invalided home in December, 1775, and saw no further military service. After the Revolution, he held various minor offices, such as assessor and justice of the peace, and did some public surveying, but most of his time was spent looking after his farm. He was twice married, had twelve children, and died February 29, 1828.

Mr. Livingston seems to have been a genial and cultivated gentleman, and all his life he had a fondness for writing playful rhymes for the amusement of his family. Some of these were published in contemporary newspapers and magazines, as were also a number of prose articles on such subjects as "Antiquity and Universality of the English Language," "Journal of an Asiatic Expedition," or descriptive of plates made from the author's drawings. He was evidently very proud of these drawings, which though rude are not without merit, for he always carefully signed them.

A manuscript book containing forty-four of his poems written between 1784 and 1789 is in the possession of Dr. Thomas. In addition to the evidence which these poems furnish, and the persistence of the legend itself, the belief that Mr. Livingston wrote "A Visit from St. Nicholas" is supported by a number of family letters, the most important of which, as explaining how the poem came to be attributed to Dr. Moore, is by Mrs. Edward Livingston Montgomery and is as follows:

The little incident connected with the first reading of "A Visit from St. Nicholas" was related to me by my grandmother, Catherine Breese, the eldest daughter of Henry Livingston. As I recollect her story there was a young lady spending the Christmas holidays with the family at Locust Grove. On Christmas morning, Mr. Livingston came into the dining-room, where the family and their guests were just sitting down to breakfast. He held the manuscript in his hand and said it was a Christmas poem that he had written for them. He then sat down at the table and read aloud to them "A Visit from St. Nicholas." All were delighted with the verses and the guest, in particular, was so much impressed by them that she begged Mr. Livingston to let her have a copy of the poem. He consented and made a copy in his own hand, which he gave to her. On leaving Locust Grove, when her visit came to an end, this young lady went directly to the home of Clement C. Moore, where she filled the position of governess to his children.

The inference to be drawn from this is, of course, that the young lady showed the poem to Dr. Moore, who made a copy of it and subsequently read it to his children (not necessarily as his own), and that Miss Butler, who

68

was present at the time and who sent the copy to the Troy *Sentinel,* supposed him to be the author and so informed Editor Holley when that gentleman questioned her about it. In this way, the belief that Dr. Moore was the author might have started without any complicity on his part.

But Mrs. Montgomery's story is vitiated by the fact that in 1805, when Mr. Livingston supposedly wrote the poem, Dr. Moore was only twenty-six years old, unmarried, without children, and consequently in no need of a governess. Nor were there any children at "Chelsea Farm," Dr. Moore having been an only child. His first child was not born until 1815. Various attempts have been made to explain away this discrepancy, but with no great success.

However, there is another letter written in 1879 by Henry Livingston's daughter Eliza, who married Judge Smith Thompson of the New York Supreme Court. Here it is:

DEAR ANNIE:

Your letter has just been received and I hasten to tell you all I know about the poem "Night before Christmas."

It was supposed and believed in our family to be Father's and I well remember our astonishment when we saw it claimed as Clement C. Moore's many years after my Father's decease, which took place more than forty years ago.

69

At that time my brothers in looking over his papers found the *original* in his own handwriting with his many fugitive pieces which he had preserved. And then too the style was so exactly his, when he felt in a humorous mood, and we have often said could it be possible that another could express the same originality of thought and use the same phrases so familiar to us as Father!

I remember my brother Charles took the poem home with him. He was then living in Ohio and I have an indistinct idea that he intended to have it published, but I am not at all sure on this point, so don't like to assert it as fact.

My Father had a fine poetical taste, and wrote a great deal, both prose and poetry, not for publication but for his own amusement. He also had a great taste for drawing and painting. When we were children, he used to entertain us on winter evenings by getting down his paint box, we seated around the table. First he would portray something very pathetic which would melt us to tears, the next thing would be so comic that we would be almost wild with laughter; and this dear good man was your great greatgrandfather, Henry Livingston.

Now my dear, give Mama and Grandmama my warmest love. Yours very truly,

E. L. THOMPSON.

Elvie Cottage, 8 Court Street,
    March 4, 1879.

Still another letter from Henry Livingston, of Babylon, L. I., tells what became of the original draft:

A Visit from St. Nicholas

My father, as long ago as I can remember, claimed that his father (Henry, Jr.), was the author; that it was first read to the children at the old homestead near Poughkeepsie, when he was about eight years old, which would be about 1804 or 1805. He had the original manuscript, with many corrections, in his possession for a long time, and by him it was given to his brother Edwin, and Edwin's personal effects were destroyed when his sister Susan's house was burned at Waukesha, Wisconsin, about 1847 or 1848.

Still another bit of evidence is supplied by Mrs. Rudolph Denig, the wife of a retired commodore of the navy. Her grandmother was Eliza Clement Brewer, who married Charles Livingston, son of Henry Livingston, in 1826. The Brewers and the Livingstons were neighbors, and Mrs. Denig states that her grandmother told her that in 1808, while visiting at the Livingston home, she heard Mr. Livingston read the poem as his own.

But the greatest emphasis in the Livingston argument is laid on the internal evidence of the poem itself, on its resemblance to the acknowledged poems of Henry Livingston, and the contrast between it and anything else Dr. Moore ever wrote. Of the forty-four poems in Mr. Livingston's book, one third are in the same anapæstic meter as "A Visit from St. Nicholas," and they abound in the same tricks of rhyme and

71

phrase. The most significant of them, so far as the present controversy is concerned, was written in 1786 and is here given in full:

LETTER TO MY BROTHER BEEKMAN

WHO THEN LIVED WITH MR. SCHENK AT NEW LEBANON

To my dear brother Beekman I sit down to write
Ten minutes past eight and a very cold night;
Not far from me sits with a baullancy cap on
Our very good cousin, Elizabeth Tappan.
A tighter young sempstress you'd ne'er wish to see
And she (blessings on her) is sewing for me.
New shirts & new cravats this morning cut out
Are tumbled in heaps and lye huddled about.
My wardrobe (a wonder) will soon be enriched
With ruffles new hemmed and wristbands new
    stitched.
Believe me, dear brother, the women may be
Comparèd to us, of inferior degree.
Yet still they are useful, I vow with a fegs,
When our shirts are in tatters & jackets in rags.

Now for news, my sweet fellow, first learn with a
    sigh
That matters are carried here gloriously high.
Such gadding, such ambling, such jaunting about—
To tea with Miss Nancy—to sweet Willy's rout;
Now parties at coffee—then parties at wine—
Next day all the world with the Major must dine.

A Visit from St. Nicholas

Bounce, all hands to Fishkill must go in a clutter
To guzzle bohea and destroy bread and butter!
While you at New Lebanon stand all forlorn
Behind the cold counter from evening to morn.
The old tenor merchants push nigher and nigher
Till fairly they shut out poor Baze from the fire.

Out, out, my dear brother, Aunt Amy's just come
With a flask for molasses and a bottle for rum.
Run! Help the poor creature to light from her
    jade,
You see the dear lady's a power afraid.
Souse into your arms she leaps like an otter
And smears your new coat with a piggin of butter.

Next an army of shakers your quarters beleager
With optics distorted and visages meagre,
To fill their black runlets with brandy and gin—
Two blessed exorcists to drive away sin.

But laugh away sorrow nor mind it a daisy
Since it matters but little, my dear brother Bazee,
Whether here you are rolling in pastime and pleasure
Or up at New Labanon taffety measure.
If the sweetest of lasses, CONTENTMENT, you find,
And the BANQUET enjoy of an undisturb'd mind,
Of friendship & love let who will make a pother
Believe me, dear Baze, your affectionate brother
Will never forget the fifth son of his mother.

P. S. If it suits your convenience, remit if you
    please
To my good brother Paul an embrace and a squeeze.

73

The resemblance to "A Visit from St. Nicholas" is very marked. To be sure, all anapæstic verse sounds much alike, but here there are the same tricks of expression, the same fondness for detail—in a word, the same style.

No doubt Mr. Livingston kept on writing such lively verse to the end of his life, since it seems to have been his favorite amusement, but none survives which is known to have been written later than 1789.

As to the internal evidence of the poem, it is pointed out that its setting fits admirably the old stone house at "Locust Grove," with its broad lawn and wide fireplaces, that Mr. Livingston always addressed his wife as "mama," and that she was in the habit of wearing a 'kerchief on her head at night; that he was born, reared and lived among villagers of Dutch descent, who retained many of the customs and traditions of their fathers, and that it "is manifestly more probable that the poem was composed by a country gentleman reared among Dutch surroundings, than by a Biblical scholar and linguist of the city."

On the other hand, Dr. Moore's poems are as different as possible from this light-hearted, airy and dashing rhyme. He frequently essays to be airy, it is true, and perhaps a third of the poems in his volume might fairly be called *vers de société,* but it is written laboriously with a

heavy hand. For instance, with a pair of gloves
to a young lady he sends some lines beginning:

> Go envied glove, with anxious care,
> From scorching suns and withering air,
>   Belinda's hand to guard.
> And let no folds offend the sight;
> Nor let thy seams, perversely tight,
>   With hasty rents be marred.

He invokes the Muses, celebrates various
nymphs, apostrophizes Hebe, Apollo, Terpsich-
ore, Pallas and numerous other gods and god-
desses, and capitalizes Fancy, Hope and so on,
all in the good old way. He castigates the fol-
lies of the times, especially the freedom with
which young ladies display their charms; decries
the wine-bibber and exalts the drinker of water;
writes at length (fifty pages) of a family ex-
cursion to Saratoga; tells of his sorrow at the
death of his wife, and includes a few translations from classic poets.

In a word, the volume is entirely characteristic of the times, when writing verses was a sort
of courtly accomplishment with which the grav-
est men were supposed to amuse their leisure
hours. That it was often a painful amusement
is witnessed by Dr. Moore himself, for he explains that his poems were not heedlessly thrown
off, but cost him much time and thought, and
were carefully and correctly composed. It is

there that they differ so radically from "A Visit from St. Nicholas," which, very evidently, was not composed carefully and correctly at all, but bubbled up in high spirits from the inspiration of the moment.

Only one other poem in the book bears any discoverable resemblance to "A Visit from St. Nicholas." That is an effusion called "The Pig and the Rooster," and a sub-title states that "the following piece of fun was occasioned by a subject for composition given to the boys of a grammar school attended by one of my sons— *viz.:* 'Which are to be preferred, the pleasures of a pig or a chicken?'" It starts off as follows:

On a warm sunny day, in the midst of July,
A lazy young pig lay stretched out in his sty,
Like some of his betters, most solemnly thinking
That the best things on earth are good eating and
  drinking.

These four lines are the best in the poem, which, as a whole, is vastly inferior to "A Visit from St. Nicholas," and entirely lacking in the spontaneity and sprightly fancy which make the latter so delightful. But it at least proves that Dr. Moore could, when he wished, write very passable anapæsts—a meter which he would naturally not employ for the didactic poems to which he was generally addicted.

76

A Visit from St. Nicholas

It will be remembered that it is admitted that the poem was taken from Dr. Moore's house to Troy by Miss Butler; that she might have supposed him to be the author without any specific claim on his part; and that it was probably she who gave his name to Editor Holley; consequently that the first connection of his name with the poem might have been wholly without his connivance. It is argued by Dr. Thomas that in the end Dr. Moore very possibly came to believe he really wrote it. "Having at last permitted his name to become connected with the poem, perhaps after denials which became successively fainter, before actual acquiescence took their place, it was possibly natural to find detailed evidence in support of a claim which at last may well have been really sincere. It is not difficult to believe that Dr. Moore actually came to think, as time went on, that the poem was really his own." That his claim was not at once disputed was due, it is alleged, to an entirely natural reluctance on the part of the Livingstons to call into question the veracity of the son of a Bishop and a professor of Biblical Learning.

There is a certain plausibility about all this, though it should be pointed out that there is no single written document extant to show that Henry Livingston ever claimed the authorship of "A Visit from St. Nicholas," even after its appearance in the Troy *Sentinel;* and it seems strange that, if he really wrote it and found every one to whom he read it so delighted with it, he did not himself, in the years following 1805, send it to some paper for publication. If we are to believe the Livingston chronology it remained unpublished for eighteen years. As to the surroundings of the two men, no doubt "Chelsea Farm" had a lawn and wide fireplaces as well as "Locust Grove," and Mrs. Moore was just as likely to be called "Mama" and to wear a 'kerchief over her head at night as was Mrs. Livingston!

Familiarity with the Saint Nicholas legend was also, of course, common to both men, and one is inclined to think that the solution of the riddle may be that Henry Livingston really did write a Christmas jingle to read to his children in 1805—and so did Clement Clarke Moore seventeen years later. These may very easily have been enough alike both in theme and treatment to create confusion in the memories of the Livingston family, and to cause them honestly to believe that the poem which subsequently became so famous and which was attributed to the New York theologian was the same one they had first heard in childhood from their father's lips. Charges of plagiarism have very often originated in just this way.

However, if no one else had ever claimed it,

and if its authorship had to be decided on internal evidence alone, "A Visit from St. Nicholas" might fairly be held to resemble the work of Henry Livingston much more closely than it resembles the work of Clement C. Moore—though, as another writer has pointed out, it must be remembered that *Alice in Wonderland* was written by a professor of mathematics, and that the *Nonsense Novels* and *The Elements of Political Science* are by one and the same hand.

But in the face of Dr. Moore's explicit claim, something more than indirect evidence of this sort is required. In 1844, when he included it among his published works, he was only sixty-three years of age, in full possession of all his faculties, and if the poem was not his, he was committing a theft of the basest and meanest sort, of whose nature he must have been fully conscious. To suppose that he would stoop so low for so paltry a purpose is to imply that he was really only a whited sepulcher. There is absolutely nothing else in his life to warrant such a supposition. He was a man of unblemished reputation, of high repute for integrity, of wide beneficence, of upright and kindly life, and rich in honors.

Conclusive indeed must be the proof to convince any one that he would soil himself by the theft of another man's poem in order to add one more leaf to his wreath of laurel. The only final and absolute proof would be the discovery of the poem in some published form prior to 1822. Until such proof is forthcoming, Dr. Moore's claim to its authorship cannot be justly denied, and the children whom it has delighted need not hesitate to gather around his grave, as heretofore, on Christmas eve, to do him honor.

THERE IS NO UNBELIEF

THERE IS NO UNBELIEF

There is no unbelief;
Whoever plants a seed beneath the sod
And waits to see it push away the clod,
He trusts in God.

There is no unbelief;
Whoever says, when clouds are in the sky,
"Be patient, heart; light breaketh by and by,"
Trusts the Most High.

There is no unbelief;
Whoever sees, 'neath winter's field of snow,
The silent harvest of the future grow—
God's power must know.

There is no unbelief;
Whoever lies down on his couch to sleep,
Content to lock each sense in slumber deep,
Knows God will keep.

There is no unbelief;
Whoever says "to-morrow," "the unknown,"
"The Future," trusts that power alone
He dares disown.

There is no unbelief;
The heart that looks on when dear eyelids
    close,
And dares to live when life has only woes,
    God's comfort knows.

There is no unbelief;
For thus by day and night unconsciously
The heart lives by the faith the lips deny.
    God knoweth why.

Lizzie York Case

THERE IS NO UNBELIEF

EUGENE BULMER, of "somewhere in Illinois" —was he a myth? Or was he really an industrious plagiarist, copying other people's verses and signing his name to them, with the result that they were all, in the end, attributed to Bulwer-Lytton because, sooner or later, some proofreader took it for granted that Bulmer was a misprint for Bulwer and changed it accordingly?

It was in that way, so John Luckey McCreery averred, that his poem, "There Is No Death," came to be attributed to Bulwer.

And years later Mrs. Lizzie York Case made precisely the same explanation with respect to another poem, "There Is No Unbelief," of which she claimed to be the author, but to which Bulwer's name was usually signed.

In the story of McCreery's struggle for recognition as the author of "There Is No Death," the remark was hazarded that, for some reason, Bulmer, the villain of the piece, was not altogether convincing. There was about him a certain puzzling elusiveness and insubstantiality. All that McCreery knew about him was his

85

name and that he lived "somewhere south of Dixon, Illinois."

Mrs. Case, apparently, knew even less; but really the only way to have her tell her story is to resort to the deadly parallel:

JOHN LUCKEY MCCREERY in *Songs of Toil and Triumph*, 1883:

One E. Bulmer, of Illinois, copied it ["There Is No Death"], signed his own name to it, and sent it as his own to the *Farmer's Advocate*, Chicago. The editor of some Wisconsin paper, whose name I have forgotten, if I ever knew, clipped it from the *Farmer's Advocate* for his own columns; but supposing that there was a misprint in the signature, changed the *m* therein to a *w*, and thus the name of "Bulwer" became attached to the poem.

LIZZIE YORK CASE in the Detroit *Free Press*, August 1, 1905:

But then began the strange appropriation by others and false ascribing of my little poem ["There Is No Unbelief"]. A man named Bulmer, of Illinois, copied the poem and sent it under his own name to the *Farmer's Advocate* of Chicago. A Wisconsin paper copied it, changing the name to Bulwer, assuming that "Bulmer" was a misprint. That accounts, I suppose, for its being accredited to Bulwer-Lytton.

Poor Bulmer! What sins were committed in thy name!

Or perhaps the real villain of the piece is that Wisconsin editor who, whenever he came across Bulmer's name attached to a poem, seems to have taken a fiendish delight in changing it to Bulwer. It may even be that Bulmer wrote some poems of his own which were reft from him in the same way and added to his British rival's already plethoric list.

Consider, too, the trusting nature of the editor of the *Farmer's Advocate*, who apparently never suspected that his favorite contributor was a thief, in spite of the activities of that other editor in Wisconsin.

, Consider, finally, the impossibility of both the above stories being true; and yet, in spite of them, there is every reason to believe both that McCreery wrote "There Is No Death," and that Mrs. Case wrote "There Is No Unbelief."

Their mistake seems to have been that they were overeager to prove it; or perhaps it was only Mrs. Case who was overeager, for McCreery promulgated the story first. It was originally told by him in 1869, and repeated *ad infinitum* until he died. Whether he invented Bulmer will never be known. Perhaps not, since the thing might have happened once. But it is inconceivable that it should have happened twice in exactly the same way. Undoubtedly Mrs. Case had read McCreery's story somewhere and adopted it, consciously or unconsciously, as her own. She was nearly seventy years old when her story was published in the *Free Press*, and perhaps her mind had failed a little.

Biographical data about Lizzie York Case are exceedingly scant. In 1905 she visited at Oak

Park, Illinois, at the home of a Mrs. M. L.
Rayne, with whom she apparently had a friendship of long standing, since Mrs. Rayne included one of her poems in a book entitled
What Can a Woman Do? published twenty
years previously. Mrs. Rayne's daughter, Mrs.
Lulu G. Niles, of Oak Park, gives the following information:

I do not know when or where Mrs. Case was
born. She died when she was a little over seventy
years old, and I am quite sure it was in Baltimore.
In a short introduction before a poem among others
in my mother's book, *What Can a Woman Do?*
[Detroit, 1884], my mother wrote:

"Mrs. Lizzie York Case is a Southern lady, a resident of Baltimore and vicinity for many years, and
at present living at Mobile, Alabama, where her
husband, Lieutenant Madison J. Case, is stationed in
the service of the United States navy. Mrs. Case
is descended from Quaker ancestry, and much of
the grace and versatility of character she possesses
is derived from that source. Many of her poems
have been published in household collections and
school readers, and are much admired for their high
educational standard."

The poem under the foregoing was "Faith and
Reason." This was in 1884, and her poem, "There
Is No Unbelief," was written many years later, I believe. Mrs. Case had it printed on cards that were
sent out to many of her friends. I cannot believe
that she would have done this if she had not been

88

There Is No Unbelief

the author. To hear Mrs. Case talk was like listening to a poem—she certainly was capable of writing "There Is No Unbelief."

One of the cards above referred to, autographed by Mrs. Case, is now in the possession of Mr. Vincent Starrett, of Chicago, and it is from this that the version of the poem herewith given is taken.

A little further information about Mrs. Case is contained in a letter from one of her friends, Mr. Daniel Gibbons, of Brooklyn, N. Y.:

Mrs. Case was the wife of Chief Engineer James Madison Case, U. S. Revenue Marine—now known as the Revenue Cutter Service. He was stationed on inspection duty, overseeing the construction of the U. S. Fish Commission steamer *Fish Hawk*, at the yards of the Pusey & Jones Co., Wilmington, Delaware, in 1881, and it was there that I knew him. He was a little bit of a man not much if any above five feet in height, making up by a large manner for his deficiency in inches. I never heard that Mrs. Case was a Friend. She was an uncommonly fine and refined woman.

A letter from Mrs. Mary E. Marshall, of New York City, adds the following:

During the winter of 1870, my husband and I boarded in a hotel in Cleveland, Ohio, and at this

89

time Mrs. Case was there. Her husband, Lieutenant Case, was on a revenue cutter on Lake Erie. I remember her telling me she was married during the Civil War and did not see her husband for months at a time. Mrs. Case was very blond and exceedingly pretty. I know she was a Southerner, but do not remember whether she was from Baltimore or somewhere in Virginia. I have always remembered vividly her vivacity, wit and charm.

It was presumably while Mrs. Case was visiting at Oak Park in 1905 that she wrote her story for the *Free Press,* and she also at that time met Dr. William E. Barton, pastor of the First Congregational Church there. Dr. Barton was to become one of her most redoubtable champions. He drew from her the story of "There Is No Unbelief," together with a few facts about her life, which he embodied in an article published in the *Advance,* a Congregationalist paper printed in Chicago, in its issue of April 1, 1915.

Dr. Barton did not learn from Mrs. Case either the date or place of her birth. She had been a widow for many years and was quite old when he met her in 1905. From a portrait of that date, which accompanies his article, she appears to be somewhere between sixty-five and seventy. It is not really a portrait—it is just a snap-shot showing her seated beneath some palms in California, where she had been living. The face is decidedly prepossessing, though a little pathetic, and there is pathos in the way she holds her head. Mrs. Case stated to Dr. Barton that in 1878 she was on the staff of the Detroit *Free Press*, and had been for several years. About 1880, her husband was transferred to Wilmington, Delaware, and later to California. Mrs. Case lived in California for a number of years, but finally came east again, and died, presumably in Baltimore, in 1911.

For many years "There Is No Unbelief" went the rounds of the press, and was read from hundreds of pulpits, and included in scores of compilations. It was usually accredited to Bulwer-Lytton, but sometimes Elizabeth Barrett Browning was named as its author, sometimes Charles Kingsley—sometimes even John Luckey McCreery! Finally, on August 1, 1905, Mrs. Lizzie York Case told, in the Detroit *Free Press*, the whole story of how she was inspired to write the poem.

Briefly, her story was this:

One morning, "about twenty-seven years ago"—that is to say, about 1878—she was breakfasting with a zealous young clergyman, who questioned her as to her religious belief. She told him that she had always clung to the faith of her fathers and was a Quakeress. Upon which her companion hastened to assure her that she was an unbeliever and would undoubtedly be damned.

"I am not afraid of that," Mrs. Case replied, "for there is no unbelief. The thing is unthinkable. I believe in everything that is good and beautiful and true; in God and man and nature; in love and life and joy. There is no unbelief."

The clergyman's rejoinder is not recorded. Probably he was vanquished by this eloquence. That night, Mrs. Case tossed upon a sleepless pillow and next morning, instead of preparing the regular weekly article which she states she was at that time contributing to the *Free Press,* she "dashed off the poem that had been framing in my mind all night."

"The *Free Press* published it," Mrs. Case continues, "and soon after letters came pouring in to me from all over the country thanking me for the verses and for the consolation which had been induced in many cases by them. They were copied by numberless newspapers and magazines. They were translated into many foreign languages. I heard of them being read from pulpits and quoted far and wide. Frances E. Willard and others set the verses to music. In short, the little poem which had been dashed off under the sting of a cruel word had touched a responsive chord in thousands of human hearts."

And then she tells the story of the mythical

92

There Is No Unbelief

Bulmer, as quoted above, adding that she had
always bitterly resented the fact that she was
robbed of credit for the poem, which she cherished "with the fondness of a mother for her
offspring." And she showed Dr. Barton, with
much pride, a book of poems by James Whitcomb Riley which he had sent her after inscrib-
ing it:

To
Mrs. Lizzie York Case,
Who lit the lone world's darkness, doubt and grief,
With truth's own song—"There Is No Unbelief."

There was one obvious way to confirm Mrs.
Case's story. That was to make a search of
the files of the Detroit *Free Press*. This bit of
bibliographical service was courteously undertaken by the custodian of the Burton Historical
Collection in the Detroit Public Library, and
the poem was discovered in the issue for
August 18, 1878. It is signed with Mrs. Case's
name, and of course settles the controversy.

It is interesting to compare the first version
with the later one. Both consist of seven
stanzas, and the first three are the same in both.
The earlier version then continues:

There is no unbelief,
Whoever says to-morrow, the unknown,
The future, trusts that power alone
He dare disown.

93

There is no unbelief,
O skeptic proud! light comes but from on high,
And so in grief, like faith, *you* turn your eye
　　Upward unconsciously.

There is no unbelief,
The heart that looks on when dear eyelids close
And dares to live when life has only woes,
　　Some comfort knows.

There is no unbelief,
The soul survives though all its loves may die;
The heart lives by the faith the lips deny,
　　God knoweth why.

It will be seen that, for once, revision was also improvement.

Eight other poems by Mrs. Case were found in the columns of the *Free Press*, as follows:

"God as a Thinker," in the issue of July 7, 1878.

"The Balance Sheet," in the issue of January 1, 1879.

"The Year's Immortality," in the issue of January 1, 1880.

"Florence," in the issue of September 29, 1880.

"We All Do Fade as a Leaf," in the issue of October 29, 1880.

"Mysterious Message," in the issue of October 29, 1880.

"Silence," in the issue of January 3, 1881.

"The Last Skylark," in the issue of January 19, 1881.

94

There Is No Unbelief

Three of these, it will be noted, are New Year's poems, their subject-matter being the usual banal moralizing, without any hint of poetic thought. The others show some skill at versification, and a happy phrase or two, but the only one which possesses even a germ of what may truly be termed poetry is the shortest of all:

WE ALL DO FADE AS A LEAF

You leaves that through the summer long
　　Such vernal beauty made,
It is your time for fading now:
　　O! leaves, *how do you fade?*

Why, in gold and crimson splendor
　　Ye flutter from the trees.
Great God, we thank Thee evermore
　　That we *do fade* like these.

And does such radiant glory
　　Go with us to the tomb?
Fade! Why if this it is to fade,
　　God, what is it to bloom?

The earliest discoverable book publication of "There Is No Unbelief" is in a little volume called *Flowers by the Wayside,* which appeared at Columbus, Ohio, in 1892. Two poems signed by Mrs. Case are included. One is "No Unbelief," of which only five stanzas are given,

95

and the other is fourteen lines of doggerel entitled "A Persian Fable," telling the story of a mythical bird with one wing which could fly only when its mate came along and hooked on to the wingless side!

Flowers by the Wayside is an octavo volume of 194 pages, gorgeously bound in crimson morocco, and was published by The Co-operative Publishing Co.—which probably means that the contributors paid for the privilege of having their poems included, and were perhaps to divide the profits, if any. At least the volume has all the earmarks of a book of that sort, and the verses which adorn its pages are almost without exception incredibly bad. "No Unbelief" is easily the best of the lot, and this was, perhaps, its first appearance between the covers of a book.

Six poems by Mrs. Case in addition to those which appeared in the *Free Press* are listed in Granger's *Index to Poetry and Recitations,* so that her complete works as they now survive consist of sixteen poems. "No Unbelief" is the only one which ever became widely known, and that of course was due not to its poetic merit but to its sentimental appeal. It has traveled hand in hand with McCreery's "There Is No Death." The two poems are spiritual twins.

It should be noted in passing that Mrs. Case never signed her first name Elizabeth, but always Lizzie.

There Is No Unbelief

Mrs. Case's article in the *Free Press* in 1905 by no means settled the question of the poem's authorship, and she was kept busy defending her claim until the day of her death. This she always did most vigorously. In 1908 she had a spirited controversy with a magazine which credited her poem to Bulwer and which refused to make any correction until she employed a lawyer and threatened to bring suit for damages.

And the controversy has outlived her. On January 15, 1915, the Chicago *Record-Herald* printed the poem, crediting it to Mrs. Case. Some readers objected, and a few days later the paper apologized for its mistake and explained that the poem was really written by Owen Meredith. Then Mrs. Case's friends unlimbered their batteries, and in the end a second apology was forthcoming and the credit restored to Mrs. Case. This is but one example of the merry dance which the question of the poem's authorship has led anthologists and editors for many years. Even in so recent and carefully edited a collection as *Songs of Challenge,* published in 1922, it is credited to Owen Meredith!

Let it be hoped that the discovery of the poem in the *Free Press,* under Mrs. Case's name, will settle the controversy once for all, and that her child will never again be snatched from its fond mother's arms.

CASEY AT THE BAT

CASEY AT THE BAT

The outlook wasn't brilliant for the Mudville
    nine that day:
The score stood four to two, with but one inning
    more to play,
And then when Cooney died at first, and Bar-
    rows did the same,
A pall-like silence fell upon the patrons of the
    game.

A straggling few got up to go in deep despair.
    The rest
Clung to that hope which springs eternal in the
    human breast;
They thought, "If only Casey could but get a
    whack at that—
We'd put up even money now, with Casey at
    the bat."

But Flynn preceded Casey, as did also Jimmy
    Blake,
And the former was a hoodoo, while the latter
    was a cake;
So upon that stricken multitude grim melancholy
    sat,
For there seemed but little chance of Casey get-
    ting to the bat.

But Flynn let drive a single, to the wonderment
    of all,
And Blake, the much despisèd, tore the cover off
    the ball;
And when the dust had lifted, and men saw
    what had occurred,
There was Jimmy safe at second and Flynn a-
    hugging third.

Then from five thousand throats and more
    there rose a lusty yell;
It rumbled through the valley, it rattled in the
    dell;
It pounded on the mountain and recoiled upon
    the flat,
For Casey, mighty Casey, was advancing to the
    bat.

There was ease in Casey's manner as he stepped
    into his place;
There was pride in Casey's bearing and a smile
    lit Casey's face.
And when, responding to the cheers, he lightly
    doffed his hat,
No stranger in the crowd could doubt 'twas
    Casey at the bat.

Ten thousand eyes were on him as he rubbed
    his hands with dirt;
Five thousand tongues applauded when he
    wiped them on his shirt;

Casey at the Bat

Then while the writhing pitcher ground the ball
 into his hip,
Defiance flashed in Casey's eye, a sneer curled
 Casey's lip.

And now the leather-covered sphere came hurt-
 ling through the air,
And Casey stood a-watching it in haughty gran-
 deur there.
Close by the sturdy batsman the ball unheeded
 sped—
"That ain't my style," said Casey. "Strike
 one!" the umpire said.

From the benches, black with people, there went
 up a muffled roar,
Like the beating of the storm-waves on a stern
 and distant shore;
"Kill him! Kill the umpire!" shouted some
 one on the stand;
And it's likely they'd have killed him had not
 Casey raised his hand.

With a smile of Christian charity great Casey's
 visage shone;
He stilled the rising tumult; he bade the game
 go on;
He signaled to the pitcher, and once more the
 dun sphere flew;
But Casey still ignored it, and the umpire said,
 "Strike two!"

"Fraud!" cried the maddened thousands, and
    echo answered "Fraud!"
But one scornful look from Casey and the
    audience was awed.
They saw his face grow stern and cold, they
    saw his muscles strain,
And they knew that Casey wouldn't let that ball
    go by again.

The sneer has fled from Casey's lip, his teeth
    are clenched in hate;
He pounds with cruel violence his bat upon the
    plate.
And now the pitcher holds the ball, and now
    he lets it go,
And now the air is shattered by the force of
    Casey's blow.

Oh, somewhere in this favored land the sun is
    shining bright;
The band is playing somewhere, and somewhere
    hearts are light,
And somewhere men are laughing, and little
    children shout;
But there is no joy in Mudville—great Casey
    has struck out.

                      Ernest L. Thayer

CASEY AT THE BAT

MENTION has been made of the comfortable and consoling theory held by many optimists that every great work of art possesses an immortal soul which ensures its survival through the ages, and that consequently nothing which has passed from human ken is worth lamenting, since the very fact that it died proves that it was not immortal, and therefore not a masterpiece. Francis W. Halsey, in *Our Literary Deluge,* stated this theory with much eloquence:

We may be absolutely certain that whatever is good will not die. Wherever exists a book that adds to our wisdom, that consoles our thought, it cannot perish. Nothing is so immortal as mere words, once they have been spoken fitly or divinely. A good book die! We shall sooner see the forests cut away from the hillside . . .

and so on.

Which is just empty rhetoric. Of course one cannot say definitely and finally that anything is lost so long as the world continues to support the human race, for there is always a possibility of finding it. Perhaps another Vermeer may be discovered some day, or a statue by Praxiteles, or the Gospel of St. Matthew. But the chances are against it. And it is just as certain that modern literature is built upon a foundation of forgotten masterpieces as that modern life moves over an earth compounded of the forgotten dead.

Indeed, the survival of masterpieces, far from being due to any inherent quality, is largely the result of accident. A few statues catch the conqueror's eye in the captured city and he carries them off—the rest are destroyed; the fleeing inmates snatch a few pictures from the walls of the burning house—the others go up in smoke; the anthologist chooses a few poems from among many to publish in his "Reliques" or "Pastorals," and the others vanish into darkness. We can only hope that, in each case, the best ones were selected, but there is no way to prove it.

And even when a masterpiece does survive, it very often needs a press agent before it is generally recognized as such. It was Chaplain McCabe who advertised the "Battle Hymn of the Republic" by singing it in his incomparable voice, Captain Coghlan who called the world's attention to "Hoch! der Kaiser" by reciting it at the psychological moment, and De Wolf Hopper who furnished the publicity which made a household word of "Casey at the Bat."

And yet Mr. Hopper does not deserve the

credit so much as Archibald Clavering Gunter, for it was the latter who discovered the poem in a newspaper, perceived its merits, and gave it to Mr. Hopper with the suggestion that he recite it. Now this was an extraordinary thing. It is easy enough to recognize a masterpiece after it has been carefully cleaned and beautifully framed and hung in a conspicuous place and certified by experts; but to stumble over it in a musty garret, covered with dust, to dig it out of a pile of junk and know it for a thing of beauty—only the true connoisseur can do that.

That is what Mr. Gunter did when he dug "Casey at the Bat" out of the smudgy columns of a newspaper more than thirty years ago. His novels have fallen into undeserved neglect, for some of them are rattling good yarns—who that met her will ever forget the beautiful flower-girl of the Jardin d'Acclimatation, with her white and red roses? At least let it be remembered that to him the American public owes its introduction to the supreme classic of baseball.

For every one has now agreed that that is what "Casey" is. But classics have a way of being despised or ignored by their contemporaries, and when the poem first appeared in the San Francisco *Examiner* nobody hailed it with shouts of joy or suspected that the great Casey was to become immortal. In fact, the *Examiner*

107

staff was rather proud that the New York *Sun* should think well enough of the poem to copy the last eight stanzas. The first five were remorselessly lopped off—but it has always been one of the inalienable rights of exchange editors to mutilate masterpieces, so nobody even thought of protesting, and it was in this acephalous form that Casey started on his travels through the east—a fact whose relevance will appear later on. Luckily it was in the *Examiner* and not in the *Sun* that Mr. Gunter saw it, so he got the complete poem. He cut it out and put it in his pocket and bided his time.

De Wolf Hopper was appearing at Wallack's Theater in New York City in a comic opera called *Prince Methusalem*. He was not then the public institution he has since become, but just a rising young comedian for whom "Wang" had not yet been written. However, even then, he had a wide circle of acquaintances, of whom Mr. Gunter was one. It chanced that one morning, as he was looking over the paper, Mr. Gunter saw the announcement that the New York and Chicago baseball clubs were to be at Wallack's that night as Mr. Hopper's guests. He bethought him of "Casey at the Bat," hunted up Mr. Hopper and gave it to him with the suggestion that he recite it. He added that it was a really great poem and was certain to make a hit with the baseball people.

108

Casey at the Bat

But the lengthy comedian regarded it with dismay, for it seemed to him even longer than himself. But when he read it over he saw its possibilities, pitched into it and mastered it in a couple of hours. He had no need to study its atmosphere, for he had always been a baseball fan himself and could visualize every line.

When the curtain went up that night the two teams, headed by Anson and Ewing, were in the boxes, and in the course of the show Mr. Hopper, as he puts it, "pulled Casey on them." Any one who has ever heard him recite it can imagine the effect. It brought down the house, and then and there took its place in his repertoire.

After the performance he hunted up Mr. Gunter and asked him who wrote "Casey," for it seemed only fair that the author should have a share of the glory; but Mr. Gunter did not know. It was not until four or five years later, after Mr. Hopper had recited the poem during a performance of "Wang" at Worcester, Mass., that a note was sent in to him asking him to come around to a club and meet the author of "Casey." Of course he went, and was introduced to Ernest L. Thayer. "Over the details of the wassail that followed," says Mr. Hopper, "I will draw the veil of charity."

Meanwhile, as is usually the case with famous fugitive poems, many claimants to the authorship had appeared, and some of them had even tried to compel Mr. Hopper to pay a royalty for the privilege of reciting it. The basis of most of these claims was exceedingly fantastic, but one man, at least, succeeded in building an elaborate structure of evidence in support of his own contention, and to this day there is no little confusion in the public mind as to when and by whom the poem was written.

The first person to whom it was ascribed with some appearance of authority was Joseph Quinlan Murphy. In 1902 Frederic Lawrence Knowles edited an anthology called *A Treasury of Humorous Poetry*, and included an early version of "Casey at the Bat," crediting it to Mr. Murphy. The only information about him was given in the index of authors, where it was stated that he died in 1902. By the time anybody thought to question this, Mr. Knowles himself was dead, and his publishers could say nothing more than that he had always been very careful to trace the authorship of anything of which he was in doubt.

Richter's *History and Records of Baseball* states, in a chapter on "Writers on Baseball," that Joseph Murphy was at one time on the staff of the St. Louis *Globe-Democrat*, but the editor of that paper writes that "the oldest members of our editorial staff do not recall any person named

110

Joseph Quinlan Murphy ever being connected with this paper. Joseph A. Murphy, nationally known racehorse judge, was sporting editor of the *Globe-Democrat* in the early 'eighties, but he has never been credited with the authorship of the poem, 'Casey at the Bat.'" So who Joseph Quinlan Murphy was, as well as Mr. Knowles's reasons for attributing the poem to him, remain a matter of conjecture. The publishers of *A Treasury of Humorous Poetry,* after some investigating of their own, evidently concluded that Mr. Knowles had made a mistake, for in recent editions of the book the poem is credited to Ernest L. Thayer.

Another man to whom the poem has been attributed was an Irishman named William Valentine, who died in the late 'nineties while on the staff of the New York *World.* The basis for his claim rests largely upon the evidence of Mr. Frank J. Wilstach, the compiler of the *Dictionary of Similes.* Here is the story as Mr. Wilstach has told it in two recent letters:

Will Valentine, a young Irishman, came up from the Kansas City *Star* to the Sioux City (Iowa) *Tribune* in 1885 to be city editor. He was constantly writing verse. On the back page of the *Tribune* I was at that time conducting a column which, shamefacedly I may say, was supposed to be like Eugene Field's "Sharps and Flats" in the Chicago *Record*. It was bad; but Valentine every once in a while would hand me a bit of verse which I would run, he signing it "February 14," being St. Valentine's day, as 'twere.

Valentine and I were roommates. My brother Walter sent me a set of Macaulay's works and one Sunday evening, reading "Horatius at the Bridge," I said to Valentine that here was a good opportunity to parody "Horatius" by a poem about a Mick at the Bat. We were then baseball crazy. Valentine read the Macaulay poem and went ahead and wrote a piece he called "Casey at the Bat."

It is rather curious that all the claimants for this poem have been seemingly unaware that "Casey at the Bat" is a parody on "Horatius at the Bridge," with the same meter and the end of each stanza very nearly the same.

I left Sioux City in 1887 and never heard of Valentine or thought anything of his poem until one night I met him on lower Broadway in 1898. I was then press agent at the Broadway Theatre and Valentine was employed on the New York *World*. He promised to come to see me at the Broadway Theatre. About the first thing he mentioned to me at this meeting was that De Wolf Hopper, who was reciting his poem "Casey at the Bat," was giving credit for its authorship to a man named Thayer. He asked me if I didn't recall the fact that I had suggested "Casey at the Bat" to him in consequence of reading "Horatius at the Bridge." I told him that I did recall it, but that I had forgotten all

112

about it during the years intervening. I subsequently learned that Will Valentine died of typhoid fever while an employee of the New York *World* a few months after I met him.

This is a clear-cut narrative, but it is modified a little in Mr. Wilstach's second letter, in which he says:

This matter of "Casey at the Bat" is so nebulous that I would really like to withdraw from it. However, I am certain of two things: first, that I suggested to Will Valentine that he write a burlesque of Macaulay's "Horatius at the Bridge"; second that he did write this burlesque and that it was called "Casey at the Bat." I was present in the room when he wrote it. I haven't seen his copy since that afternoon, or a day or two afterwards, when it appeared in the *Tribune*. Whether the present "Casey at the Bat" is a re-write of Valentine's I can't say.

An inquiry of the Sioux City *Tribune* had previously elicited the information that Mr. Valentine had indeed been employed on the paper in 1887, but that there was no apparent foundation for the statement that he had written "Casey at the Bat." It was also stated (by Mr. Thayer) that Mr. Valentine's claim had been investigated about 1905 by the San Francisco law firm of Lent & Humphrey, who had

sent an agent to Sioux City especially for that
purpose, and that no evidence had been found
to support it. But in view of the letters from
Mr. Wilstach, it was evident that the only way
to settle the question definitely was by a careful
search of the *Tribune* files. Mr. John H.
Kelly, the editor of the *Tribune,* was accordingly requested to have such a search made. He
did so, and the following letter from him is
self-explanatory:

We have had one of our men go over every copy
of the *Tribune* during 1885-1888 inclusive, and he
found the column referred to in your letter in numerous forms; but did not find the much sought
"Casey at the Bat." It would have been a very
real pleasure and distinction to have claimed the
great "Casey."

So, whatever the poem was that Mr. Valentine
wrote at Mr. Wilstach's suggestion, it was evidently not the present "Casey at the Bat." Indeed, this might fairly be inferred from Mr.
Wilstach's own letters, in which he emphasizes
the fact that Mr. Valentine's poem was written
as a parody on "Horatius at the Bridge." "Casey
at the Bat" in no way suggests "Horatius"—except perhaps by a very faint similarity in the
basic idea. But its form and character are entirely different, as the first stanza of "Horatius"
will show:

Casey at the Bat

Lars Porsena of Clusium
By the Nine Gods he swore
That the great house of Tarquin
Should suffer wrong no more.
By the Nine Gods he swore it,
And named a trysting-day,
And bade his messengers ride forth,
East and west and south and north,
To summon his array.

There is still a third aspirant. A man with the extraordinary name of D'Vys—George Whitefield D'Vys—of Cambridge, Mass., has been a persistent and undiscouraged claimant for many years; he has related the circumstances of the composition of the poem repeatedly and at great length; he has even, at the instance of the late Dr. Harry Thurston Peck, who discussed the question of authorship in the *Scrap Book* for December, 1908, gone before a notary public and sworn that his story was true. This story, much condensed from D'Vys's diffuse narrative, but with all its essential details, is as follows:

On the first or second Sunday of August, 1886, D'Vys and a friend named Edward L. Cleveland were loitering about the ball grounds at Franklin Park, Boston, when a sudden inspiration seized D'Vys, and he started to write "Casey" on the margin of a Boston *Globe* he found flying across the field. "I was fairly wild as I mapped it out," he says, "and when I

115

got home I wrote it, 'There was ease in Casey's manner,' etc., and the thirty-two lines I sent to Mr. O. P. Caylor, of the New York *Sporting Times,* of which I held his red card credentials as correspondent." He adds that the poem appeared in the *Sporting Times* within the following week.

In another statement D'Vys says, "It went bearing the word 'Anon.' as a signature because of the great antipathy held by my stern parent toward all things literary." As D'Vys says he was born in 1860, and was consequently twenty-six years old in 1886, one might suppose he would have somewhat outgrown his awe of the stern parent. But apparently he never did—at least he never wrote any more poetry!

Unfortunately no file of the *Sporting Times* of 1886 is known to exist, and Mr. Caylor has long been dead. Also unfortunately D'Vys's evidence was lost. His story is that in 1897, while he was ill, the Boston *Globe* (the same paper whose margin, by a singular coincidence, had recorded the first draft of "Casey" eleven years before!) printed the poem, with five additional stanzas, and attributed it to Ernest L. Thayer. Being too ill to go himself, he sent his mother around to the *Globe* office next day with his one and only copy of the *Sporting Times* containing the eight original stanzas, and also two letters from Mr. Caylor confirming

116

his authorship. The *Globe* people assured Mrs. D'Vys that her son would receive full justice, but no correction was ever made.

"Unfortunately," continues D'Vys, "the little mother left with the gentleman with whom she talked the proof positive, and unfortunately she failed to ask his name"; and for the third time unfortunately D'Vys was never able to get his evidence back; yes, and even for the fourth time unfortunately D'Vys further records that a notebook filled with all his other rhymes about baseball and Mudville was carelessly left by him on a seat in Cambridge Common and could never again be found. From which it would appear that D'Vys certainly had a run of bad luck!

Out of this farrago one fact emerges: that D'Vys claims to have written the last eight stanzas of "Casey at the Bat" some time in August, 1886. He was always complaining about the fellow who had spoiled his poem by prefixing five other stanzas to it. Now let it be recalled that in the summer of 1888 the New York *Sun* had introduced the poem to the East by quoting the last eight stanzas only. Then finally consider a letter from Edward L. Cleveland, of Shelby, Montana, to the effect that he was indeed with Mr. D'Vys on that memorable Sunday at Franklin Park, and that D'Vys had really written out a part at least of "Casey at the Bat,"—but that the Sunday was in the latter part of September, *1889.* The inference is obvious.

James V. McClaverty, of Cambridge, Mass., who had kept for many years a complete file of *Sporting Life,* to which he made an index, and had also in his possession many copies of the *Sporting Times,* subsequently produced further evidence—if any were needed—to disprove D'Vys's claim.

D'Vys alleged that he sent his poem at once to O. P. Caylor, editor of the New York *Sporting Times;* but in *Sporting Life* for October 23, 1897, there is an obituary of Mr. Caylor, who died in that month and year, in which it is stated that he did not become editor of the *Sporting Times* until 1890.

D'Vys also asserted that his poem was published in the *Sporting Times* some time during August, 1886; but in an editorial in the issue of that paper for August 26, 1888, it is distinctly stated that its first issue was dated March 6, 1887.

Finally, in the issue for Sunday, July 29, 1888, the *Sporting Times* actually contains the last eight stanzas of "Casey at the Bat," in what is substantially the correct form, except that the name "Casey" is changed to "Kelly," "Mudville" to "Boston," and the poem is entitled, "Kelly at the Bat," with a sub-title which

118

states that it was "Adapted from the San Francisco *Examiner*."

Surely, after all this, it is perfectly safe, so far as the falsity of Mr. D'Vys's claim is concerned, to write: Q. E. D.

But the adaptation in the *Sporting Times* added one more snarl to the tangle. "Mike" Kelly, "the $10,000 beauty," "the Only Mike," "King Kelly," to mention only a few of his nicknames, was at that time the bright particular star of the Boston team, which had paid the then unprecedented sum of $10,000 for him. He was already the hero of a very popular song, "Slide, Kelly, Slide!" The Boston fans worshiped him, and his prowess at the bat had more than once pulled his team out of a hole. The poem fitted him perfectly and to change "Casey" to "Kelly" and "Mudville" to "Boston" was to give it a point which every baseball enthusiast at once understood. So it became increasingly popular with exchange editors, and many old-time devotees of the diamond still treasure it in its adapted form, believing it to be the original one.

Now for the real story of the poem.

When the late George Hearst decided to run for senator from California in 1885, he realized the need of an influential organ, and bought the San Francisco *Examiner* to promote his political ambitions. When the campaign was over, he had no further use for the paper, and presented it to his son, William Randolph Hearst, who had just graduated from Harvard College. The latter had already shown some journalistic leanings, having been associated with the Harvard *Lampoon,* and when he started west to demonstrate to the people of California how a newspaper should be run, he took along three members of the *Lampoon* staff to help him do it. They were Eugene Lent, F. H. Briggs and Ernest L. Thayer. Thayer had been president of the *Lampoon* during his last three years in college, and was Ivy Orator of his class.

Of course they all had nicknames. "Genie" Lent was to assist with the editorial work; "Fatty" Briggs was to do the cartoons; "Phin-nie" Thayer was to conduct a humorous column. Thayer signed his column "Phin," and his most successful contributions to it were a series of ballads begun in the fall of 1887, and continuing every Sunday for two or three months. During the winter his health failed, and he was compelled to return to his home at Worcester, Mass. He continued, however, to write the ballads, and in the spring of 1888 wrote "Casey at the Bat" and sent it on. It was published by the *Examiner* on Sunday, June 3, 1888, signed, as usual, "Phin." There it is to this day for anybody to see.

120

Casey at the Bat

Every newspaperman in San Francisco, of course, knew who "Phin" was, but nobody else did, and so when the poem was copied by other papers, the meaningless signature was usually lopped off. Meanwhile, Mr. Thayer had quit the newspaper business and gone into the more profitable vocation of manufacturing woolen goods at Worcester, and people gradually forgot that he had once been a humorist. But after Mr. D'Vys's claims had been given a wide publicity, he went before a notary public at Worcester and made an affidavit to the facts of the case—although, as he remarks, the affidavit "left D'Vys quite undiscouraged." He too had made an affidavit!

But Mr. Thayer's story is supported by a great deal of outside evidence. Eugene Lent, who went west with him and was a member of the *Examiner* staff when "Casey" was written, became afterwards one of the best known lawyers in San Francisco, the senior member of the firm of Lent & Humphrey, and on more than one occasion has borne testimony to his personal knowledge that Mr. Thayer wrote the poem; Theodore F. Bonnet, who was covering baseball for the *Examiner* at the time, has also told the story of the poem's first appearance; in 1896, Mr. Hearst asked Mr. Thayer to write another series of ballads, this time for the New York *Journal*, and he contributed four

121

during the following winter, all but one of which, "Oppenheimer's Barbecue," appeared in the Sunday supplement; many persons have testified to their long acquaintance with Mr. Thayer, to their familiarity with his verse, and to its similarity in style and quality to "Casey at the Bat."

In May, 1908, the New York *Sun* published a somewhat imaginative interview with a San Francisco newspaperman (name not given), which, although inaccurate in some of its details, gives a little further information about Mr. Thayer.   It says in part:

Genie Lent's father wanted him to be a lawyer, and he is a lawyer now, and Thayer's father wanted him to go into the wool business at Worcester. He's there now.   But both rich papas could be made to yield to a touch now and then, and at such times journalism did not greatly concern that bunch of Harvard stars.

Then there were times when papas were obdurate, and Briggs would draw some pictures to illustrate Phinnie Thayer's verses.   Thayer could write rhymes while thinking about anything else that pleased him.   One day he wrote "Casey at the Bat." He didn't think much of it, but he sat up and took notice when the *Sun* praised it.

I guess it was the *Sun's* praise that started trouble.   The verses began to appear in the backwoods and mountain-top papers signed with the names of

local bards. Then the song birds on the city papers
began to sign their names to it, and pretty soon you
could get a rise out of Phinnie by asking which of
the poets he lifted it from.

In final proof of Mr. Thayer's claim there
is the internal evidence of the poem itself, and
if there were no affidavits or other evidence at
all, it would be sufficient. Mr. D'Vys claims
that he wrote the last eight stanzas, and that
somebody else tacked on the first five; he even
made the remarkable assertion that he was convinced that the person who had written those
five stanzas was the same one who had picked
up the notebook full of his verses which he
(D'Vys) had carelessly left lying on a bench
in Cambridge Common, "because he used the
names I ever used in all my baseball rhymes."
This, of course, is too puerile for words; and
an examination of the poem will convince any
one that it was written by one man. It is an
entity in style and manner. More than that,
the poem is incomplete without the first five
stanzas, which describe the situation at the moment Casey goes to bat and are necessary to an
understanding of it.
So the case seems complete.
The only rift in it is furnished by the reminiscences of De Wolf Hopper. He writes:

"Casey at the Bat" first appeared in the San Francisco *Examiner* in the early eighties. It was found by Archibald Clavering Gunter, who gave it to me. I recited it in New York City at Wallack's Theatre. I should think about '85. I did not find out until four years later that the initials E. L. T. at the bottom of the article were those of Mr. Ernest L. Thayer of Worcester, Mass. I met him very pleasantly and he gave me some manuscripts of other works of his, which are just as good as "Casey" but not so appealing to the public. Many people have claimed the authorship of "Casey," but I know beyond the peradventure of a doubt that Mr. Thayer was the one. I have recited it heaven knows how many thousand times, and shall probably continue so to do until the end of my terrestrial career, and probably in the Great Beyond.

In an interview published in *Caste*, some years ago, Mr. Hopper names 1887 definitely as the year in which he began to recite the poem, and here again he says that the copy which Mr. Gunter gave him was signed E. L. T. Now of course he could not have recited it either in 1885 or 1887 if Mr. Thayer wrote it; and if the version Mr. Gunter gave him was signed E. L. T. it could not have been cut from the *Examiner*, or been copied from the *Examiner*, because the verses there were signed "Phin."

When these discrepancies were pointed out

to Mr. Hopper, he replied that very possibly it was not until 1888 he first recited the poem, but he adds quite positively, "the initials E. L. T. were at the foot of the copy Mr. Gunter gave me. The nom de plume 'Phin' did not appear." This is probably a slip of memory, but if Mr. Hopper is right, it is one more item in Mr. Thayer's favor. In his book, *Once a Clown Always a Clown,* Mr. Hopper says that he first recited the poem at Wallack's Theatre, on May 13, 1888; but a subsequent letter from Mrs. Hopper states that it was really sometime in August, 1888, which is probably the correct date.

It is worth pointing out that the poem has sometimes been ascribed to "Phineas Thayer"— it is easy to see why.

Mr. Thayer was born at Lawrence, Mass., in 1863, but his family shortly thereafter moved to Worcester, and he was graduated from the Worcester high school in 1881. Four years later he graduated from Harvard College, engaged in journalistic work, as has been said, in San Francisco until the winter of 1887, when he returned to Worcester and went into his father's woolen business. He retired some years later, and after traveling widely, settled down at Santa Barbara, Cal., where he now lives. He has never thought it worth while to gather his verse together in book form.

"Please to understand that I never had any pretensions as a writer of verse," Mr. Thayer writes. "During my brief connection with the *Examiner*, I put out large quantities of nonsense, both prose and verse, sounding the whole newspaper gamut from advertisements to editorials. In general quality 'Casey' (at least in my judgment), is neither better nor worse than much of the other stuff. Its persistent vogue is simply unaccountable, and it would be hard to say, all things considered, if it has given me more pleasure than annoyance. The constant wrangling about the authorship, from which I have tried to keep aloof, has certainly filled me with disgust."

The version of "Casey at the Bat" which accompanies this article is the one supplied by Mr. Thayer to the *Bookman* some years ago. It is not as good in some respects as the earlier version—revision has destroyed a little of its spontaneity and vim. But it is used here in accordance with the specific request of the author. There have been numberless imitations, and parodies, and sequels, the best of which is perhaps "Casey's Revenge," by Grantland Rice, but none of them possesses the rich humor and masterly rhythm of the one and only original.

IF I SHOULD DIE TO-NIGHT

IF I SHOULD DIE TO-NIGHT

If I should die to-night,
My friends would look upon my quiet face
Before they laid it in its resting-place,
And deem that death had left it almost fair;
And, laying snow-white flowers against my hair,
Would smooth it down with tearful tenderness,
And fold my hands with lingering caress,—
Poor hands, so empty and so cold to-night!

If I should die to-night,
My friends would call to mind with loving
    thought
Some kindly deed the icy hands had wrought,
Some gentle word the frozen lips had said,
Errands on which the willing feet had sped;
The memory of my selfishness and pride,
My hasty words would all be put aside,
And so I should be loved and mourned to-night.

If I should die to-night,
Even hearts estranged would turn once more
    to me,
Recalling other days remorsefully;
The eyes that chill me with averted glance
Would look upon me as of yore, perchance,

And soften in the old familiar way,
For who could war with dumb, unconscious
    clay?
So I might rest, forgiven of all to-night.

Oh, friends! I pray to-night,
Keep not your kisses for my dead, cold brow:
The way is lonely, let me feel them now.
Think gently of me; I am travelworn;
My faltering feet are pierced with many a
    thorn.
Forgive, oh, hearts estranged, forgive, I plead!
When dreamless rest is mine I shall not need
The tenderness for which I long to-night.

              Arabella Eugenia Smith.

IF I SHOULD DIE TO-NIGHT

If I should die to-night,
And you should come to my cold corpse and say,
Weeping and heartsick o'er my lifeless clay—
If I should die to-night,
And you should come in deepest grief and
    woe—
And say: "Here's that ten dollars that I owe,"
I might arise in my large white cravat
And say, "What's that?"

If I should die to-night,
And you should come to my cold corpse and
    kneel,
Clasping my bier to show the grief you feel,
I say, if I should die to-night,
And you should come to me, and there and then
Just even hint at paying me that ten,
I might arise the while,
But I'd drop dead again.

Ben King.

IF I SHOULD DIE TO-NIGHT

THERE are a few poems in the English language which possess the dubious distinction of having been made famous by a parody. Southey's "Father William" is perhaps the classic example. It was Lewis Carroll who turned the poet laureate's labored homily upon the advantages of a well-spent youth into the delightful nonsense which Alice repeated at the command of the Caterpillar. And similarly, in America, it was Ben King who put so much pep and point into a joyous parody of some pensive verses by Arabella Eugenia Smith that he effectively rescued them from the oblivion which otherwise would certainly have been their portion.

Under date of July 24, 1916, an Associated Press dispatch from Santa Barbara, Cal., announced the death at the age of seventy-two of the author of "If I Should Die To-night," and thereby awoke the echoes of an old controversy—for not only was this Miss Smith's one published poem, but, as has been the case with so many of the ewe lambs of literature, the honor of being its author was disputed by many claimants.

132

If I Should Die To-night

Miss Smith—so far as known—never told the story of the inspiration or impulse which produced "If I Should Die To-night," and the facts of her life are shrouded in the obscurity of the undistinguished. But if she was seventy-two years old in 1916, she must have been born in 1844, and Stedman & Hutchinson, in their *Cyclopedia of American Literature*, state that this event took place at Litchfield, Ohio. Apparently her family soon moved west, for it is likewise stated that she resided at Percival, Iowa, from 1850 to 1874. She graduated from Tabor College, and afterwards became an instructor there—and that is all.

It is from the same authority one learns that "If I Should Die To-night" appeared first in the *Christian Union* of June 18, 1873. Its sentiment was absolutely in tune with that sentimental era, and it was soon being copied by all the exchange editors of the country. It became a favorite recitation at church fairs and Sunday school entertainments. It was set to music, replete with minors, and so found its way to many a heart. In a word, the poem was a great success.

As usual, its author's name soon became detached from it as something of no importance. After all, what did it matter who wrote it? As Eugene Field so eloquently put it, "Homer's harp is broken and Horace's lyre is unstrung, and the voices of the great singers are hushed; but their songs, their songs are imperishable! Oh, friend, what moots it to them or to us who gave this epic or that lyric to immortality? The singer belongs to a year, his song to all time!"

Which would be all very well but for the fact that there are always a lot of pirates sailing the literary seas ready to spring upon and claim as a prize any poem whose author is unknown. It was so in this case, and the question of the authorship of "If I Should Die Tonight" was soon inextricably confused—a confusion which has persisted to the present day. The latest edition of Granger's *Index to Poetry and Recitations* attributes it to Robert C. V. Meyers, of Philadelphia, on what authority does not appear. Mr. Meyers died a few years ago, and has no discoverable representative to whom an appeal for further information can be made; but he was not born until 1858, and was consequently only fifteen years old in 1873. "If I Should Die Tonight" is, indeed, juvenile—but it is not as juvenile as that!

Mr. Meyers was not the only claimant—if he really was a claimant. It was at various times attributed, among others, to Alice Cary and Father Abram J. Ryan, but the most persistent aspirant was Irvine Dungan, of Jack-

son, Ohio, and at one time the controversy was
quite a cause célèbre throughout the Middle
West.

About 1890, the Jackson *Standard* published
a page of local poetry to prove that as an abode
of the Muses Jackson was singularly favored.
Among these poems, which had, of course, been
contributed by the authors, was "If I Should
Die To-night," signed with Mr. Dungan's
name.

Jackson is an altogether undistinguished
Middle Western town of a few thousand in-
habitants, with a Main Street where most of
its business is transacted, and various side
streets bordered by the unpretentious homes of
its citizens. There were no poetry experts
among them, so when Mr. Dungan asserted
that he had written "If I Should Die To-
night," nobody thought of contradicting him.
For he was one of Jackson's most prominent
men—a lawyer, and sufficiently powerful in
local politics to secure the nomination for Congress and actually to be elected for two or three
terms in the early 'nineties. The verses with
his name attached were copied by first one Ohio
paper and then another, for local patriotism is
strong among the Buckeyes; and the only un-
toward development was the announcement by
Colonel William Betts, also prominent in Ohio
politics in those days, that he had at last dis-

covered who stole his pocketbook during the
Republican State Convention at Columbus, because it had in it that very poem.

However, his intimation that Mr. Dungan
had stolen the poem as well as the pocket-book
was vitiated by the fact that the latter was able
to prove that he never attended Republican con-
ventions, being himself a staunch Democrat, as
befitted the resident of a town named after the
the greatest democrat of them all! So his
laurels seemed secure.

But when, in 1911, the Ohio *State Journal*
published the poem, at the request of a correspondent, with Mr. Dungan's name attached
as usual, some sharp on the staff of the Gallipolis *Tribune* dug up the poem in Stedman
& Hutchinson's compilation and found it attributed to Miss Smith, together with the date
of its first appearance in the *Christian Union*
in 1873. The *Tribune* thereupon animad-
verted editorially upon literary thieves and
credulous editors, and challenged the *State
Journal* to prove that Mr. Dungan was really
what he claimed to be.

The *Journal*, of course, accepted the challenge and a few days later published the following statement:

We showed the *Tribune* article to Mr. Dungan,
who, after laughing heartily over it, said: "Why, I

read that poem from the original manuscript in 1867, before a large audience in the courthouse in Jackson. Let's see: there are some men now living who were there and heard me read it. There were Horace Chapman, now living in Columbus; Arch Mayo, now of Los Angeles; Tom Moore, G. David of Jackson, and others whom I might recall. Ask them."

We are not insistent upon the claim that Mr. Dungan is the author. We gave him credit because his name has been attached to the poem for forty years. If it is so grand a poem that his authorship may be doubted, why give the claim to Belle Eugenia Smith? Are her credentials any better? If Longfellow's or Lowell's name had been attached to the poem no one would have doubted the authorship. Of course it comes natural when a fameless name is accorded the credit to hesitate. We hope the Gallipolis *Tribune* will pursue the matter further.

The *Tribune* did pursue it, and in the course of time fired a veritable broadside by publishing a letter from Elmer C. Powell, a fellow-Jacksonian of Mr. Dungan, which, as it put it, did not leave the *Journal* a leg to stand on.

Mr. Powell, who seems to have been of a methodical mind, ranged his proofs in the following order:

1. Of the persons mentioned by Mr. Dungan as having been present when he read his poem before a large and appreciative audience in the Jackson

county courthouse in 1867, only two were living. One was seven years old at the time and lived in Pike county, while the other did not become a resident of Jackson county until twenty years later.

2. The Jackson county courthouse burned down in 1860, and was not rebuilt for many years. There was no courthouse in 1867.

3. A book called *The History of the Scioto Valley*, published in 1884, contained a very laudatory sketch of Mr. Dungan's life (presumably written by himself), but strangely enough made no mention of the fact that he was the author of "If I Should Die To-night."

4. Mr. Powell had persuaded Mr Dungan to read to him some of his original poetry, which proved to be so sadly deficient in rhyme, rhythm and content that he could not persuade even the local paper to print it—which was saying much!

5. Mr. Powell had known Mr. Dungan for thirty-three years, and in all that time had never known him to get a line of poetry published, in spite of the most industrious efforts to that end.

6. Mr. Powell challenged Mr. Dungan to submit a sample of his verse to the *State Journal*, agreeing, if the *Journal* published it, never again to question his authorship of "If I Should Die To-night."

After which withering assault the *State Journal* confessed that it did indeed feel shaky in the legs, and begged to be excused from meddling in the matter any further. Nor, so far as the record shows, did any rejoinder ever come from Mr. Dungan. What he did to Mr. Powell is also unrecorded, but the subsequent relations between the two men were undoubtedly somewhat strained.

Enter, then, Ben King.

It is a curious fact that, although a volume of Ben King's verse was published after his death for the benefit of the family he left behind him, he is almost as much a one-poem man as Miss Smith is a one-poem woman, and practically his sole claim to remembrance is based upon his parody of her poem.

There has always been a great deal of confusion in the public mind as to who was the author of which. In fact not long ago "A Constant Reader" sent the following note to a well-known literary weekly, which solemnly published it:

I notice "M. D." asked for the words to Ben King's poem, "If I Should Die To-night." You published a parody on it. Inclosed find the poem as recited by him at a banquet in Bowling Green, Ky. He was found dead in bed the next morning.

And the words of Miss Smith's poem followed.

Now Ben King was indeed found dead one morning in a hotel room in Bowling Green— but that was in 1894, so that it would be nearly as impossible to ascertain what he really did recite as it would be to substantiate Irvine Dungan's description of that literary evening at the Jackson county courthouse in 1867. Of course he might have recited the original and followed it with his parody, and his auditors might have jumped to the conclusion that he wrote both of them, but all this is shrouded in the mists of three decades—to say nothing of the potations which no doubt accompanied the banquet.

In the volume of Ben King's collected poems published shortly after his death, there is an introduction by John McGovern which gives an admirable picture of the man.

"He began," writes Mr. McGovern, "as the expositor of 'The Maiden's Prayer' on the piano, where each accented note was flat or sharp, and the music flowed rapidly, or over great difficulties, as the score might determine. He arose, and looking half-witted, recited with unapproachable modesty the stammering delight which he would feel 'If He Could Be by Her.' He frowsled his hair and became Paderewski, who forthwith fell upon the piano tooth and nail, tore up the track, derailed the symphony, went downstairs and shook the furnace, fainted at the pedals, and was carried out rigid by supers—the greatest pianist of any age.

"He wrote 'If I Should Die To-night'—a

parody that was accepted as the true original, the sum, the center of the great If-I-should-die-to-night system of thought and poetry. He wrote the poet's lament—that there was nothing to eat but food, and nowhere to fall but off. He was coldly, then not coldly, then warmly received by the church fairs, the clubs, and the Elks, where he got a supper—if any were left. At last he charged a small sum for appearing publicly, and this sum was rapidly enlarging and his fortune was in sight, when the hotel porter found him dead in his room at Bowling Green."

Not very much is known about his life. Opie Read wrote a short biography of him to follow Mr. McGovern's appreciation in his book of verses, but beyond recording that his full name was Benjamin Franklin King, that he was born at St. Joseph, Mich., March 17, 1857, that he was a sort of musical genius in his youth, and was survived by a widow and two sons, it is singularly empty of information.

"If I Should Die To-night" is the first poem in the book. For the rest, the verses are the usual run of mediocre humorous chaff, which filled the "columns" of that period. Most of them are in dialect, and with two exceptions, there is nothing about any of them to be remembered. One of the exceptions is this parody on Longfellow:

HOW OFTEN

They stood on the bridge at midnight,
  In a park not far from town;
They stood on the bridge at midnight
  Because they didn't sit down.

The moon rose o'er the city
  Behind the dark church spire;
The moon rose o'er the city
  And kept on rising higher.

How often, oh! how often
  They whispered words so soft;
How often, oh! how often,
  How often, oh! how oft.

The second exception is the first two quatrains of "The Pessimist":

Nothing to do but work,
  Nothing to eat but food,
Nothing to wear but clothes
  To keep one from going nude.

Nothing to breathe but air,
  Quick as a flash 'tis gone;
Nowhere to fall but off,
  Nowhere to stand but on.

These represent the sum of Ben King's achievement—the best that was in him.

WAITING

WAITING

Serene, I fold my hands and wait,
  Nor care for wind, or tide, or sea;
I rave no more 'gainst Time or Fate,
  For lo! my own shall come to me.

I stay my haste, I make delays,
  For what avails this eager pace?
I stand amid the eternal ways,
  And what is mine shall know my face.

Asleep, awake, by night or day,
  The friends I seek are seeking me;
No wind can drive my bark astray,
  Nor change the tide of destiny.

What matter if I stand alone?
  I wait with joy the coming years;
My heart shall reap where it hath sown,
  And garner up its fruits of tears.

The waters know their own, and draw
  The brook that springs in yonder heights;
So flows the good with equal law
  Unto the soul of pure delights.

The stars come nightly to the sky;
  The tidal wave unto the sea;
Nor time, nor space, nor deep, nor high,
  Can keep my own away from me.

John Burroughs.

WAITING

It is, of course, well known that the saddest poems are written by the youngest poets; that it is youth which breaks its heart over the tragedies of fate, which finds in life nothing but despair, which delights to muse upon death and even to sigh for it, and which has a generally gorgeous time playing with its emotions. It is only with age and experience that understanding comes, or at least a certain induration which enables one to defy more or less successfully fortune's slings and arrows. Bryant wrote "Thanatopsis" at the mature age of eighteen; Keats's first poem (at nineteen) was entitled "On Death," and Lowell's first one (at twenty) was a "Threnodia" with a refrain of "Nevermore!" as lugubrious as Poe's.

Nevertheless, it is with something of a shock one learns, from the recently-published "John Burroughs Talks" of Mr. Clifton Johnson, that Burroughs's one famous poem, "Waiting," was written not as one might suppose in the ripe placidity of age, but in the year 1862 when its author was twenty-five years old.

Twenty-five does seem rather an early age

147

at which to sit down and fold one's hands and wait—at least to an American. To an Arab or a Hindu it would doubtless appeal as the wisest course of all; certainly it is the course recommended by all their saints and prophets— to devote oneself to contemplation in order to win through to that high serenity where the world and its stings seem petty and far away, to that Nirvana which is the supremest good the gods bestow on man.

As a matter of fact, that is exactly what Burroughs did, in so far as circumstance and environment permitted, and he seems to have been fairly successful in winning for himself a placid and happy life, with no great excitements, to be sure, no high and passionate experiences, but also with no greater annoyances than an occasional lack of money and a wife with a mania for cleaning house. Both of these irritations he escaped in his later years, for his writings brought him an income adequate to his simple needs, and he evaded his wife by building himself a cabin in the woods where, with an utter disregard of the neighborhood gossip, he could live by himself and be as untidy as he pleased.

The poem did, then, in a way, voice his inner convictions, though he himself points out that it was not so much the outgrowth of any spiritual experience or reasoned philosophy as of

148

the religious beliefs which his parents fiercely held and which they had labored to impress upon him. Perhaps the real truth is that, as the years passed, he gradually grew up to it.

John Burroughs's people were all what were commonly known as Hardshell Baptists—though they preferred to call themselves by the more dignified title of Primitive Baptists. Their principal dogma seems to have been that the Methodists, or Arminians as the Baptists loved to designate them, were headed straight for hell because they believed that everybody had a chance to get to heaven: faith and repentance being the only things necessary. Whereas the Hardshell Baptists were firm believers in predestination. If a man was meant to be saved, he would be saved no matter how bad he was; if he was meant to be damned, he would be damned no matter how good he was; and it was not only useless but unfair, once the Lord had settled these matters to His own satisfaction, to annoy Him with prayers and petitions in an effort to warp His will. This has always been the creed of good old fighting Christians such as the Calvinists and the Covenanters and the Puritans, and the Hardshell Baptists were also a militant people.

Burroughs had started his career as a wage earner at the age of seventeen. After a frag-

mentary education, he had secured a job as a
teacher in a little red schoolhouse in the village
of Tongore, New York. He received ten dollars a month and was boarded around among
the families of his pupils. Eight years later, he
was still teaching, having in the meantime acquired a wife, but nothing else worth mention-
ing.

By this time he had come to the very reasonable conclusion that he would never get anywhere as a teacher, and finally, as a possible
solution of life's difficulties, decided to become
a doctor. He had no especial predilection for
doctoring, but he thought he might be able to
make a better living that way, so he began to
read such books of medicine as the local prac-
titioner happened to own. It is worth noting
that he had not, as yet, developed any interest
in that study of nature which was to occupy all
his later years. He was just blindly groping
around trying to find some way to earn enough
money to support his wife decently. It was
under these circumstances that "Waiting" was
written. But let him tell the story.

"I wrote considerable poetry as a young
man," he says, "but the verse form of expression hampered my thought. Rhyme and rhythm
never flowed through my mind easily. My
poems seemed to me manufactured rather than
spontaneous, and a time came when I wrote no

150

more poetry and destroyed most of what I had done previously.

"Three of my early poems found their way into print. One of them was addressed to a friend who had been visiting me at the old farm. When he went away it left me kind of sentimental and lonesome, I suppose, and I put my feelings into verse. Another poem entitled 'Loss and Gain' came out in the *Independent*. 'Waiting' was the name I gave the third and that has become well known. I can't say as much for any of the other verses I have written, either in my youth or later when I resumed writing poetry. So I am practically a man of a single poem.

" 'Waiting' dates back to 1862, when I was twenty-five. I was not prospering, the outlook was anything but encouraging, and it was a very gloomy period of my life. Besides, the Civil War was raging; I was thinking I ought to join the army, but my wife was very much opposed to that, and so were my folks. I was teaching school at Olive in Ulster county and was reading medicine in the office of the village doctor with the notion of becoming a physician. One evening, as I sat in the little back room of the doctor's office, I paused in my study of anatomy and wrote the poem, which begins:

Serene, I fold my hands and wait.

"The poem was written as a comfort to myself and it was more felt and more spontaneous than anything else I ever put into verse. Because it voiced a real feeling, it has touched others. The ideal that what is good for us will come, and that we need not be uneasy or in haste, has proved true in my own case. Much good has come to me that I had no reason to expect—came just as a matter of luck in the unfolding of the great world life.

"The theme of the poem accorded with the religious ideas of my people. They were Old School Baptists who believed in predestination, foreordination, and all that sort of thing. I inherited their feeling, but I wasn't so theological. It took the shape with me that you see in the poem. It is predestination watered down, or watered up.

" 'Waiting' was published in the *Knickerbocker Magazine,* but it attracted no attention until, many years later, Whittier put it in his *Songs of Three Centuries.* Since then it has kept floating around and has won wide popularity. Every once in a while it makes a tour of the newspapers. Sometimes they give it a new title, or drop my name, or change lines, or add verses, or subtract them. Recently the *Congregationalist* printed it under the title 'Serenity' and credited it to the *British Weekly.* In the usual version there is one less verse than

Waiting

in the original. But that verse was unnecessary and the poem is stronger without it.

"Some time ago a Rhode Island manufacturer printed the poem in a leaflet to hand about. I suppose doing that was a relief to him from the grind of business. I understand that the Theosophists swear by the poem. I hear from it a great deal. People say to me, 'That poem has been more to me than anything else in my life.' "

The poem as usually quoted, and as Burroughs himself used it as a preface to his book, *The Light of Day*, has six stanzas, but as originally published in the *Knickerbocker Magazine* in 1863 (Vol. 61, page 201), it had seven, the extra stanza (the sixth in the original version) being as follows:

> Yon floweret nodding in the wind
> Is ready plighted to the bee;
> And, maiden, why that look unkind?
> For, lo! thy lover seeketh thee.

A few years ago Joel Benton wrote a warm letter to the New York *Times* protesting against the dropping of this stanza as an act of vandalism.

"This poem," he said, "is one of the very few specific poems of the nineteenth century that grasps an idea of supreme importance and gives it a supreme setting and expression. It has had, however, one misfortune, that of being 'improved' by a meddlesome interference that should be put in the list of legal torts. Some squeamish person has elided the following stanza and set the lyric afloat in a mangled form," and he quotes the stanza which is given above.

"Why a symbolic reference," continues Mr. Benton, "to the most enormous element and force in nature should require this self-assumed fissiparous performance would trouble a Philadelphia lawyer to tell. The grannified impulse that does this mean surgery is not uncommon, and even Longfellow's 'Excelsior' has been subjected to it. The verse omitted from that by false prudery is the following, if I may quote again from memory:

> " 'Oh, stay,' the maiden said, 'and rest
> Thy weary head upon this breast!'
> A tear stood in his bright blue eye,
> But still he answered, with a sigh,
> Excelsior!"

All of which gives rather the impression of fighting windmills. The stanza from "Excelsior" has never been omitted from any version of the poem which has come under the observation of the present scribe, who can detect nothing in it to offend the most prudish. Who dropped the sixth stanza from "Waiting" has never been discovered, but it was probably cut out not by a Mr. Bowdler but by some intelligent critic. It is far more reasonable to suppose that it was dropped, not because of any squeamishness, but because, as any one can see, it is distinctly inferior to the remainder of the poem. Burroughs was quite right in saying that the poem is stronger without it.

Also, it is entirely contrary to the facts of life, as another correspondent in the *Times* subsequently pointed out. "Maidens are not in the habit of looking unkindly on the lovers who seek them," she observes, quite justly, "unless there are good reasons!" Indeed, the complaint of the moralists has always been that 'maidens, all too often, are far kinder than they should be!

Nowhere in his talks does Burroughs make any reference to the fact that he subsequently wrote a concluding stanza to the poem, which perhaps sums up the philosophy of his later life:

> The law of love threads every heart
> And knits it to its utmost kin,
> Nor can our lives flow long apart
> From souls our secret souls would win.

This stanza has fortunately been preserved by Mrs. Alice Cleary Sutcliffe. "Several years ago," she writes, "while spending a never-to-be-forgotten day at Slabsides, the poet inscribed this stanza for one of our party, and explained that he had composed it after his famous poem was committed to print. It adds an important element of psychic force to the fateful prophecy, 'Mine own shall come to me.' "

So far as known, this stanza has not been preserved elsewhere; but it furnishes an altogether worthy conclusion to the poem and should perhaps be added to it.

Long before his death John Burroughs completely outgrew the iron-bound tenets of the Hardshell Baptists, and this was due, in no small degree, to his constantly growing intimacy with nature, and his observation of her moods.

"I didn't start in the bird business until the spring of 1863," he says in one of his talks. "I was twenty-five or twenty-six years old before birds began to interest me." But from that time on, they interested him more and more—and not birds only, but all the manifestations of the world about him. It was characteristic of him that nothing seemed to him too minute or too commonplace to be unworthy his attention; but this study gave him an ever increasing sense of his own isolation.

As he phrases it, he became more and more

conscious as he grew older of "the great cosmic chill." For years he had watched the tremendous processes of nature going on entirely independent of man, often seemingly contemptuous of him; he had come to realize that he was not shut in by any protecting walls, but that he was naked in the universe and that he had to "take his chance and warm himself as best he could."

He had never had that vivid realization of hell which was part and parcel of his father's religion, and had never had the slightest belief in the devil. He refused to speculate about the Trinity, which seemed to him just a puzzle which men had set up for their own confusion. Evil, he thought, was merely a phase of good, and seemed evil only because of man's limited and imperfect understanding.

"I have never accepted the creed of any church," he adds. "I have given my heart to Nature instead of to God, but that has never cast a shadow over my mind or conscience. I believe God is Nature. I also believe that there is some sort of omnipotent intelligence underlying the manifestations of power and the orderliness that we see in the universe. Personal immortality has never seemed to me probable, though I can't say that it is impossible. What Nature's ends are, or God's ends, I often have but a faint idea. Most of our preachers seem much too sure; but however much I differ with

157

them, I think we can agree that it is always fitting to preach the gospel of beauty in the commonplace. Look about your own vicinity and find heaven. The grand and beautiful are there if you have eyes for them."

And that was the gospel which John Burroughs preached to the very end of his days.

BEN BOLT

BEN BOLT

Don't you remember sweet Alice, Ben Bolt,—
　Sweet Alice whose hair was so brown,
Who wept with delight when you gave her a
　　smile,
　And trembled with fear at your frown?
In the old churchyard in the valley, Ben Bolt,
　In a corner obscure and alone,
They have fitted a slab of the granite so gray,
　And Alice lies under the stone.

Under the hickory tree, Ben Bolt,
　Which stood at the foot of the hill,
Together we've lain in the noonday shade,
　And listened to Appleton's mill.
The mill-wheel has fallen to pieces, Ben Bolt,
　The rafters have tumbled in,
And a quiet which crawls round the walls as
　　you gaze
Has followed the olden din.

Do you mind of the cabin of logs, Ben Bolt,
　At the edge of the pathless wood,
And the button-ball tree with its motley limbs,
　Which nigh by the doorstep stood?

The cabin to ruin has gone, Ben Bolt,
  The tree you would seek for in vain;
And where once the lords of the forest waved,
  Are grass and the golden grain.

And don't you remember the school, Ben Bolt,
  With the master so cruel and grim,
And the shaded nook in the running brook
  Where the children went to swim?
Grass grows on the master's grave, Ben Bolt,
  The spring of the brook is dry,
And of all the boys who were schoolmates then
  There are only you and I.

There is change in the things I loved, Ben Bolt,
  They have changed from the old to the new;
But I feel in the depths of my spirit the truth,
  There never was change in you.
Twelvemonths twenty have passed, Ben Bolt,
  Since first we were friends—yet I hail
Your presence a blessing, your friendship a
      truth,
  Ben Bolt of the salt-sea gale.

                              Thomas Dunn English.

BEN BOLT

THE story of the poet who struggles long years to convince the public that he wrote some poem which, quite possibly, he really did write, is not an uncommon one; but the writer who lives, decade after decade, in the hope that eventually the public will forget a metrical indiscretion of his youth, only to die at last, an old man, with the hope unfulfilled—that is far more unusual, and perhaps also far more tragic.

The history of the distressing controversies waged by John Luckey McCreery and Lizzie York Case has already been recounted in these pages. Set against this the story of Thomas Dunn English, who spent the last sixty years of his life striving vainly to make the public understand that he had claims upon fame far more serious (as he thought) than a sentimental ballad written at the age of twenty-three.

The labors of Hercules were as nothing beside the task of getting an idea out of the public mind once it has found firm lodgment there, and McCreery and Mrs. Case and English all died defeated and disappointed. To-day there are apparently as many people as ever who believe that Bulwer wrote "There Is No Death" and "There Is No Unbelief," and few indeed who remember that English ever wrote anything except "Ben Bolt."

Nothing is more devastating to a literary career than for a writer, early in it, to gain a reputation for a certain kind of work. He has started out, let it be supposed, to be a serious novelist; his aim is, of course, the novel of character; his ambition is to set upon paper a searching interpretation of life. But before one can interpret life one must understand it, and understanding requires experience and observation, which in their turn require time. Meanwhile he happens upon a plot, and, just to keep his hand in—or perhaps to keep the pot boiling—he casts it into the form of a detective story and sends it off. If it is a success, his fate is sealed. Ever afterwards, in the public mind, he will be labeled as a writer of detective stories, and his publishers will do all they can to persuade him to keep on writing them.

For the public is like a child—it insists on its stories being told "just-so," and its authors must perform the same tricks over and over again. So Chesterton must keep on being witty and Shaw paradoxical and Barrie whimsical; nothing is wanted from Conan Doyle except Sherlock Holmes. When Mark Twain wrote a serious book, he was compelled to publish it anonymously to prevent it being treated as a joke. De Wolf Hopper might make an admirable Othello, but he would be greeted with shrieks of laughter. The audience would go into hysterics when he smothered Desdemona, and yell for "Casey at the Bat." Such is the force of habit.

The poet is in peculiar peril. Perhaps in an unguarded moment he contributes some jingles to a comic weekly, or writes a sentimental song to oblige a friend, little suspecting the awful fate he is inviting. For it is quite within the range of possibility that those jingles or that song may dog his footsteps the remainder of his life and harry him into his grave.

There are many examples in American literature of promising novelists straying away along the primrose paths of crime or of sex, but the most horrible example of the poet overshadowed by an early bit of doggerel is undoubtedly Thomas Dunn English.

Now English was in no sense a great writer, nor even an important one, but he was industrious and he believed in his work. He produced a dozen novels, fifty plays and perhaps a thousand poems. Some of the poems are of considerable merit—as witness "The Charge by the Ford." And yet, practically all his life, he was identified in the public mind only with a single song.

Famous Single Poems

If it had been a good song, this would not have been so galling—Lovelace would, no doubt, be happy to know that he has come down through the ages as the author of "To Althea from Prison." But "Ben Bolt" is unutterable bosh, and English knew it was bosh. He had written it at the very outset of his literary career, being in need presumably of the ten dollar bill which the editor of the New York *Mirror* was in the habit of handing out for poems of this sort.

In other words, he produced a pot-boiler and sold it in a good market—a thing which almost any needy young author would be glad to do if he could, and which has been done by many who were neither young nor needy, without incurring any special reprobation. One recalls that the Jove-like Sir Edwin Arnold once upon a time wrote some verses to be used in advertising Bovril (in consideration of an extra price), and that George du Maurier's most widely circulated drawing is the one which adorns the Apollinaris bottle! Indeed, many of the world's great masterpieces have been pot-boilers, written solely because their authors were in desperate need of money, and had to work or starve. Thomas Bailey Aldrich, who ought to know, went so far as to assert that it was only under such circumstances a poet could hope to be visited by the Muse:

166

Ben Bolt

A man should live in a garret aloof,
  And have few friends and go poorly clad,
With an old hat stopping the chink in the roof,
  To keep the Goddess constant and glad.

Most pot-boilers, of course, are not master-pieces and are soon forgotten, having served their purpose of providing their creators with a little ready cash. The Muse was certainly not present when English wrote "Ben Bolt," and in the ordinary course of events, oblivion would have been its portion, but a strolling player named Nelson Kneass happened to see the verses and set them to an air adapted from a melancholy German melody. Kneass had gaged his public with a fiendish accuracy, verses and air exactly suited the taste of the day, and the song swept through America and England on such a wave of popularity that it netted its publishers over $60,000—of which neither English nor Kneass received any share. Maudlin sentimentality was the prevailing, the indispensable, note in the popular songs of that epoch, but "Ben Bolt" outmaudlined the worst of them. Sweet Alice with her smiles and tears, her early grave and gray tombstone, the old mill, the ruined cabin, the little school, the purling brook—all the old tried properties are there, wedded to a mournful tune which suits them exactly—just the sort of tune to appeal

167

not only to the tightly-laced, semi-hysterical, sex-suppressed denizens of the drawing-room, but also to the gay celebrants at stag parties when those present had reached that stage of inebriety where they longed to put their heads on the table and weep over their sins. Its range was not too exacting, its rhythm was slow and soothing, and its minors gave opportunity for pleasing variations by the bass and tenor. The present scribe recalls another song of a later generation called "The Picture That Is Turned to the Wall." It was about a girl driven out into the storm by a relentless father, and it was in its day almost as popular as "Ben Bolt," for exactly similar reasons; but its author had been wise enough to remain anonymous!

Poor English had had no such forethought, and he could not deny his child after he had given it his name. It confronted him at every turn; he was everywhere referred to as the author of "Ben Bolt." It was popularly regarded as his supreme achievement, if not his only one. Think of a poet, a novelist, a dramatist, who took himself and his work seriously, being continually reminded that his only hold upon fame was as the author of a doggerel song!

Such, then, was the awful fate which English had unthinkingly brought upon himself. But even the worst reputation may in time be lived

down, and as the years passed, new favorites
crowded "Ben Bolt" off the programs and out
of public recollection. So English picked up
heart of hope and labored away at his plays
and his poetry in the fond belief that he had at
last managed to outlive that miserable song.
Fifty years had passed since it appeared in the
New York *Mirror;* surely it was buried beyond
any possibility of resurrection, and his last
years would be unshadowed by it.

But Fate held in reserve a truly terrific stroke.

In 1894, *Harper's Magazine* began the publication of a story of Paris student life entitled
Trilby, by George du Maurier, the great car-
toonist of *Punch.* (These details are here set
down because nobody reads *Trilby* nowadays,
more's the pity!) Its heroine, Trilby O'Ferrall
—a light-hearted daughter of the Quarter, with
all the virtues but one, who drifted in and out
of the studios on the left bank posing for everything from a hand to the "altogether," but
chiefly remarkable for her feet which were
masterpieces—happened to be the daughter of a
convivial Irishman, Patrick Michael O'Ferrall,
one-time fellow of Trinity, Cambridge. He,
too, had all the virtues but one: he was a
drunkard. So, after disgracing himself at home,
he had drifted to Paris, married a bar-maid and
found congenial haven behind her bar, where, in

his cups, he had doted on "Ben Bolt," and often sang it to the delight of his only child.

"Do you know 'Ben Bolt'?" asks Trilby of the Three Musketeers of the Brush, after listening without enthusiasm to the "Rosemonde" of Schubert, as beautifully played by Svengali.

"Oh, yes, I know it well," answers Little Billee. "It's a very pretty song."

"I can sing it," announces Miss O'Ferrall with pride. "Shall I?"

"Oh, certainly, if you will be so kind," says Little Billee in his best drawing-room manner.

So, gazing up at the ceiling with a sentimental smile, Trilby sings it with an utter absence of tune which stupefies her audience.

"It's the only song I know," she explains. "My father used to sing it just like that, when he felt jolly after hot rum and water. It used to make people cry; he used to cry over it himself. *I* never do."

And when she has taken herself off, Little Billee sings the song in "his pleasant little throaty English barytone"; and then Svengali and Gecko play it as only those two great artists could, until "their susceptible audience of three was all but crazed with delight and wonder; and the masterful Ben Bolt, and his over-tender Alice, and his too submissive friend, and the old schoolmaster so kind and so true, and the rustic porch and the mill, and the slab of granite so

170

gray, were all magnified into a strange, almost holy poetic dignity and splendor."

And behold, "Ben Bolt" was once more the rage. For *Trilby* swept the country from end to end, and even contributed a new word to the language. Everybody, once again, after the lapse of half a century, was singing, or whistling, or playing "Ben Bolt."

"That unsophisticated little song," Du Maurier calls it, "which has touched so many simple British hearts that don't know any better." He little suspected that he was almost to break a simple American heart by resurrecting it! And yet, of course, it was exactly the song which Patrick Michael O'Ferrall would have sung in the circumstances mentioned. The vogue of the book ceased with a suddenness which still remains one of the puzzles of the publishing business, but a play had been made from it and lasted for several seasons—was even revived from time to time. It helped to keep "Ben Bolt" before the public, for a portion of the song was sung off-stage during the third act. And when the book got into the movies, "Ben Bolt" of course was part of the musical program.

Thomas Dunn English died in 1902, at the age of eighty-three, knowing that his song had outlived him. His collected works would fill many volumes; but of his fifty plays only one,

The Mormons, was ever published, while his novels, *Walter Woolfe, Ambrose Fecit, Jacob Schuyler's Millions,* and the rest, have long since dropped from public ken. Sometimes a collection devoted to patriotic or historical poetry will include one or two of his Civil War verses; but only one of his poems has achieved the sort of immortality which a general anthology can give. There, under the head of *Old Favorites* or *Songs of Yester-Year,* one always finds "Ben Bolt."

There is a moral to this tale:

The only safe rule for the aspiring author is to publish everything he writes either anonymously or under a pen-name. Then, when his creative days are over, he can amuse his declining years by gathering together such of his work as he wishes to be associated with his name, and claim it as his own.

But if authors did that, how thin that final volume would often be!

BEAUTIFUL SNOW

BEAUTIFUL SNOW

Oh! the snow, the beautiful snow,
Filling the sky and the earth below;
Over the house-tops, over the street,
Over the heads of the people you meet;
    Dancing,
        Flirting,
            Skimming along,
Beautiful snow! it can do nothing wrong.
Flying to kiss a fair lady's cheek;
Clinging to lips in a frolicsome freak.
Beautiful snow, from the heavens above,
Pure as an angel and fickle as love!

Oh! the snow, the beautiful snow!
How the flakes gather and laugh as they go!
Whirling about in its maddening fun,
It plays in its glee with every one.
    Chasing,
        Laughing,
            Hurrying by,
It lights up the face and it sparkles the eye;
And even the dogs, with a bark and a bound,
Snap at the crystals that eddy around.
The town is alive, and its heart in a glow
To welcome the coming of beautiful snow.

How the wild crowd goes swaying along,
Hailing each other with humor and song!
How the gay sledges like meteors flash by—
Bright for a moment, then lost to the eye.
    Ringing,
        Swinging,
            Dashing they go
Over the crest of the beautiful snow:
Snow so pure when it falls from the sky,
To be trampled in mud by the crowd rush-
    ing by;
To be trampled and tracked by the thousands
    of feet
Till it blends with the horrible filth in the
    street.

Once I was pure as the snow—but I fell:
Fell, like the snow-flakes, from heaven—to
    hell:
Fell, to be tramped as the filth of the street:
Fell, to be scoffed, to be spit on and beat.
    Pleading,
        Cursing,
            Dreading to die,
Selling my soul to whoever would buy,
Dealing in shame for a morsel of bread,
Hating the living and fearing the dead.
Merciful God! have I fallen so low?
And yet I was once like this beautiful snow!

Beautiful Snow

Once I was fair as the beautiful snow,
With an eye like its crystals, a heart like its
    glow;
Once I was loved for my innocent grace—
Flattered and sought for the charm of my face.
        Father,
            Mother,
                Sisters all,
God, and myself I have lost by my fall.
The veriest wretch that goes shivering by
Will take a wide sweep, lest I wander too nigh,
For of all that is on or about me, I know
There is nothing that's pure but the beautiful
    snow.

How strange it should be that this beautiful snow
Should fall on a sinner with nowhere to go!
How strange it would be, when the night comes
    again,
If the snow and the ice struck my desperate
    brain!
        Fainting,
            Freezing,
                Dying alone,
Too wicked for prayer, too weak for my moan
To be heard in the crash of the crazy town,
Gone mad in its joy at the snow's coming down;
To lie and to die in my terrible woe,
With a bed and a shroud of the beautiful snow!

John Whitaker Watson.

177

BEAUTIFUL SNOW

THE human race is incurably romantic. It
longs to believe that, however drab life may be
in the immediate vicinity, somewhere else, in
some happier clime, hearts are always light,
virtue always rewarded, and high and passionate
love the rule instead of the rare exception.
Romance, romance—it is what every one sighs
for and endeavors to experience—if not in person, at least by proxy; if not in one's own life,
then in a novel or a play or a movie.

Sometimes even in a poem!

Thousands and thousands of simple hearts
have been wrung by Whittier's pastoral of
Maud Muller and the sentimental Judge, who
used to sit and dream of her

> In his marble hearth's bright glow

after he had ridden away and

> wedded a wife of richest dower,
> Who lived for fashion, as he for power.

and millions of sighs have been evoked by the
concluding lines:

Beautiful Snow

Alas for maiden, alas for Judge,
For rich repiner and household drudge!

God pity them both! and pity us all,
Who vainly the dreams of youth recall.

For of all sad words of tongue or pen,
The saddest are these: "It might have been!"

Yet every sane person who stops to think of
it knows that the Judge was wise to ride away
back to his own circle and manner of life, and
that if he had not done so, if he had tarried and
married, instead of a little tender melancholy,
he would have had a lifelong tragedy on his
hands. Bret Harte perceived this, and had the
courage, in a poem called "Mrs. Judge Jen-
kins," to describe clearly and accurately what
would undoubtedly have happened had the
Judge led Maud back to his "garnished rooms"
—the twins who looked too much like the men
who raked the hay on old Muller's farm, Maud
growing broad and red and stout—

And looking down that dreary track,
He half regretted that he came back;

For, had he waited, he might have wed
Some maiden fair and thoroughbred;

For there be women as fair as she,
Whose verbs and nouns do more agree.

179

Alas for maiden! alas for Judge!
And the sentimental,—that's one-half "fudge";

For Maud soon thought the Judge a bore,
With all his learning and all his lore;

And the Judge would have bartered Maud's fair face
For more refinement and social grace.

If, of all words of tongue and pen,
The saddest are, "It might have been,"

More sad are these we daily see:
"It is, but hadn't ought to be."

But this is not the stuff of which romance is made, the public will have none of it; and Maud Muller and the Beggar Maid and others of that ilk will always be popular heroines.

The task of the patient historian whose duty it too often is to puncture these pleasant fictions is a thankless one. To tear the halo of wifely devotion from the head of the Empress Josephine, to show that Queen Victoria was at bottom only an obstinate and narrow-minded woman—these are acts which to the multitude savor of sacrilege. Purveyors of mental food for popular consumption have long since discovered that a picturesque lie is far more convincing than a drab fact, and that it is a great mistake to permit a slavish regard for the truth

to spoil a good story. The only sensible rule is
to emulate Barney McGee!

American literature is overlaid with romantic
fictions which, originating in the brain of some
lecturer desperately endeavoring to keep his
auditors awake, or of some newspaperman hard
up for a story, accumulate detail after detail
as they roll along until the minute grain of fact
upon which they were sometimes founded becomes hopelessly lost amid imaginative accre-
tions. It is with such a story that the present
article is concerned.

The two decades from 1870 to 1890 were
chiefly remarkable for sentimental balderdash.
It was the taste of the time; it is, of course, the
half-baked taste of all times, but the songs that
were sung in "genteel" drawing-rooms and the
verse which was read and recited and widely-
acclaimed amid the same surroundings touched
depths of imbecility which have never since
been equaled. One of the most popular of
such recitations was entitled "Beautiful Snow,"
and purported to be the tragic revery of an outcast as she makes her way along the wintry
streets of a great city in the midst of a driving
snow-storm. It was "sure-fire stuff," especially
when recited by one of the gentler sex, because
to the hopeless melancholy which was once so
popular in pieces of this sort it added discussion,
or at least mention, of a subject strictly taboo.

The Scarlet Woman was a phenomenon to which polite society at that time not only shut its eyes, but of which it pretended to be unaware. If she was pictured at all, it was as despairing and hopeless, ceaselessly bemoaning her fall from virtue, drinking the dregs of misery and want, with remorse ever gnawing at her heart, and finally dying of starvation amid wretched surroundings.

The idea that a woman who had taken the wrong turning could ever come back was anathema. In fact, society was banded together to prevent her coming back. To contend that such a woman had any claim to consideration, that she might be a good sort at bottom, and that she might eventually make a success of her life and be happy and contented in her last days was to incur grave suspicion. French fiction was held to be vicious and degraded because it occasionally developed such a theme. The fact that she died of consumption was the one thing that palliated the sins of Camille. Nobody knew exactly what to make of Trilby, though her death, too, was to her credit; but everybody agreed that for Little Billee to have married her would have been a crime against good morals. For sin must be punished.

"Beautiful Snow" laid the colors on exactly as society liked to imagine them. It was real movie stuff—the only wonder is that it has never been made into a picture! The attention of the producers is called to it without charge.

Every once in a while a pathetic story connected with this poem starts anew on a round of the press. This tale as dressed-up by some resourceful sob-master so far surpasses the abilities of the present scribe that the only thing for him to do is to quote:

During the early part of the Civil War, one dark Saturday night in midwinter, there died in the Commercial Hospital at Cincinnati, a young woman over whose head only two and twenty summers had passed. She had once been possessed of an enviable share of beauty, and had been, as she herself said, "flattered and sought for the charms of her face," but, alas! upon her fair brow was written that terrible word—prostitute.

Highly educated and of accomplished manners, she might have shone in the best society. But the evil hour that proved her ruin was the door from childhood, and having spent a young life in disgrace and shame, the poor friendless one died the melancholy death of a broken-hearted outcast.

Among her personal effects was found in manuscript a poem entitled "The Beautiful Snow," which was immediately carried to Enos B. Reed, at that time editor of the *National Union*. In the columns of that paper, on the morning of the day following the girl's death, the poem appeared in print for the first time. When the paper containing the poem came out on Sunday morning, the body of the victim had not yet received burial. The attention of Thomas Buchanan Read, one of the first American poets, was so taken with its stirring pathos that he immediately followed the corpse to its final resting place, and reverently placed upon the grave a wreath of laurel.

Such are the plain facts concerning her whose "Beautiful Snow" will long be remembered as one of the brightest gems in American literature.

No doubt that sentimental journey gave Mr. Read a good feeling at the heart, which amply repaid him for the cost of the laurel-wreath, but the unfortunate girl whom he thus honored was not the author of "Beautiful Snow." It is strange how many people consider the possession of a manuscript poem to be prima facie evidence that the possessor is its author. If it shows one or two corrections, the case is popularly regarded as absolutely settled! It is sometimes very difficult to untangle such a controversy and to get at the truth, but in this case it is easy, for "Beautiful Snow" was published by *Harper's Weekly* in its issue for November 27, 1858, some years before the death of the beautiful unknown.

Anonymity was the rule and the curse of the early American magazine. Just what useful end was supposed to be served by suppressing an author's name is difficult to guess, but very few names were ever published. "Beautiful Snow" was unsigned, and no indication of the author was given either in the table of contents or in the index to the volume. It was not until 1869, when John Whitaker Watson published at Philadelphia a volume of verse called "Beautiful Snow and Other Poems," that any authoritative indication was given as to who had written it.

Not that the publication of Mr. Watson's book settled the matter. By no means! Probably no other poem in American literature has been so fought over. No less than seven people are said at one time or another to have claimed the high honor of being its author—Richard H. Chandler, William A. Silloway, William H. Sigourney, John McMasters, Dora Shaw, Dora Thorne and Henry W. Faxon—and some of them, at least, described in detail the circumstances under which it was composed.

A diverting anthology could be made of these narratives, but two of them will suffice here.

Richard H. Chandler alleged that Mr. Watson had stolen the poem from him in revenge for a practical joke—and had even carried this revenge to the point of having the poem published in *Harper's Weekly*. Mr. Chandler had not hitherto been known as a poet, but he disclosed the fact that he had written much, and added that the only reason no other poem of his had ever been published was because "the publishers sent them all back." This he seemed

to consider an ample and satisfying explanation
—as, indeed, it was!

William Allen Silloway insisted that he had
published the poem in a New England paper
(name not given) four years prior to its appearance in *Harper's Weekly,* but the files had unfortunately been destroyed. He had been inspired to its composition through the degrada-
tion of his wife, "a niece of Millard Fill-
more," who had fallen a victim to the Demon
Rum, and who had been found dead by a po-
liceman in a snowdrift in Leonard street, New
York City, in the winter of 1854. This catas-
trophe had so worked upon him that, for the
first time in his life, he had broken into verse—
the verse in question being "Beautiful Snow."
This story he seemed to regard as proving conclusively that he wrote the poem.

It is the hard fate of anthologists that they
have to decide such controversies as this, and
when William Cullen Bryant was compiling
his *Library of Poetry and Song,* he assembled
all the evidence and decided in favor of Mr.
Watson. There has never been any serious reason to question his verdict.

John Whitaker Watson was a prolific writer,
a hack of Grub Street, but "Beautiful Snow" is
the only thing of his that still lives—if it can
be said to live. He was born in New York City

on October 14, 1824, graduated at Columbia College and studied medicine, but drifted into journalism and eventually developed into a writer of sentimental verse and of sensational serials for the popular weeklies. He died in New York, July 18, 1890.

About 1884, a reporter for the New York *World* discovered that Mr. Watson lived in "a neat brick house on Twenty-second Street," and secured from him the story of his famous poem. It was written in November, 1858, at the house of Mr. Sam Colt, at Hartford, Conn., and was mailed next morning to *Harper's Weekly*. The *Weekly* accepted it and sent the author a check for $15, which he considered very liberal. In 1868, he sold the copyright to it and twenty-five other poems to Turner Brothers & Co., of Philadelphia, for the sum of $500, and these poems were published in the volume referred to above. The book was very successful and more than 30,000 copies were sold the first year. But various other ventures proved so disastrous that the firm failed, and Mr. Watson's volume passed into the hands of T. B. Peterson & Co., also of Philadelphia. They, so Mr. Watson alleged, gathered up enough of his poems to make a second volume, altered the title of the leading one, and published them wholly without his knowledge. He knew nothing of the book until he happened upon it in a Broadway bookstore, and he never received a cent for it.

But it is when he relates his experiences with the various claimants of the honor of having written this masterpiece that he is most interesting.

"There have been so many authors of 'Snow,'" says Mr. Watson, "that I only admit myself to myself as one of them. The first who came prominently to the front was one McMasters, a portrait painter, who wrote a letter to the Sunday *Times* modestly admitting that he was the long-sought author. Accompanied by a friend, I went around to see him, and he repeated his assertion to me, declaring that he could produce proofs of it in two weeks. I gave him two months, and I guess he is looking for them yet. That was twenty years ago, and I have never heard of him since.

"Then Elizabeth Akers and Dora Shaw and Hen Faxon took spells at it through the newspapers, not exactly claiming it, but letting it be known that the author was not a great distance off. I believe the poem has never yet been openly claimed by any one possessing any real literary talent," Mr. Watson added, thoughtfully, though of course without any suspicion of why this was so!

"But the most wonderful of all these claimants," Mr. Watson pursued, "and the one who

188

gave me the most serious annoyance was a rascal calling himself William H. Sigourney, and professing to be a nephew of the husband of Lydia Huntley Sigourney. He somehow secured an endorsement from the *Galaxy Magazine,* and on the strength of this traveled through the country making addresses at country fairs, reciting 'Beautiful Snow' and swindling the country people out of anything he could. He ran his career for several years, and every little while my eyes were gratified by a newspaper paragraph to the effect that the author of 'Beautiful Snow' had been arrested somewhere for obtaining goods under false pretenses, or picking pockets.

"There wasn't much inducement for me at that time to proclaim myself as the author; but one day I saw in the Philadelphia *Ledger* the announcement that the author of 'Beautiful Snow' had shot himself and died on the Bloomingdale road the day before. I fancied I was rid of the fellow at last, but when I came back to New York I was disappointed to find that the report had originated with the *Evening Post,* and had been written by a man who had claimed to be the author of the poem and who, when threatened with arrest for some rascality, took this means of avoiding it.

"A few months later the papers announced that the author of 'Beautiful Snow' had been arrested for robbing a Mr. Page of $300. I had the curiosity to go to the Tombs to see him, and he told me his real name and history. What happened to him after that I don't know."

Like all other one-poem men, Mr. Watson was convinced that Fate had done him a great injustice by linking his name to a single poem, and consigning all his other work to oblivion.

"I am not only the author of 'Beautiful Snow,'" he protested, "but of 'The Dying Soldier,' 'Farmer Brown,' 'Ring Down the Drop,' and of many others as good or better. Why they are not equally famous I cannot imagine. I think I can say without egotism that my poems originated a new taste or school, of which Trowbridge, Carleton and a few others are worthy followers."

But a careful examination of the contents of "Beautiful Snow and Other Poems," reveals nothing but a dreary waste. And yet, an editorial note at the back of the volume, dated March, 1871, proclaims the sixth edition, and calls attention to the interesting fact that two of the poems contained in the book, "Beautiful Snow" and "The Dying Soldier," "were read upon one night, a few months since, to audiences varying from one thousand to four thousand, in seven of the great cities of the country, including New York, Philadelphia and Boston!"

Yes, it was the Age of Plush!

NOTHING TO WEAR

NOTHING TO WEAR

AN EPISODE OF CITY LIFE

Miss Flora McFlimsey, of Madison Square,
Has made three separate journeys to Paris,
And her father assures me, each time she was
    there,
That she and her friend Mrs. Harris
(Not the lady whose name is so famous in
    history,
But plain Mrs. H., without romance or mys-
    tery)
Spent six consecutive weeks without stopping
In one continuous round of shopping,—
Shopping alone, and shopping together,
At all hours of the day, and in all sorts of
    weather,—
For all manner of things that a woman can put
On the crown of her head or the sole of her
    foot,
Or wrap round her shoulders, or fit round her
    waist,
Or that can be sewed on, or pinned on, or laced,
Or tied on with a string, or stitched on with a
    bow,
In front or behind, above or below;

For bonnets, mantillas, capes, collars, and
    shawls;
Dresses for breakfasts and dinners and balls;
Dresses to sit in and stand in and walk in;
Dresses to dance in and flirt in and talk in;
Dresses in which to do nothing at all;
Dresses for winter, spring, summer, and fall;
All of them different in color and pattern,
Silk, muslin, and lace, crape, velvet, and satin,
Brocade, and broadcloth, and other material,
Quite as expensive and much more ethereal;
In short, for all things that could ever be
    thought of,
Or milliner, *modiste*, or tradesman be bought of,
    From ten-thousand-francs robes to twenty-
    sous frills;
In all quarters of Paris, and to every store,
While McFlimsey in vain stormed, scolded, and
    swore,
    They footed the streets, and he footed the
    bills.

The last trip, their goods shipped by the steamer
    Arago,
Formed, McFlimsey declares, the bulk of her
    cargo,
Not to mention a quantity kept from the rest,
Sufficient to fill the largest-sized chest,
Which did not appear on the ship's manifest,

Nothing to Wear

But for which the ladies themselves manifested
Such particular interest, that they invested
Their own proper persons in layers and rows
Of muslins, embroideries, worked underclothes,
Gloves, handkerchiefs, scarfs, and such trifles as
    those;
Then, wrapped in great shawls, like Circassian
    beauties,
Gave *good-by* to the ship, and *go-by* to the
    duties.
Her relations at home all marveled, no doubt
Miss Flora had grown so enormously stout
    For an actual belle and a possible bride;
But the miracle ceased when she turned inside
    out,
    And the truth came to light, and the dry-
        goods beside,
Which, in spite of collector and custom-house
    sentry,
Had entered the port without any entry.

And yet, though scarce three months have passed
    since the day
This merchandise went, on twelve carts, up
    Broadway,
This same Miss McFlimsey, of Madison
    Square,
The last time we met was in utter despair,
Because she had nothing whatever to wear!

NOTHING TO WEAR!   Now, as this is a true
   ditty,
    I do not assert—this, you know, is between
    us—
That she's in a state of absolute nudity,
    Like Powers' Greek Slave, or the Medici
    Venus;
But I do mean to say, I have heard her declare,
    When, at the same moment, she had on a
    dress
    Which cost five hundred dollars, and not a
    cent less
    And jewelry worth ten times more, I should
    guess,
That she had not a thing in the wide world to
    wear!

I should mention just here, that out of Miss
    Flora's
Two hundred and fifty or sixty adorers,
I had just been selected as he who should throw
    all
The rest in the shade, by the gracious bestowal
On myself, after twenty or thirty rejections,
Of those fossil remains which she called her
    "affections,"
And that rather decayed, but well-known work
    of art,
Which Miss Flora persisted in styling "her
    heart."

Nothing to Wear

So we were engaged. Our troth had been
    plighted,
Not by moonbeam or starbeam, by fountain or
    grove,
But in a front parlor, most brilliantly lighted,
Beneath the gas-fixtures we whispered our
    love.
Without any romance or raptures or sighs,
Without any tears in Miss Flora's blue eyes,
Or blushes, or transports, or such silly actions,
It was one of the quietest business transactions,
With a very small sprinkling of sentiment, if
    any,
And a very large diamond imported by Tiffany.
On her virginal lips while I printed a kiss,
She exclaimed, as a sort of parenthesis,
And by way of putting me quite at my ease,
"You know, I'm to polka as much as I please.
And flirt when I like,—now, stop, don't you
    speak,—
And you must not come here more than twice
    in the week,
Or talk to me either at party or ball,
But always be ready to come when I call;
So don't prose to me about duty and stuff,
If we don't break this off, there will be time
    enough
For that sort of thing; but the bargain must
    be
That, as long as I choose, I am perfectly free,

For this is a sort of engagement, you see,
Which is binding on you but not binding on
me."

Well, having thus wooed Miss McFlimsey
and gained her,
With the silks, crinolines, and hoops that con-
tained her;
I had, as I thought, a contingent remainder
At least in the property, and the best right
To appear as its escort by day and by night;
And it being the week of the Stuckups' grand
ball,—
Their cards had been out for a fortnight
or so,
And set all the Avenue on the tiptoe,—
I considered it only my duty to call,
And see if Miss Flora intended to go.
I found her,—as ladies are apt to be found,
When the time intervening between the first
sound
Of the bell and the visitor's entry is shorter
Than usual,—I found—I won't say, I caught
her,—
Intent on the pier-glass, undoubtedly meaning
To see if perhaps it didn't need cleaning.
She turned as I entered,—"Why, Harry, you
sinner,
I thought that you went to the Flashers' to
dinner!"

Nothing to Wear

"So I did," I replied; "but the dinner is swal-
    lowed
  And digested, I trust, for 'tis now nine and
    more,
So being relieved from that duty, I followed
  Inclination, which led me, you see, to your
    door;
And now will your ladyship so condescend
As just to inform me if you intend
Your beauty and graces and presence to lend
(All of which, when I own, I hope no one will
    borrow)
To the Stuckups', whose party, you know, is
    to-morrow?"

The fair Flora looked up with a pitiful air,
And answered quite promptly, "Why, Harry,
    mon cher,
I should like above all things to go with you
    there;
But really and truly—I've nothing to wear."

"Nothing to wear! go just as you are;
Wear the dress you have on, and you'll be by
    far,
I engage, the most bright and particular star
  On the Stuckup horizon"—I stopped—for
    her eye,
Notwithstanding this delicate onset of flattery,
Opened on me at once a most terrible battery

Of scorn and amazement. She made no
    reply,
But gave a slight turn to the end of her nose
    (That pure Grecian feature), as much as to
    say,
"How absurd that any sane man should sup-
    pose
That a lady would go to a ball in the clothes,
    No matter how fine, that she wears every
    day!"

So I ventured again: "Wear your crimson bro-
    cade,"
(Second turn-up of nose)—"That's too dark by
    a shade."
"Your blue silk"—"That's too heavy." "Your
    pink"—"That's too light."
"Wear tulle over satin"—"I can't endure
    white."
"Your rose-colored, then, the best of the
    batch"—
"I haven't a thread of point lace to match."
"Your brown *moire antique*"—"Yes, and look
    like a Quaker."
"The pearl-colored"—"I would, but that
    plaguey dressmaker
Has had it a week." "Then that exquisite lilac
In which you would melt the heart of a Shy-
    lock."

Nothing to Wear

(Here the nose took again the same elevation)—
"I wouldn't wear that for the whole of crea-
tion."
  "Why not? It's my fancy, there's nothing
  could strike it
As more *comme il faut*"—"Yes, but, dear me!
  that lean
Sophronia Stuckup has got one just like it,
And I won't appear dressed like a chit of six-
teen."
"Then that splendid purple, that sweet Maza-
rine,
That superb *point d'aiguille,* that imperial green,
That zephyr-like tarlatan, that rich *grena-
dine*"—
"Not one of all which is fit to be seen,"
Said the lady, becoming excited and flushed.
"Then wear," I exclaimed, in a tone which
  quite crushed
  Opposition, "that gorgeous *toilette* which you
  sported
In Paris last spring, at the grand presentation,
When you quite turned the head of the head of
  the nation;
  And by all the grand court were so very
  much courted."
  The end of the nose was portentously tipped
  up,
And both the bright eyes shot forth indignation,

As she burst upon me with the fierce exclama-
    tion,
"I have worn it three times at the least calcu-
    lation,
    And that and the most of my dresses are
        ripped up!"
Here I ripped *out* something, perhaps rather
    rash,
    Quite innocent, though; but, to use an ex-
        pression
More striking than classic, it "settled my hash,"
    And proved very soon the last act of our
        session.
"Fiddlesticks, it is, sir? I wonder the ceiling
Doesn't fall down and crush you—oh! you men
    have no feeling;
You selfish, unnatural, illiberal creatures,
Who set yourselves up as patterns and preachers,
Your silly pretense,—why, what a mere guess
    it is!
Pray, what do you know of a woman's neces-
    sities!
I have told you and shown you I've nothing to
    wear,
And it's perfectly plain you not only don't care,
But you do not believe me" (here the nose went
    still higher).
"I suppose, if you dared, you would call me a
    liar.
Our engagement is ended, sir—yes, on the spot;

202

Nothing to Wear

You're a brute and a monster, and—I don't
    know what."
I mildly suggested the words—Hottentot,
Pickpocket, and cannibal, Tartar, and thief,
As gentle expletives which might give relief;
But this only proved as spark to the powder,
And the storm I had raised came faster and
    louder;
It blew and it rained, thundered, lightened, and
    hailed
Interjections, verbs, pronouns, till language
    quite failed
To express the abusive, and then its arrears
Were brought up all at once by a torrent of
    tears,
And my last faint, despairing attempt at an obs-
Ervation was lost in a tempest of sobs.

Well, I felt for the lady, and felt for my hat,
    too,
Improvised on the crown of the latter a tattoo,
In lieu of expressing the feelings which lay
Quite too deep for words, as Wordsworth would
    say;
Then, without going through the form of a
    bow,
Found myself in the entry—I hardly knew
    how,—
On doorstep and sidewalk, past lamp-post and
    square,

At home and up stairs, in my own easy-chair;
  Poked my feet into slippers, my fire into
    blaze,
And said to myself, as I lit my cigar,
Supposing a man had the wealth of the Czar
  Of the Russias to boot, for the rest of his
    days,
On the whole, do you think he would have
    much to spare,
If he married a woman with nothing to wear?

Since that night, taking pains that it should not
    be bruited
Abroad in society, I've instituted
A course of inquiry, extensive and thorough
On this vital subject, and find, to my horror,
That the fair Flora's case is by no means sur-
    prising,
  But that there exists the greatest distress
In our female community, solely arising
  From this unsupplied destitution of dress,
Whose unfortunate victims are filling the air
With the pitiful wail of "Nothing to Wear."
Researches in some of the "Upper Ten" dis-
    tricts
Reveal the most painful and startling statistics,
Of which let me mention only a few:
In one single house, on Fifth Avenue,
Three young ladies were found, all below
    twenty-two,

Nothing to Wear

Who have been three whole weeks without any-
    thing new
In the way of flounced silks, and, thus left in
    the lurch,
Are unable to go to ball, concert, or church.
In another large mansion, near the same place,
Was found a deplorable, heartrending case
Of entire destitution of Brussels point lace.
In a neighboring block there was found, in
    three calls,
Total want, long continued, of camel's-hair
    shawls;
And a suffering family, whose case exhibits
The most pressing need of real ermine tippets;
One deserving young lady almost unable
To survive for the want of a new Russian
    sable;
Another confined to the house, when it's windier
Than usual, because her shawl isn't India.
Still another, whose tortures have been most
    terrific
Ever since the sad loss of the steamer *Pacific*,
In which were engulfed, not friend or relation
(For whose fate she perhaps might have found
    consolation
Or borne it, at least, with serene resignation),
But the choicest assortment of French sleeves
    and collars
Ever sent out from Paris, worth thousands of
    dollars,

And all as to style most *recherché* and rare,
The want of which leaves her with nothing to
    wear,
And renders her life so drear and dyspeptic
That she's quite a recluse, and almost a skeptic;
For she touchingly says that this sort of grief
Cannot find in Religion the slightest relief,
And Philosophy has not a maxim to spare
For the victims of such overwhelming despair.
But the saddest by far of all these sad features
Is the cruelty practised upon the poor creatures
By husbands and fathers, real Bluebeards and
    Timons,
Who resist the most touching appeals made for
    diamonds
By their wives and their daughters, and leave
    them for days
Unsupplied with new jewelry, fans, or bouquets,
Even laugh at their miseries whenever they have
    a chance,
And deride their demands as useless extrava-
    gance;
One case of a bride was brought to my view,
Too sad for belief, but, alas! 'twas too true,
Whose husband refused, as savage as Charon,
To permit her to take more than ten trunks to
    Sharon.
The consequence was, that when she got there,
At the end of three weeks she had nothing to
    wear,

Nothing to Wear

And when she proposed to finish the season
  At Newport, the monster refused out and out,
For his infamous conduct alleging no reason,
  Except that the waters were good for his
  gout.
Such treatment as this was too shocking, of
  course,
And proceedings are now going on for divorce.

But why harrow the feelings by lifting the
  curtain
From these scenes of woe?   Enough, it is cer-
  tain,
Has here been disclosed to stir up the pity
Of every benevolent heart in the city,
And spur up Humanity into a canter
To rush and relieve these sad cases instanter.
Won't somebody, moved by this touching de-
  scription,
Come forward to-morrow and head a subscrip-
  tion?
Won't some kind philanthropist, seeing that
  aid is
So needed at once by these indigent ladies,
Take charge of the matter?   Or won't Peter
  Cooper
The corner-stone lay of some splendid super-
Structure, like that which to-day links his name
In the Union unending of honor and fame;
And found a new charity just for the care

Of these unhappy women with nothing to wear,
Which, in view of the cash which would daily
    be claimed,
The *Laying-out* Hospital well might be named?
Won't Stewart, or some of our dry-goods im-
    porters,
Take a contract for clothing our wives and our
    daughters?
Or, to furnish the cash to supply these distresses,
And life's pathway strew with shawls, collars,
    and dresses,
Ere the want of them makes it much rougher
    and thornier,
Won't some one discover a new California?

Oh, ladies, dear ladies, the next sunny day
Please trundle your hoops just out of Broad-
    way,
From its whirl and its bustle, its fashion and
    pride,
And the temples of Trade which tower on each
    side,
To the alleys and lanes, where Misfortune and
    Guilt
Their children have gathered, their city have
    built;
Where Hunger and Vice, like twin beasts of
    prey,
  Have hunted their victims to gloom and de-
    spair;

Nothing to Wear

Raise the rich, dainty dress, and the fine broid-
 ered skirt,
Pick your delicate way through the dampness
 and dirt,
 Grope through the dark dens, climb the rick-
 ety stair
To the garret, where wretches, the young and
 the old,
Half-starved and half-naked, lie crouched from
 the cold.
 See those skeleton limbs, those frost-bitten
 feet,
All bleeding and bruised by the stones of the
 street;
Hear the sharp cry of childhood, the deep groans
 that swell
 From the poor dying creature who writhes
 on the floor,
Hear the curses that sound like the echoes of
 Hell,
 As you sicken and shudder and fly from the
 door;
Then home to your wardrobes, and say, if you
 dare,—
Spoiled children of Fashion,—you've nothing
 to wear!

And oh, if perchance there should be a sphere
Where all is made right which so puzzles us
 here,

Where the glare and the glitter and tinsel of
Time
Fade and die in the light of that region sublime,
Where the soul, disenchanted of flesh and of
sense,
Unscreened by its trappings and shows and pre-
tense,
Must be clothed for the life and the service
above,
With purity, truth, faith, meekness, and love;
O daughters of Earth! foolish virgins, beware!
Lest in that upper realm you have nothing to
wear!

William Allen Butler.

NOTHING TO WEAR

"I confess," writes William Allen Butler, in his *Retrospect of Forty Years*, "that I have sometimes felt a pang, or at least a thrill, of mortification that, after many years of toil to attain a desired place in my profession, my chief, if not only, claim to public recognition has been the writing of a few pages of society verse."

When Mr. Butler died, twenty years ago, many learned societies passed resolutions of respect and regret, and panegyrics upon his legal attainments were pronounced in many courts; but he was quite right in thinking that all these would quickly fade. They are almost as though they had never been, and the great public still remembers him—in so far as it remembers him at all—only as the author of a single poem.

That poem, of course, is "Nothing to Wear," published in 1857—the first bit of genuinely American rhymed satire in our literature. There had been satire before it from American pens, but the inspiration was that of Pope and Dryden. Here was a new note, something indigenous and original, a definite breaking away

211

from the classic formulas of the eighteenth century—the Nymphs, the Muses, the Pierian
Springs. How fresh and delightful it must
have seemed!

William Dean Howells has told how he
was entranced by it. At the time of its appearance in *Harper's Weekly* in February, 1857, he
was editing the *Ohio State Journal* at Columbus, and in an introduction to a collection of
Mr. Butler's poems published in 1899, he tells
the story thus:

"In the year 1857," he says, "prairie fires
were still punctual with the falling year on the
plains which farms and cities now hold against
them; and when one said that this thing or that
was sweeping the country like a prairie fire,
every one else knew what one meant, and
visualized the fact with quick intelligence. But
if I say now that in 1857 a new poem, flashing
from a novel impulse in our literature, and gay
with lights and tints unknown before, swept the
country like a prairie fire, how many, I wonder, will conceive of the astonishing success of
'Nothing to Wear'? . . .

"But, after all, one must have lived in the
year 1857, and been, say, in one's twenty-first
year, to have felt the full significance of its
message and shared the joyful surprise of its
amazing success. If to the enviable conditions
suggested one joined the advantage of being a

212

newspaperman in a growing city of the Middle West, one had almost unequaled privileges as a spectator and participator of the notable event. Upon the whole, I am inclined to think that prairie fire suggests a feeble image of the swift spread of Mr. Butler's poem under the eye of such a witness; and I begin to prefer a train of gunpowder.

"I do not know where the piece first appeared, but I remember that with the simple predacity of those days we instantly lifted the whole of it out of a New York paper, hot from the mail, and transferred it to our own columns about midnight, as if it were some precious piece of telegraphic intelligence. I am not sure but that it was for us something in the nature of a scoop or beat. At any rate, no other paper in town had it so early; and I think it appeared on our editorial page, and certainly with subheads supplied by our own eager invention, and with the prefatory and concurrent comment which it so little needed."

What happened in that newspaper office, happened in scores of others. "Nothing to Wear" swept the country; Miss Flora McFlimsey became a type, and "nothing to wear" a phrase with satiric implications which it has never lost. Its permanence, indeed, is due in no small part to its universality, for its message is as intelligible and apropos to-day as the day it was written.

The moral at the close may be found old-fashioned and banal, and the puns sometimes a little forced, but, as a whole, the poem has lost none of its sparkle.

Mr. Howells hazarded the opinion that "but for the professional devotion of the able lawyer, we might have counted in him the cleverest of our society poets." But this may be doubted. He was a one-poem man, visited once and once only by genuine inspiration. His other poems show a certain whimsicality and facility in rhyme, but none of them approaches "Nothing to Wear." They are written out of the air, not out of experience, and time has worn them as thin as ghosts.

William Allen Butler was not a born poet— he was a born lawyer; his career proves that. Indeed one has only to look at the photograph which he had taken in 1857 and includes in his book. Nothing could be more typically legalistic than the face and figure there portrayed. But both in his father's family and in his wife's family the feminine sex was in a large majority. He had five sisters and his wife had four sisters. Consequently whenever the families got together, the usual subject of discussion was clothes, and the phrase "nothing to wear," in connection with proposed entertainments or social festivities, was continually in his ears. This was the inspiration. It was of this

mental reaction that the poem was the pre-
cipitant.

Curiously enough, Mr. Butler himself believed that he was inspired to write, not this portion of the poem, but the very portion which has
least inspiration in it.   Here is what he says:

The idea of giving a moral turn to the subject
did not occur to me until I had made considerable
progress in my work on the poem, which occupied
odd moments of leisure in a very busy winter, and
I remember that it was while I was walking one
evening that the thought expressed in the closing
lines of "Nothing to Wear" came to me, a sudden,
and, I must believe, a genuine inspiration.

But it was not the mind of the poet, it was
the mind of the lawyer which devised the
closing lines, and the lawyer is also betrayed in
other places by a stilted phrase or a legal reference.   Mr. Butler continues:

Having finished the poem, and after reading .it
to my wife, I took it to my friend, Evert A.
Duyckinck, whom I found in his accustomed place
in the basement of his house, No. 20 Clinton Place,
surrounded by the books which afterwards, under
his will, went to the Lenox Library.   I read him
the poem, to which he listened with lively interest;
but, much to my disappointment, he did not appre-
ciate as keenly as I had hoped what I believed and

what afterwards proved to be the elements of its popularity. While Duyckinck was the most genial of companions and the most impartial of critics, he was too much of a recluse, buried in his books, almost solitary in his life, and entirely removed from the circle of worldly and fashionable life, to judge of my work as a possible palpable hit.

However, he immediately possessed himself of it for publication in *Harper's Weekly*, then recently started, and I at once acquiesced, making the single condition that they should publish it in columns wide enough to prevent breaking of the lines. No thought of securing the copyright or of retaining any control in reference to the publication of it occurred to me, and the check for fifty dollars which in due course I received from Harper's, represented the entire pecuniary benefit that ever came to me from "Nothing to Wear."

The poem as it went to Harper's contained 305 lines. When I received the proof sheets they were accompanied by a note stating that the addition of 24 lines would fill out the last page, and I wrote the required number, inserting them in the body of the poem, which appeared very handsomely printed in the number of *Harper's Weekly* for February 7, 1857."

Mr. Butler never stated where these twenty-four lines were added, but it is fairly safe to guess that they comprise the section beginning

But why harrow the feelings by lifting the curtain,

for this section is not only rather loosely connected with the rest of the poem, but it is here
that the inspiration is most obviously being
flogged along.

"Nothing to Wear" became almost instantly
popular in England as well as in this country. It
was published in book form in London; Harriet
Martineau quoted it entire in an article on
"Female Dress" in the *Westminster Review;* it
invaded the continent, and was translated into
French, with a foot-note explaining that the
Mrs. Harris referred to in the opening lines as
"famous in history," was a lady who had lost
her life at Niagara Falls; a German translation
with illustrations appeared in the Almanach de
Gotha. Evidently it appealed to all peoples, for
of course there were Flora McFlimseys in Bel-
gravia and on the Avenue du Bois de Boulogne,
as well as on Madison Square—and equally, of
course, there still are.

"It does not indeed find her posterity in
Madison Square," says Mr. Howells; "the
fashion that once abode there has fled to upper
Fifth Avenue, to the discordant variety of handsome residences which overlook the Park. But
there it finds her descendants quite one with her
in spirit, and as little clothed to their lasting
satisfaction. Still they shop in Paris, still they
arrive in all the steamers with their spoil, still
it shrinks and withers to nothing in their keep-

ing. Probably there are no longer lovers so
simple-hearted as to fancy any of them going
to a function in a street costume, or in a dress
which has already been worn three times, but,
if there were, their fate would be as swift and
dire. In such things the world does not change,
and the plutocrats of imperial New York spell
their qualities with the same characters as the
plutocrats of Imperial Rome."

On the basis of all this popularity, Mr.
Butler tried to persuade the Harpers to publish
the poem in book form, but they refused on the
ground that they had sold 80,000 copies of the
Weekly which contained it, and there could be
no possible demand for the book. They were
so sincere in this belief, that when the firm of
Rudd & Carleton, just starting in the publishing
business, asked permission to publish "Nothing
to Wear," the Harpers granted it, without asking any payment and also without any consulta-
tion with Mr. Butler. The book,[1] with illustrations by Augustus Hoppin, was a great success
and assisted materially in placing the new firm
on its feet. Mr. Butler, of course, received
nothing, not even credit, for nowhere in the
book does his name appear.

He soon found, indeed, that not only was he

[1] *Nothing to Wear. An Episode of City Life.*
(From *Harper's Weekly.*) Illustrated by Hoppin.
New York: Rudd & Carleton, 310 Broadway,
MDCCCLVII.

to get no material benefit from the poem, but that he was in danger of having the laurels of authorship snatched from his brow. He had not signed his name to the poem when he sent it to *Harper's Weekly,* and it had appeared there anonymously. That was the general custom in those days, and Mr. Butler had an added reason for withholding his name—or thought he had! As he himself puts it, "I feared that if I were known to be the writer of verses, it might injure my standing as a lawyer. Members of my profession were permitted to make politics an adjunct of their practice at the bar, but dalliance with the Muse and dabbling in verses were apt to come under the ban of a commercial clientage."

The consequence was that a number of claimants to the authorship soon came forward. The most annoying of these—annoying because her youth and her sex gave her an advantage and won a certain sympathy—was a girl of fifteen named Peck. Her story, confirmed by her father, was to the effect that about a year previously she had been wandering through the woods near her home in the outskirts of New York, and accidentally tore the skirt of her dress. "There, now, I have nothing to wear!" she had exclaimed vexedly, but this exclamation was followed by the reflection, "How many are in the habit of declaring that they have nothing

219

to wear, who really have no just reason for the complaint, while, on the other hand, multitudes might make the same complaint with truth as well as sorrow!"

When she reached home, she sat down and wrote a poem around this thought—a poem of thirty-nine lines, written on a single sheet of paper. She took it with her on a visit to New York, intending to show it to some friends, "had the manuscript in her hand on leaving the cars near Twenty-sixth Street, and passing through the crowd it was lost."

What was her astonishment to discover in *Harper's Weekly* some months later her poem incorporated in a much longer one. The first nine lines of her poem had been used as the introduction, and the other thirty lines included at the close. The inference was, of course, that the author of the poem in *Harper's Weekly* had picked up Miss Peck's verses, and found in them the inspiration for his more ambitious effort.

It would seem that a story so absurd, and put forward as this one was without the slightest effort at substantiation beyond the worthless confirmation given it by the girl's father, would drop dead of its own weight; but, as has already been remarked in the course of these pages, there are always a lot of people seemingly ready to believe anything, and a number of them rallied enthusiastically around Miss Peck, who became a sort of nine days' wonder, her partizans pointing out, quite justly, what a remarkable achievement it was for so young a girl to have written even thirty-nine lines of such a poem.

But her triumph was short-lived, for Mr. Butler soon decided that the only thing for him to do was to disclose his authorship, which he did in a card stating "in the most explicit and unmistakable terms that every line and word in 'Nothing to Wear' was original with him and branding the claim as utterly false." Horace Greeley, who lived next door to Mr. Butler (and kept a goat in the back yard, much to the annoyance of his neighbors), came to his defense in an editorial in the *Tribune*, and *Harper's Weekly* confirmed Mr. Butler's statement and denounced Miss Peck as a fraud. Thereafter, no sensible person ever questioned his authorship of the poem, though a few very silly ones still affected to regard him as a thief and impostor.

Mr. Butler, as has been said, was always proud of the moral twist he had given the poem at the end, but a more discerning judgment was well expressed by a French reviewer, M. Étienne, who admired the poem as a true expression of American humor until he came to its last lines. "Then," says he, "I am brought back against my will to the memory of those old Puritans who founded the American nation. The idea of damnation dissipates all my gaiety, and I look to see if I have really before me a humorist or a son of Calvin."

SOLITUDE

SOLITUDE

Laugh, and the world laughs with you;
　　Weep, and you weep alone,
For the sad old earth must borrow its mirth,
　　But has trouble enough of its own.
Sing, and the hills will answer;
　　Sigh, it is lost on the air,
The echoes bound to a joyful sound,
　　But shrink from voicing care.

Rejoice, and men will seek you;
　　Grieve, and they turn and go.
They want full measure of all your pleasure,
　　But they do not need your woe.
Be glad, and your friends are many;
　　Be sad, and you lose them all,—
There are none to decline your nectared wine,
　　But alone you must drink life's gall.

Feast, and your halls are crowded;
　　Fast, and the world goes by.
Succeed and give, and it helps you live,
　　But no man can help you die.
There is room in the halls of pleasure
　　For a large and lordly train,
But one by one we must all file on
　　Through the narrow aisles of pain.
　　　　　　　　Ella Wheeler Wilcox

SOLITUDE

In May, 1883, there was published at Chicago a thin little volume containing about fifty poems of very second-rate quality which, in the ordinary course of events, would have quickly dropped from sight and been forgotten. But some adroit advertising, combined with an astounding absence of humor on the part of certain editors and reviewers, changed all that, and this little book not only made a great splash in the literary mill-pond, but convinced many Americans for all time that its author was an abandoned creature, a slave to passions quite oriental in their character, and the heroine of various torrid love adventures.

The book bore the daring title *Poems of Passion,* but its author, far from being an adventuress, was a little Wisconsin girl named Ella Wheeler, the daughter of a poor farmer, who had lived all her life in the cramped environment of a tiny hamlet called Johnson Centre, whose knowledge of the world was bounded by a few short visits to Madison and Milwaukee, and whose acquaintance with literature was confined to the menus furnished by the New York *Mercury* and the New York

Ledger, and to the novels of Ouida, Mary J.
Holmes and Mrs. Southworth—with a later
smattering of Gautier, Shakespeare, Swinburne
and Byron.

All this is evident enough in the book itself,
for the verses it contained were exactly the sort
of sentimental rot that a Mary J. Holmes
heroine would write; but most readers jumped
to the conclusion that Miss Wheeler must herself have undergone the emotional experiences
which she described, and her image as a Woman
with a Past was then and there fixed permanently
in the public mind.

The volume had started off with the immense
advantage of a lot of advertising such as is now
supplied by the Vice Society to certain fortunate
books. McClurg, of Chicago, had declined to
publish it on the ground that it was immoral;
Miss Wheeler, quite outraged, told a friend in
Milwaukee about it, and this friend in turn
told one of the Milwaukee papers, which thereupon published a column article headed,

TOO LOUD FOR CHICAGO
The Scarlet City by the Lake Shocked by a Badger
Girl, whose Verses out-Swinburne Swin-
burne and out-Whitman Whitman.

Another Chicago publisher, less fastidious
than McClurg, at once saw the opportunity to

make some money, offered to publish the book and brought it out with great éclat. He sent review copies, no doubt with cleverly worded blurbs, to various guardians of public morals, and then sat back and waited results.

They were not long in coming. A terrific cyclone of public indignation burst about the author's head. Her friends turned away from her in disapproval, and many of them expressed the opinion that she should have waited until she was dead, or at least married, before permitting the poems to appear, since they dealt with matters with which no decent girl could possibly be familiar. Charles A. Dana devoted two sizzling columns to a sweeping condemnation of the book which, he announced, threatened to undermine all morality and should be suppressed. The Chicago *Herald*, after pointing out the poisonous character of the book's contents, ventured the hope "that Miss Ella Wheeler will relapse into *Poems of Decency* now that the New York *Sun* has voiced the opinion of respectability that her *Poems of Passion* are like the songs of half-tipsy wantons." Nowhere was a voice raised in her defense.

The most embarrassing feature of the situation was that she had just become engaged to be married to a man who, as it turned out, was to be her lifelong lover and husband; but she dared not announce the engagement for fear of the

228

storm of Rabelaisian laughter which would sweep the press—what, the author of *Poems of Passion* posing as a shy maiden approaching her first experience of love? And the man—what sort of fool was he?

"Were I to live my life over again," says Mrs. Wilcox in her autobiography, "with the wisdom of years and knowledge of the world to start with, I surely would not publish *Poems of Passion.*" However, on the other side of the ledger it should be recorded that financially the book was a great success and the proceeds enabled her to put a new roof on the house, to buy her father a new suit of clothes, and to help the family generally.

It seems strange now, looking through the book, to remember what forbidden fruit it was thirty years ago, how it was excluded from the shelves of public libraries, and read surreptitiously by young Lydia Languishes, who thrust it hastily under a cushion when any one entered; how daring it was considered to mention it at all, and what a zest it gave to any entertainment if somebody recited something from it. The sensation was precisely the same as it is to-day when the cocktails are passed around. Cocktails created no sensation then; but Bayard Taylor's "Bedouin Love Song" and Shelley's "Lines to an Indian Air" and anything from *Poems of Passion* were considered so daring that

229

it was very difficult for Lydia to decide whether
she should blush without smiling, or smile without blushing, or blush and smile simultaneously,
or just sit with downcast eyes and seem not to
understand. How times do change!

The poem which called forth the loudest
reprobation was entitled "The Farewell of
Clarimonde," and was suggested by Gautier's
famous story, which Miss Wheeler had somewhere happened upon and devoured with avidity.
Here are four stanzas—the worst ones:

Adieu, Romauld! But thou canst not forget me,
Although no more I haunt thy dreams at night,
Thy hungering heart forever must regret me,
And starve for those lost moments of delight.

Naught shall avail thy priestly rites and duties—
Nor fears of Hell, nor hope of Heaven beyond:
Before the Cross shall rise my fair form's beauties—
The lips, the limbs, the eyes of Clarimonde.

I knew all arts of love: he who possessed me
Possessed all women, and could never tire:
A new life dawned for him who once caressed me:
Satiety itself I set on fire.

Inconstancy I chained: men died to win me;
Kings cast by crowns for one hour on my breast,
And all the passionate tide of love within me
I gave to thee, Romauld. Wert thou not blest?

Solitude

No one to-day would consider this especially shocking; but it shows that, whatever the deficiencies educational and otherwise of this rustic Wisconsin girl, lack of imagination of a certain sort was not one of them.

Not all the poems in the book were concerned with the tender passion. That special source of inspiration failed at page ninety-five, and the concluding sixty pages are devoted to "Miscellaneous Poems." They are for the most part quite frankly juvenile—indeed, Mrs. Wilcox's verse never outgrew a certain immaturity—moralizing upon "Courage," "Progress," "Regret," "Creation," and other well-worn topics of similar character; and it is with one of these, entitled "Solitude," that the present article is concerned.

Mrs. Wilcox has herself told in detail the circumstances of its composition. On the forenoon of a February day in 1883 she boarded the train for Madison, having been honored with an invitation to attend the governor's inaugural ball that evening, and being in consequence in a flutter of excitement. She had in her bag a pretty white dress, made especially for the occasion, and was very happy; but as she took her seat in the coach, she saw a young woman clad in black and shaking with sobs, sitting across the aisle. It was, as Mrs. Wilcox characteristically puts it, "the bride of a year, the widow of a week, a lovely girl I had last seen radiant with happiness."

The young poetess sat down beside the mourning girl, her own gaiety all forgotten, and did what she could to console her. She left the train at Madison feeling very blue, and certain that all the pleasure had been taken out of her visit. But she soon forgot the incident in the excitement of getting ready for the ball, she had underestimated the resilience of her own young spirits, and it was not until she was standing in her room before her mirror putting the last touches to the white toilet of which she was so proud, that a vision of that young widow clad all in black flashed before her. With something like remorse, she compared her own radiant figure with that other one bowed under its sorrow, and the first four lines of the poem which was to be called "Solitude" sprang into her mind:

> Laugh and the world laughs with you,
> Weep and you weep alone.
> For the sad old earth must borrow its mirth,
> It has trouble enough of its own.

She knew at once that they were the nucleus of a longer poem, tucked them away in a pigeon-hole of her brain and went on to the ball, where she thoroughly enjoyed herself.

Solitude

But the next morning the quatrain recurred to her at the breakfast-table, and she recited it to her host and hostess, telling them at the same time the story of the young widow. Both of her hearers were enthusiastic, and the host remarked that if she could keep the remainder of the poem up to the epigrammatic standard of these first four lines she would produce something really worth while.

Two nights later, on coming home from a theater-party, she told her friends that she was going to sit up and finish the poem, and did so in a very short time after getting to her room. When, next morning, she took the poem down to breakfast with her and read it aloud, she warned her hearers that she felt she had not kept up to the standard of the first lines, but, she adds, "I can still see the look on the very handsome face of the Judge as he listened with increasing interest, and I can still hear his deep voice lifted in quick spontaneous praise, in which his fair young wife joined."

She sent the poem to the New York *Sun* and received five dollars for it. The *Sun* published it February 21, 1883, and it was then added to the "Miscellaneous Poems" needed to fill out *Poems of Passion.*

Almost at the same time with *Poems of Passion,* a man by the name of John A. Joyce had published a volume of reminiscences entitled

Famous Single Poems

A Checkered Life, written, so Mrs. Wilcox afterwards asserted, while Joyce was serving a term in prison for complicity in certain whisky frauds. The book purported to tell the story of Joyce's career from youth to maturity, and included the following remarkable memorandum:

Eastern Kentucky Lunatic Asylum,
Lexington, Kentucky.
The records of this asylum show No. 2,423, John A. Joyce, 18 years of age; occupation, farmer; habit, temperate; original disposition and intellect good; cause, heredity; form of mania, perpetual motion. Admitted June 20, 1860; discharged September, 1860.

W. A. BULLOCK, M. D.
Medical Superintendent.

This memorandum was supposed to prove that Joyce had entirely recovered from the mental trouble which had clouded his youth.

At the back of the book were twenty-three extremely mediocre poems, supposedly all that he had ever written.

In 1885 another edition of the book was published with some additions and revisions, and one of the additions was the poem, "Laugh and the World Laughs with You." Ten years later Joyce published another book entitled *Jewels of Memory,* also including a number of his poems, "Laugh and the World Laughs with

You" among them, and telling the following story of how this particular poem was written.

In January, 1863, when he was twenty-one years old and adjutant of the Twenty-fourth Kentucky regiment, at that time camped at the "Oaklands," near Louisville, Ky., he secured a forty-eight hours' pass and went in to Louisville to call on George D. Prentice, the editor of the Louisville *Journal,* whose poem, "The Closing Year," Joyce says he considered the finest in American literature. Joyce had had some correspondence with Prentice, who had published a few of his poems, so he proceeded to the *Journal* office, introduced himself and indulged in some cheap wit which he faithfully records.

"Do you drink?" Prentice asked.

"Never," Joyce replied, like a flash, "except when alone or in company."

Uplifted by this brilliant exchange, the two proceeded to the Galt House and were ushered into a wine-room back of the bar where Prentice was very much at home, and where Major Silas Miller, the proprietor of the house, and two or three friends joined them. Two bottles of Piper Heidseick were ordered by Prentice and presently two more by Joyce, who was unusually rich with four months' back pay in his pocket, and the talk was so clever that Joyce says he imagined himself "at the club with Johnson, Garrick, Beauclerc and Goldsmith."

"Prentice then began his badinage," he continues, "and spurred me about presuming to think I was a poet, and finally defied me to write something off-hand and prove to his friends that I was not a pretender.

"I said, 'All right; what shall I write about?'

" 'Oh,' said Prentice, 'write about anything— write about us, wine, feasting, fun, or philosophy.'

"I asked for paper, and it was furnished. I then turned around to a side table, pulled my memories together, thought of Horace, the Falernian wine poet, and one of his odes, where he speaks of people joining you when you laugh, but declining to cling to you when you weep. Then, too, the suggestions of Prentice and the surrounding scene anchored in my mind and inspired my lines.

"I immediately pulled a pencil from my pocket and wrote the following verses inside of fifteen minutes, while my companions were dumping down wine with hilarious vociferation:

(He here quotes Mrs. Wilcox's poem, word for word, the only change being that he has transposed the quatrains of the second and third stanzas.)

"I threw these lines to Prentice. He read them to the revelers and then exclaimed: 'Sir,' speaking to Miller, 'didn't I tell you that fellow was a fool? Now I know he's crazy.'

"Well, the world has had the benefit of my brain baby for thirty years," Joyce concludes, "although 'Exchange,' 'Anonymous,' and other literary robbers have claimed it. What care I? Mankind can make the most of it. More than a dozen other of my verses have gone the rounds of the press under the colors of some plagiarist.

"The glorious Prentice has slept beneath the sod for nearly a quarter of a century, but the grand thoughts he uttered in life will spread over the years like perfume from an unseen censer and thrill the heart of mankind when the memory of his social and literary critics are washed into the waters of oblivion."

It is unfortunate that Prentice died before Joyce made this story public. There might then have been some confirmation of it. As it is, there is none; nor does memory recall any ode of Horace, "the Falernian wine poet," to whom Joyce refers in such off-hand fashion, dealing with the subject of Mrs. Wilcox's poem. There can be no doubt, indeed, that Joyce's story was manufactured out of whole cloth. If he wrote the verses in 1863 they would certainly have appeared somewhere before they were published over Ella Wheeler's name twenty years later, and he would undoubtedly have included them among the poems printed in the first edition of his book.

In 1901 he published another book which purported to be a biography of Edgar Allan Poe, but which is really a strange farrago of nonsense, and he took occasion to include "Solitude" under the title "Love and Laughter." It is dedicated to George D. Prentice, and is accompanied by this comment:

My own poem, "Love and Laughter," written for George D. Prentice, Journalist and Poet, in Louisville, Kentucky, January, 1863, might well be inserted here for the information and education of the rushing world.

The reader can do no better than memorize it and act upon its precepts. The idea of the poem can be found in Homer, Horace, Shakespeare, and the Bible, but not in such rhythmic, epigrammatic and synthetical form. It is a philosophic sermon and will be repeated on the lips of mankind as long as Truth is triumphant!

This is a fair example of the style of the book, the character of whose contents indicates that the wheels of perpetual motion were still going around in Joyce's head. The portrait which serves as a frontispiece to *Jewels of Memory* confirms this impression. The face is unquestionably that of a man of unstable mentality. It is not without a certain cheap attractiveness, but it is stamped with weakness and dissipation, and the angle at which the broad-brimmed hat is worn betrays the inordinate vanity of the man who wears it.

Mrs. Wilcox, of course, indignantly denied Joyce's story from the first, but he continued to repeat it on every possible occasion, and her husband wished to start a suit for damages, but his friends very wisely dissuaded him from doing so.

"But," writes Mrs. Wilcox, "Mr. Joyce proved himself seriously annoying up to the day of his death. He never allowed more than two years to pass without finding some obscure paper in which he could again set forth his claims to my poem. I repeatedly made an offer of $5000 to be given to charity when any one could produce a copy of 'Solitude' published prior to February, 1883. I finally offered to present to any charitable institution he might select, in his name, that amount of money, when Mr. Joyce produced his proof. Of course it was never forthcoming; and yet he claimed the poem had been in circulation for twenty years before I wrote it.

"I believe my experience one which nearly every author has known at some time in his or her career," concludes Mrs. Wilcox. "Though misery may like company, the fact does not prevent one's own suffering, when made the victim of a man of this type, who belongs to the poison insect order of humanity. He is only an insect, and yet his persistent buzz and sting can produce great discomfort."

A few years later, Mrs. Wilcox had a somewhat similar experience with another poem. In December, 1886, she was shopping in New York and was shown a very beautiful opal, the first she had ever seen, by a Mr. Marcus, a dealer in precious stones, who remarked that he wished she would write a poem about it to be used in a book on gems which he was preparing. He added that the opal had always seemed to him the child of the sunbeam and the moonbeam, but though he had mentioned this idea to several New York poets, none of them had been able to make anything of it. Mrs. Wilcox said she was sure that she could, and the next morning, in about half an hour's time, wrote the following:

THE BIRTH OF THE OPAL

The Sunbeam loved the Moonbeam,
  And followed her low and high,
But the Moonbeam fled and hid her head,
  She was so shy—so shy.

The Sunbeam wooed with passion;
  Ah, he was a lover bold!
And his heart was afire with mad desire,
  For the Moonbeam pale and cold.

240

Solitude

She fled like a dream before him,
　　Her hair was a shining sheen,
And, oh, that Fate would annihilate
　　The space that lay between!

Just as the day lay panting
　　In the arms of the twilight dim,
The Sunbeam caught the one he sought
　　And drew her close to him.

But out of his warm arms, startled
　　And stirred by Love's first shock,
She sprang afraid, like a trembling maid,
　　And hid in the niche of a rock.

And the Sunbeam followed and found her
　　And led her to Love's own feast;
And they were wed on that rocky bed,
　　And the dying day was their priest.

And lo! the beautiful Opal—
　　That rare and wondrous gem—
Where the moon and the sun blend into one,
　　Is the child that was born to them.

She sent these verses to Mr. Marcus, saying she wished to publish them in the *Century Magazine*, after which he could use them, if he wished, in his book on gems. Mr. Marcus was so impressed with them that he sent her a check for twenty-five dollars, and asked to be permitted to publish them first. Mrs. Wilcox agreed, but much to her chagrin, when the book appeared, the verses had no name attached. A few months later, she included them in her *Poems of Pleasure,* and was astonished to have her authorship sharply challenged by people who claimed to have seen them published elsewhere over other names. She had no difficulty, of course, in proving her right to them, but occasionally for many years she would see them attributed to some one else.

"The Birth of the Opal" became one of the most popular poems Mrs. Wilcox ever wrote, and it is one of the best; but it served to give a fresh fillip to the reputation for daring which *Poems of Passion* had started. Many of her friends thought it too frank, and one woman, the wife of a successful author, went so far as to cut her acquaintance on the ground that in "The Birth of the Opal" she had laid bare all the secrets of married life!

ROCK ME TO SLEEP

ROCK ME TO SLEEP

Backward, turn backward, O Time, in your flight,
Make me a child again just for to-night!
Mother, come back from the echoless shore,
Take me again to your heart as of yore;
Kiss from my forehead the furrows of care,
Smooth the few silver threads out of my hair;
Over my slumbers your loving watch keep—
Rock me to sleep, mother—rock me to sleep!

Backward, flow backward, O tide of the years!
I am so weary of toil and of tears—
Toil without recompense, tears all in vain—
Take them and give me my childhood again!
I have grown weary of dust and decay,
Weary of flinging my soul-wealth away,
Weary of sowing for others to reap—
Rock me to sleep, mother—rock me to sleep!

Tired of the hollow, the base, the untrue,
Mother, O mother, my heart calls for you!
Many a summer the grass has grown green,
Blossomed and faded, our faces between;
Yet, with strong yearning and passionate pain,
Long I to-night for your presence again;
Come from the silence so long and so deep—
Rock me to sleep, mother—rock me to sleep!

Over my heart in the days that are flown,
No love like mother-love ever has shone;
No other worship abides and endures,
Faithful, unselfish, and patient, like yours;
None like a mother can charm away pain
From the sick soul and the world-weary brain;
Slumber's soft calms o'er my heavy lids creep—
Rock me to sleep, mother—rock me to sleep!

Come, let your brown hair, just lighted with gold,
Fall on your shoulders again as of old;
Let it drop over my forehead to-night,
Shading my faint eyes away from the light;
For with its sunny-edged shadows once more,
Haply will throng the sweet visions of yore;
Lovingly, softly, its bright billows sweep—
Rock me to sleep, mother—rock me to sleep!

Mother, dear mother, the years have been long
Since I last listened your lullaby song;
Sing, then, and unto my soul it shall seem
Womanhood's years have been only a dream.
Clasped to your heart in a loving embrace,
With your light lashes just sweeping my face,
Never hereafter to wake or to weep—
Rock me to sleep, mother—rock me to sleep!

Elizabeth Akers

ROCK ME TO SLEEP

MUCH has been written about the sleeping sick-
ness and the dengue fever; a vast organization
is grappling with the hookworm; the economic
losses occasioned by all three have given rise to
the direst forebodings. But they are as nothing
beside the mania for scribbling which devastates
the land. Few people are aware how much
time and money and energy are wasted by it, or
to what depths of depravity it sometimes reduces
its devotees. To have something published
somewhere, to read one's verses to an admiring
circle, to be known as a literary person—that is
the supreme ambition of countless thousands.
No effort is made to combat this dementia; on
the contrary, scores of organizations exist for
the sole object of arousing it, fanning it, keeping it going, proclaiming loudly that anybody
can write and offering (for a substantial consideration) to teach anybody how.

Since no law has as yet been enacted to put
these instigators of crime in jail, and no serum
is on the market for the cure of their victims, it may not be amiss to relate a moral tale,
after the manner of Dr. Watts or Jane Taylor,

of how a man's peace of mind was shattered and a woman's life embittered because the man, in the innocence of his heart, wanted his friends to think him a poet. And the text of this tale may very well be that justly famous couplet:

Oh, what a tangled web we weave
When first we practise to deceive!

So to the story.

In the early sixties of the last century, there dwelt in the pleasant town of Elizabeth, New Jersey, a prosperous and respected harness-maker by the name of Alexander M. W. Ball. He was a devoted husband and father, something of a personage since he had made the long voyage to California and back a few years before, well thought of by his neighbors, and possessed of enough political influence to secure an election to the New Jersey legislature.

But the thing of which he was proudest was his reputation as a poet. He was always polishing off some verses, working over them much harder than he did over his harness, and nothing pleased him more than an opportunity to read them to his friends. These opportunities were numerous, since he always had some of his verses in his pocket or lying on his desk, and his friends never failed to be impressed. But if they solicited a copy, he would explain that the verses were as yet in a rough and unfinished state entirely unsatisfactory to their author. When they were completed, he would be only too happy to oblige.

If they urged him to have them printed and permit the world to enjoy them, he would point out gently that he was entirely indifferent, even averse, to the plaudits of the public, that he wrote poetry just for the joy of it, and that it would seem to him a desecration to share the children of his brain with any but his nearest and dearest friends. The said friends drank all this in with open mouths, and in time he came to wear in their eyes not only a laurel wreath but a halo.

One of these friends happened one day to see in print a set of six stanzas entitled "Rock Me to Sleep," and signed "Florence Percy." He recognized the poem as one of Mr. Ball's—the one, indeed, which he was fondest of reading and which was admired most—and hastened to that gentleman to inform him that some brazen hussy was trying to steal his laurels. But Mr. Ball was not disturbed—his halo did not even quiver. It mattered not to him, he explained, who got the credit for the verses; he had had the pleasure of writing them, and that was enough. Let Florence Percy, whoever she might be, go in peace—her conscience would punish her.

But to this his friends would by no means agree. Without consulting him they wrote indignant letters to the papers denouncing "Florence Percy" as a shameless plagiarist, and asserting that "Rock Me to Sleep" had been written by Alexander M. W. Ball. This finally drew a tart letter from Elizabeth A. C. Akers, published in the New York *Evening Post* for June 13, 1865, in which she stated that she had written "Rock Me to Sleep" in May, 1860, while sojourning in Italy, and had sent it to the Philadelphia *Saturday Evening Post*, which had published it shortly after its receipt. She had signed it "Florence Percy," a pen-name which she had "mistakenly adopted when a girl."

"I am certainly one of the last individuals in the world," Mrs. Akers continued, "to take the humiliating position of contending in public or otherwise for a matter of literary credit; and so long as this question was merely that of ability to write the poem in dispute it was simply amusing to me.

"But when it assumes, as it has latterly done, the attitude of a slander, liable to set me wrong in the opinion of many whose regard is dearer to me than any newspaper praise could be, when I hear myself good-naturedly designated in society as the lady who pretends to have written, etc., it is high time to state the facts."

This letter unleashed the dogs of war, which

were further infuriated when "Rock Me to Sleep" was included in a volume of poems published for Mrs. Akers by Ticknor & Fields in 1866. The controversy raged in the public prints with a violence possible only in those days of smashing epithets and whole-hearted vituperation. The *Atlantic Monthly,* *The Nation,* the Providence *Journal,* the New York *Times,* the *Round Table,* the New York *Tribune,* the *Knickerbocker Magazine,* and countless others, took a hand—or, rather, a fist—in it, gave and received lusty blows, and had a gorgeous time. How deeply all this excoriated Mrs. Akers may be judged from a letter she wrote Mr. Ball in August, 1867.

"Of the utter falsity of the claim," she says to him, "which you have made to the poem, 'Rock Me to Sleep,' no two persons in the world can be so well aware as you and myself. You know that it is not yours; that you never saw it until you saw it in print. I know that it is mine, and mine only. Furthermore, you and I both know that your sin in this thing was not 'involuntary' or 'clairvoyant.' You have clearly proved, by parading before the world your so-called 'original draft' of this poem, that this claim of yours was a deliberately planned and coolly executed piece of villainy. So far as your influence reaches and convinces, I stand before the world guilty of falsehood and theft,

251

combined in the most humiliating and inexcusable form, since the crime is not a crime of necessity, nor of provocation, but of the weakest and most pitiable vanity," and after pointing out its further serious consequences for her, she asks him to repent of his wickedness, abjure his claim, and set her right before the world; otherwise she will be forced to bring suit against him.

Ball answered in a long letter dated September 6, 1867, in which he expressed himself as delighted at the prospect of threshing the question out in a court of law, and, in order that she might have explicit grounds for the suit, repeats "with an unqualified absoluteness, that you are not, and that you very well know that you are not the author of the poem published by you as your own, entitled 'Rock Me to Sleep, Mother,' but, on the contrary, that I am the author, and the sole author, of it; and I am ready to and do avouch it before God and man, here and everywhere, now and always, and in all forms that can give solemnity to statement, and bind the soul for its truth."

Poor Ball! How far he had traveled since the day when he had ingenuously read some verses to his friends and accepted their plaudits! For his claim was not at all the preconceived piece of villainy which Mrs. Akers believed; it was something into which he had been urged step by step by an Iago who was always at his elbow—the Honorable Oliver O. Morse, of Cherry Valley, New York. Morse was probably not a conscious Iago; he no doubt believed all that he wrote, but unquestionably his own *amour propre* as well as that of Ball's other friends was involved in the controversy—they had to prove they were right or confess themselves credulous fools—and his influence was as fatal to Ball as the real Iago's was to Othello. It was Morse who set the final seal to Ball's claim—committed it to imperishable bronze, as it were!—by writing a book about it, which was published by M. W. Dodd, of 506 Broadway, New York City, in 1867. It was probably at Ball's expense—or perhaps the "M. W." in both their names means that they were relatives.

This book was entitled "A Vindication of the Claim of Alexander M. W. Ball, of Elizabeth, N. J., to the Authorship of the Poem, 'Rock Me to Sleep, Mother.'" It had an introductory note from Luther R. Marsh, of New York City, and a preface by E. W. Leavenworth, of Syracuse. It is now something of a rarity. The copy in the Library of Congress, to which the present writer has had access, was given to the library in 1912, and was originally a presentation copy from Mr. Leavenworth to a cousin, Mrs. Ella E. Day. It is an octavo of seventy-two pages, with a closely-printed supplement of thirty-six pages, and is surely one of the most curious items on the shelves of that great institution. The argument which it presents is perhaps the most extraordinary and impudent in the history of American letters.

"The two accompanying articles," says the preface, "discuss a question of interest to the public, but of far deeper interest to Mr. Ball and his friends. The claim made by Mrs. Akers, and the publication as her own of six verses of his beautiful poem, 'Rock Me to Sleep,' placed him in a situation of great embarrassment. For nearly ten years previous to such publication he had from time to time read these verses to his many friends, as his own composition. They had often been commented upon, admired and enjoyed. He sought no reputation as a poet. He had never published a verse or permitted it to be published by his friends. He sought no honors from an admiring public. He neither wished his name blazoned in the public press, or his works offered for sale at the booksellers' stalls. He found his happiness in the refined enjoyments of his interesting and cultivated family circle, and in the society of his many friends."

After painting this touching picture, the writer adds that Mr. Ball was most reluctant to engage in any controversy with Mrs. Akers, "but the course to be pursued was not left en-

tirely to his decision.   His friends, knowing
that there was the most abundant and conclusive
evidence to establish his claim to the authorship,
determined that it should be vindicated."

Here, in a nutshell, is the whole plot of
what, starting as a comedy, speedily turned into
a tragedy!

It is given further elucidation in the introductory note.   "Through the zeal of his
friends," writes Mr. Marsh, "his claim to the
poem has acquired such publicity that he is now
driven to the alternative of defending his right,
or hereafter remaining clouded with the suspicion of having put forth unfounded pretensions.   A man's duty to himself and family
sometimes calls on him to wage a contest he
would else shrink from and abandon.   These
considerations, in a great measure, have been
overcome in him by a chivalric forbearance toward his chief contestant, and she would have
walked, mistress over the field," had not the
Honorable Oliver O. Morse taken the matter
in hand and prepared the "Vindication."

One can imagine the shudders which shook
the unhappy harness-maker as this work progressed, his sleepless nights, his terrific labors to
prepare his evidence and prove himself a poet.

But of all this, Iago was happily unconscious, or, if he suspected it, he regarded such
weakness with deserved contempt.   Undaunted

by the reluctance of his victim, he proceeded merrily with his task. Ball's halo was fixed so firmly upon his head that it seems never to have occurred to any of his friends that his reluctance to go into the fight might be due to something else besides chivalry and modesty; or if it did, they quickly put the thought behind them.

"The whole poem," Mr. Morse starts out by saying, "may be ranked among the gems of American literature, nor is it perhaps too much to say, that as a plaintive refrain of filial love, it is not surpassed in our language. The lines of Cowper to his mother's picture awaken the same emotions, but to a less degree than these exquisite verses, and certainly are inferior to them, as a longing and a cry that cannot be suppressed, for converse with the spirit of a beloved departed mother. It may be a question whether in Cowper's day the spiritual atmosphere of England was not such as to render impossible, even to the most refined and acute souls, any such vivid recognition and perception of beloved beings in the other world, as are manifested in these lines."

With which high proof of his competence for the task Mr. Morse proceeds with his case, using as his text the letter from Mrs. Akers published in the *Evening Post*, and producing (1) the fifteen-stanza version by Mr. Ball; (2) six letters from friends who believed they had heard Mr. Ball read portions of the poem prior to 1860; and (3) an elaborate analysis of the poem to show that it is all of one piece.

The story which this evidence is supposed to confirm is that "Mr. Ball wrote, or made a draft of the whole poem, except one verse, in the latter part of the year 1856. In February, 1857, he sailed for California, and on the steamers, on both oceans, he corrected and polished it, and added one verse," bringing home with him the finished product of fifteen stanzas.

The letters were written in 1866 or 1867, after the controversy was well under way and at Ball's solicitation. They can be explained simply by the error which most people make in trying to place from memory the date of a past event. One or two of them made a crude attempt at documenting the date, and it is possible that their authors did at some time or other hear Ball read some fragments which remotely resembled "Rock Me to Sleep." Home, Mother and Heaven have been the favorite themes of amateur poets since time began. All that any of them claims is to have heard Ball read his poem; not one possessed a copy of it.

William Dean Howells analyzed these letters in a review of the "Vindication," which appeared in the *Atlantic Monthly* for August, 1867, in a way which would be difficult to improve upon. He says:

257

These letters are six in number, including a post-script, and it is not Mr. Ball's fault if they all read a good deal like the certificates of other days establishing the identity of the Old Original Doctor Jacob Townsend. Two only of the six are signed with the writers' names, but these two have a special validity from the fact that the writer of one is a very old friend, who has more than once expressed his wish to be Mr. Ball's literary executor, while the writer of the other is evidently a legal gent, for he begins with "Relative to the controversy *in re* the authorship," etc., *like* a legal gent, and he concludes with the statement that he is able to fix the date when he heard Mr. Ball read "Rock Me to Sleep" by the date of a paper which he *thinks* he called to draw up at Mr. Ball's residence some time in the autumn of 1859. This is Mr. J. Burrows Hyde.

Mr. Lewis C. Grover, who would like to be Mr. Ball's literary executor, is more definite, and says that he heard Mr. Ball read the contested poem with others in 1857, during a call made to learn where Mr. Ball bought his damask curtains. H. D. E. is sorry that he or she cannot remember where he or she first heard Mr. Ball read it, but he or she distinctly remembers that it was in 1857 or 1858. L. P. and I. E. S. witness that they heard Mr. Ball read it in his study in 1856 or 1857, and state that the date may be fixed by reference to the time "when Mr. Ball took Maria to Dr. Cox's, and placed her in the school in Leroy," and the pamphleteer, turning to a bill rendered by the principal of the Leroy school, "fixes the date called for by the writers in February, 1857," at which time, according to the pamphleteer himself, *Mr. Ball was on his way to California in an ocean steamer!*

It appears, then, that these letters do not establish a great deal. We do not think that their writers intend deceit, but we know the rapture with which people listen to poets who read their own verses aloud, and we suspect that these listeners to Mr. Ball were carried too far away by their feelings ever to get back to their facts. We think them one and all in error, and we do not believe that any living soul heard Mr. Ball read the disputed poem before 1860, for two reasons: Mrs. Akers did not write it before that time, and Mr. Ball could never have written it after any number of trials.

Let us take one of Mr. Ball's "Christmas Carols," —probably the poem which his friends now recall as "Rock Me to Sleep, Mother,"—for all proof and comment upon this last fact:

"CHRISTMAS, 1856

And as time rolls us backward, we feel inclined to
    weep,
As the spirit of our mother comes, to rock our souls
    to sleep. . . .
It raised my thoughts to heaven, and in converse
    with them there
I felt a joy unearthly, and lighter sat world's care;
For it opened up the vista of an echoless dim shore,
Where my mother kindly greets me, as in good days
    of yore."

Here, then, is that quality of peculiarly hopeless poetasting which strikes cold upon the stomach, and makes man turn sadly from his driveling brother. Do we not know this sort of thing? Out of the rejected contributions in our waste-basket we could daily furnish the inside and outside of a dozen Balls. It *is* saddening; it *is* pathetic; it has gone on so long now, and must still continue for so many ages; but we can just bear it as a negative quantity. It is only when such rubbish is put forward as proof that its author has a claim to the name and fame of a poet, that we lose patience. The verses given in this pamphlet would invalidate Mr. Ball's claim to the authorship of Mrs. Akers's poem, even though the Seven Sleepers swore that he rocked them asleep with it in the time of the Decian persecution.

It must be admitted that Mr. Howells twisted the letters a little to suit his argument, but he was entirely right in concluding that they "do not establish a great deal"—even though the names of their authors were afterwards made public.

At a later date the Hon. George W. Wright, of Washington, D. C., who shared Mr. Ball's cabin on the voyage to California in 1857, testified that he had seen that gentleman working on his poem, that they had discussed some parts of it together, and that he had become very familiar with it. He had asked for a copy, but unfortunately Mr. Ball had not given him one, asking him (as usual) to wait until the poem was perfected. It seems that even after all the work done on it during the long sea voyage from New York to San Francisco, it still did not measure up to his high ideal of what a poem ought to be.

Ball's partisans hailed this letter with a great blare of trumpets as absolutely conclusive; but there is only one inference to be drawn from it (aside from the unfair one that it is a fabrication), and that is that Ball, as was his custom, was ostentatiously posing as a poet and tinkering at some doggerel during the voyage in order to impress his shipmates, and that Mr. Wright's imagination, after a lapse of more than ten years, did the rest.

That it was doggerel there can be no question, if one is to judge by the other specimens of Ball's versification included in the book, but before going into that, Mr. Morse's final and conclusive proof must be examined. "This," says he, "is to be found in the poem itself," the fifteen stanzas of which, he points out, "belong to the same one exquisite mosaic."

One of the commonest devices of the literary thief is to write some additional stanzas to the poem he has stolen in order to prove that he wrote all of them. It is also one of the most perilous, for seldom indeed can the pretender duplicate the flavor of the original. In Mr. Ball's case it is fatal. Mrs. Akers's "Rock Me

to Sleep" is very far from being a great poem,
but at least it shows rather unusual skill in versification, its lines are smooth and flowing, and
each of them possesses the requisite number of
feet. There are felicitous passages, a happy
use of adjectives, and an avoidance of stilted
or artificial phraseology. Mr. Ball's additional
stanzas do not possess a single one of these merits. They are uncouth, ungrammatical, in
places almost unintelligible. Here is his last
stanza, which Mr. Morse calls "a natural, simple, and harmonious finale to the whole":

> Thus with my loved ones I'll watch by your side,
> Nor weep once again, whatever betide,
> Waiting all calmly the coming of those
> Holding the signet of death's cold repose;—
> Farewell to sorrow—farewell to all ill—
> Whispers are stealing, sad heart be now still,—
> With my dear mother, kind watch I will keep,
> She charges the angels to rock me to sleep.

Surely no comment upon this is necessary;
but with Mr. Ball's claim resting upon such
evidence, there can be only one verdict, and all
the affidavits in the world could not alter it.
The blood-test proves conclusively that Mr. Ball
could never have been the parent of the stanzas
claimed by Mrs. Akers.

Mr. Morse, in spite of his laudation of Mr.
Ball's stanzas, seems to have had some dim per-

ception of this, for he adds, "On the theory
that the whole had been lost by the author, the
finder, if disposed to appropriate it, would
naturally publish only those verses which did not
so plainly repeat themselves, selecting only the
best. The very fact then of this peculiarity, or
defect, if it is one, must be taken as proof that
the whole is the work of one mind!"

This is sublime, but it is far from being Mr.
Morse's best. He easily surpasses it when he
proceeds to a dissection of the internal evidence
of the poem itself. He points out that one of
the lines stolen by Mrs. Akers is:

Come, let your brown hair just lighted with gold,

and that there can be no doubt Mr. Ball wrote
it, because his mother had exactly such hair, as
Mr. Morse himself can testify, for he has seen
a tress of it, piously preserved by her son.
Furthermore, consider these lines, also stolen by
Mrs. Akers:

Kiss from my forehead the furrows of care,
Smooth the few silver threads out of my hair.

Mr. Morse testifies that Mr. Ball's forehead
was furrowed (as well it might be!) and that
there were "silver threads in his hair not a few."
He had never seen Mrs. Akers, but she subse-

263

quently gave herself completely away in the
following damning stanza in a poem referring
to her early widowhood:

Ah, me! the red is yet upon my cheek,
  And in my veins life's vigorous currents play;
Adown my hair there shines no warning streak,
    And the sweet meeting which you paint to-day
      Seems sadly far away.

How, demands Mr. Morse triumphantly, was
it possible for Mrs. Akers to be wrinkled and
gray-haired in 1860, and blooming with youth
some years later?   Here is the conclusive, in-
escapable proof of the falsity of her high-
handed claim to "Rock Me to Sleep!"

Nor is this all.   If any one is so pig-headed
as to be still unconvinced, there is one proof
more.   Mr. Ball, it seems, was in the habit of
writing a poem to his mother's memory to cele-
brate each succeeding Christmas.   They were
really not poems, just fragments, for Mr. Ball
seemed always to have a great deal of difficulty
with his material, but the fragments for 1852,
1853, 1854, 1855 and 1856 were fortunately
preserved and are given in the book, and for
good measure certain other of Mr. Ball's verses
are included.   Unhappily, one of these poems
was afterwards discovered to be a plagiarism
from Mrs. Sarah Helen Whitman, for which
Mr. Ball apologized, saying that all uncon-

sciously Mrs. Whitman's poem "became inter-woven into my heart and mind, and, years after, found utterance as my own." The other poems are strangely reminiscent of Goldsmith and Hood, but it would scarcely be fair to charac-terize them as anything worse than that. All of them are unmitigated doggerel, the sample quoted by Mr. Howells from the effusion for 1856 being a fair specimen.

One can imagine the poor man racking his brain in the effort to satisfy his friends that he was all they thought him, and as a final bit of evidence producing the "original draft" of "Rock Me to Sleep," with all his subsequent corrections and interlineations. It was a thor-oughly puerile performance, but it was gravely examined by a solemn committee of clergymen, doctors, and literary men, among the latter being "Mr. Gilder, editor of the Newark *Daily Advertiser.*" Their verdict is not disclosed, but, as Mr. Morse points out, there could be no doubt about the date of this interesting docu-ment because, as was discovered to its author's great surprise, a portion of the draft had, by a most fortunate chance, been written upon the back of a "tradesman's bill rendered to Mr. Ball in September, 1856. Where so many bills are presented and paid as in Mr. Ball's house, the presumption is that this one was thus used by him about the time of its presentation."

There remained one more link to be forged
in the chain of evidence: it must be shown how
Mrs. Akers, who was in Italy during the winter
of 1859-1860, got hold of a poem which Mr.
Ball had brought back with him from California
a year or so before, and which had never been
published, or, presumably, been out of his possession. This was decidedly difficult, but Mr.
Morse did not falter:

"Mr. Ball himself, with the most naïve
benevolence and kindness of heart, asked
whether there might not be some occult psychological process by which Mrs. Akers could have
possessed herself, unconsciously, of these verses
from his mind or manuscript." Iago does not
altogether deny the possibility of this (though
Mrs. Akers rejected it scornfully), but he has
another and more material explanation.

"Mr. Ball," he writes, "is very careless of
his manuscript poems. When he travels he
often carries them in loose sheets of note paper
in his pockets. They lie scattered on his table.
Formerly he had a clerk, now deceased, who
used to copy for himself many of the verses.
Mrs. Akers sojourned for a while in New
Hampshire, and Mr. Ball's business often carried him there, though they never met. In a
way here hinted at, or in some other, 'Rock Me
to Sleep,' or part of it perhaps was lost, got into
some country newspaper, and floated before the

266

eye, and into the memory and poetical soul of Mrs. Akers, before she went to Italy."

And upon this lame note the "Vindication" ends.

Surely, if any man in this world ever had reason to pray to be delivered from his loving friends it was Alexander M. W. Ball, of Elizabeth, New Jersey!

Mrs. Akers, meanwhile, had also been having her troubles.

There are in the world a lot of people always ready to believe any theory, however far-fetched. In fact, their intensity of belief seems to be in direct proportion to its absurdity, and they even assume a certain superiority, as belonging to an inner circle of intelligentsia. So in any public assembly where she might appear Mrs. Akers was conscious of lifted eyebrows and ironical smiles, and could guess what was being whispered behind her back. "But, my dear, I assure you it is true—she stole it bodily —yes, a Mr. Ball—a wonderful man, so high-minded and chivalrous . . ."

Small wonder she sometimes lost her temper and wrote and said some exceedingly biting things about Mr. Ball and his friends, but fortunately she had the good sense not to bring suit, as she had threatened. When William Cullen Bryant was compiling his *Library of*

Poetry and Song, he wrote to Mrs. Akers and asked her to show cause why the poem should not be credited to the Elizabeth bard. Mrs. Akers tartly replied that there was only one reason, to wit: Mr. Ball did not write the poem and she did. This seems to have convinced Mr. Bryant, for when his collection was published the poem was credited to Florence Percy. J. T. Trowbridge came to her defense, as did the *Atlantic* and *The Nation,* and gradually the weight of expert opinion rallied behind her, and Mr. Ball and Iago and all the rest of them faded from public memory, until the whole controversy became just another literary curiosity— and a warning to plagiarists who seek to impress their admiring acquaintances!

Even yet, from time to time, its ghost flits feebly across the stage. Its most recent appearance is in the new edition of *Hoyt's Cyclopedia of Practical Quotations,* edited by Kate Louise Roberts. Miss Roberts has evidently been taken in by the same old hokum, for she credits the poem to Mr. Ball, and gives as her authority an article which appeared in the *Northern Monthly* in 1868. The *Northern Monthly* was published at Newark, N. J., which happens also to be Miss Roberts's home, and this perhaps caused her to give it more weight than it deserves. But it is unfortunate that a claim so shameless and mendacious should receive support in a compilation which will find a place in many libraries and be referred to for years to come.

Mrs. Akers has told the story of the controversy at the back of her volume, *The Sunset Song and Other Verses,* published in 1902, where "Rock Me to Sleep" appears for the first time in any of her works since its original publication in 1866. She points out how, besides causing her endless annoyance, the poem profited others much more than it did her. She received five dollars for it from the *Saturday Evening Post* and that is all it ever brought her, although it was set to music by thirty different composers and issued by fifty different music publishers, some of whom made a fortune out of it. It was featured by the Christy Minstrels, issued as an illustrated Christmas gift-book, printed on leaflets and scattered by thousands in the army during the Civil War, used in innumerable compilations, quoted in novels and sung in one well-known play—all without her consent.

In 1910, when the present writer was compiling *The Home Book of Verse,* he wrote to Mrs. Akers for permission to use certain of her poems, and her reply was extremely characteristic.

"I have no objection to your including in your compilation the poems of mine which you mention," she writes, "if you will observe two conditions, first, that you will copy them from my books instead of from possibly garbled newspaper versions, and second, that you will credit the authorship to the name of Elizabeth Akers, which is the name given on all my title-pages, and the only one which I wish to be associated with my literary work.

"You mention a poem by the title of 'The Old Story.' I do not recall that I ever gave that title to any poem, but it is possible that I may have written something that might suggest that title, and some unco' wise newspaper editor has taken the liberty of changing its name—a liberty that is sometimes taken with poems, but which is an affront to their authors, who may be supposed to know what name they prefer for their own work. If you will tell me the first two lines of 'The Old Story' I can at once decide whether the poem is mine. Of all things, I wish to avoid being credited with work that does not belong to me. It is even more unpleasant than seeing my own work stolen, as has happened many times."

So even to the end of her days the old wrong rankled in her recollection. As her publishers remark, "Truth has outlived falsehood, and the unjust claims of other years are but a cruel memory." But surely never did another poem so overshadow two lives!

THE LESSON OF THE
WATER-MILL

THE LESSON OF THE WATER-MILL

Listen to the water-mill;
  Through the livelong day,
How the clicking of its wheel
  Wears the hours away!
Languidly the autumn wind,
  Stirs the forest leaves,
From the field the reapers sing,
  Binding up their sheaves;
And a proverb haunts my mind
  As a spell is cast—
"The mill cannot grind
  With the water that is past."

Autumn winds revive no more
  Leaves that once are shed,
And the sickle cannot reap
  Corn once gatherèd;
Flows the ruffled streamlet on,
  Tranquil, deep, and still;
Never gliding back again
  To the water-mill;
Truly speaks the proverb old
  With a meaning vast—
"The mill cannot grind
  With the water that is past."

Take the lesson to thyself,
    True and loving heart;
Golden youth is fleeting by,
    Summer hours depart;
Learn to make the most of life,
    Lose no happy day;
Time will never bring thee back
    Chances swept away!
Leave no tender word unsaid,
    Love while love shall last—
"The mill cannot grind
    With the water that is past."

Work while yet the daylight shines,
    Man of strength and will!
Never does the streamlet glide
    Useless by the mill;
Wait not till to-morrow's sun
    Beams upon thy way,
All that thou canst call thine own
    Lies in thy "To-day";
Power, intellect and health
    May not always last—
"The mill cannot grind
    With the water that is past."

Oh, the wasted hours of life
    That have drifted by!
Oh, the good that might have been—
    Lost, without a sigh!

The Lesson of the Water-Mill

Love that we might once have saved
 By a single word,
Thoughts conceived, but never penned,
 Perishing unheard;—
Take the proverb to thine heart,
 Take, and hold it fast—
"The mill cannot grind
 With the water that is past."

Sarah Doudney

275

THE LESSON OF THE WATER-MILL

IT is usually the despair of single-poem men that their fame rests upon what seems to most of them so slender a foundation, and nearly all of them disclose a curious blind spot when it comes to looking at their own work, so that, just as a parent will often love his unworthiest child the best, the poet almost always thinks many of his creations are far superior to the one the public prefers, and is inclined to feel abused when they are disregarded.

"In general quality," writes Mr. Ernest Lawrence Thayer, " 'Casey at the Bat,' at least in my judgment, is neither better nor worse than much of my other stuff." Mr. Charles M. Dickinson, the author of "The Children," voices the same feeling.

"The anthologies," he writes, "seem determined that I shall go down to posterity as the author of a single poem. Now I plan to let the collectors know that I have written other verse. So I am sending you a book containing some of my other poems with the hope that you may find something in it worth copying beside 'The Children.' "

276

The Lesson of the Water-Mill

The book was examined with the best will in the world, but "The Children" remained the only poem quoted from it. The other verses were graceful, sincere, and not without poetic merit, but they lacked that quality of universal appeal which is really what has won "The Children" a place in so many anthologies. Mr. Dickinson, indeed, has some reason to be grateful to anthologists, for they have made it plain that it was he who wrote the poem, and not Charles Dickens, as some too-enthusiastic exchange editors were at one time trying to make the public believe.

So with Mr. Thayer. The anthologists have defended him valiantly against the attacks of various claimants of the authorship of "Casey at the Bat," but that remains the only poem of his which is ever quoted. His other ballads lack that touch of genius which has made "Casey" the great classic of baseball.

Many writers of verse have had another reason to despair: they were constantly receiving requests for permission for the use of certain of their poems, they saw them quoted everywhere and apparently widely popular, yet their own books, in which these poems appeared, never sold enough to keep them in postage-stamps. It is not strange that, in course of time, they should feel a resentment against all compilers, as men who were robbing them of their just reward.

277

A most interesting letter dealing with this question—interesting because so entirely frank—was written by Mrs. Elizabeth Akers Allen a year or two before her death.

"My publishers tell me that nobody buys books of poems in these days," Mrs. Allen writes, "so I have no courage to offer another volume. As most of the publishing houses seem to have changed into mere job-printing offices, publishing nothing for which they are not paid in advance, or which they cannot pick up for nothing, there seems small encouragement for verse-writers who are not prepared to hire their books printed. Considering these things, I do wonder who buys all the compilations of verse which every year brings out, if it is true that 'nobody reads poetry.'

"Another thing puzzles me. When I know that the scholarly and experienced Professor Lowell never declined a poem of mine while he edited the *Atlantic*, and that Longfellow, Bryant, Whittier, Underwood, Stedman, and many lesser lights of the literary world here and in England, have included my work in their selections, when I have over sixty sheets of music which have been written by composers (utter strangers to me) to words of mine which they have either taken from my books or have picked out of newspaper columns and appropriated without my knowledge, and when I am told that some of these songs are sung all over the English-speaking world, I cannot help wondering how it is that my books have not paid me enough to keep me supplied with stationery. If I had depended upon my verse for even the plainest living, I should have starved long ago. It is fortunate that 'poetry is its own reward,' for I judge that only the more fortunate bards find any other."

The defense of anthologists will not be undertaken here. It may be pointed out, however, that they are by no means the plutocrats Mrs. Allen supposed, and of late years they have as a class renounced piracy and become almost respectable. Poets are their debtors for two things: it is they who keep alive the single lovely songs which would be lost and forgotten in a mass of "collected works," and they are indefatigable in running down questions of authorship and in making sure that the person who wrote the poem gets the credit for it—as Mrs. Allen herself had reason to know during the violent controversy which raged in the '60's and '70's about the authorship of "Rock Me to Sleep."

Another dispute, resembling in many ways the famous one between Mrs. Allen and Mr. Ball, and involving the reputation of one of the most distinguished men of Civil War days, still starts occasionally on a fresh round of the

279

press. It was Partridge who remarked sadly of hunger that, no matter how often one subdues it, it always bobs up again; and this is equally true of literary controversies.

Every once in a while somebody happens upon a small volume published privately in Brooklyn in 1870, entitled *The Water-Mill, and Other Poems,* by D. C. McCallum, and writes triumphantly to the papers that here at last is the solution of a famous mystery. The late Dr. Washington Gladden was one of these persons, and the letter which he wrote to the *Ohio State Journal* in the fall of 1915, is so typical that it is worth quoting:

You published this morning a little poem on "The Water That Has Passed," marking it, "Author Unknown."

Permit me to remove the veil of anonymity. The author was D. C. McCallum, a resident, when this poem was written, of my old home town, Owego, Tioga County, New York. Mr. McCallum, when I first knew him, was superintendent of the Susquehanna division of the Erie Railroad; afterward he was in charge of all the bridge building on that road, and I am not sure that he was not at one time president. He was also, I think, called into the service of the government early in the Civil War. I believe that we learned to call him "General."

He was a fine, soldierly appearing man, very

quiet and domestic in his tastes, and greatly respected by all his neighbors. His children were my schoolmates.

I did not know of any other venture of his into the field of letters; but this was surely a happy one. The name of our old Dayton neighbor, Coates Kinney, will always be kept alive by his little lyric, "Rain on the Roof," and General McCallum should be remembered by this tenderly wise little poem, "The Water That Has Passed."

A few days later, a letter from Mr. Gregg D. Wolfe called Dr. Gladden's attention to the fact that "The Water That Has Passed" was written, not by General McCallum, but by Sarah Doudney, and when this was proved to Dr. Gladden's satisfaction, he hazarded the guess that a copy of the poem had been found among General McCallum's papers and mistakenly attributed to him in consequence, since it was incredible that so distinguished and respected a man would ever pose as the author of a poem which was not his.

It is, alas, impossible to place so charitable a construction upon the matter, for there the poem is in the book which General McCallum himself incautiously published. But before going into that, his career may be outlined in a few words.

Daniel Craig McCallum was born at Johnston, Renfrewshire, Scotland, January 21,

1815, and died in Brooklyn, New York, December 27, 1878. He came to America in his youth, became an architect and builder, and in 1855 was general superintendent of the Erie Railway. On February 11, 1862, he was appointed director of all the military railroads in the United States, with the staff rank of colonel, and served in that position throughout the Civil War. He seems to have been a thoroughly competent executive, his work was always referred to in the highest terms, and to him was credited in large part the efficiency which the northern railroads attained during the great struggle. He was mustered out of the service in 1866 with the rank of major-general of volunteers.

General McCallum seems to have had a fondness throughout his life, and especially in his later years, for writing verses of a moralistic character and in 1870, as has been said, gathered some of them together in a book dedicated "To My Dearest Friend." There were twenty-five poems altogether, the first being "The Water-Mill." The nature of the others may be judged from such titles as "The Creed of Life," "A Warning Voice," "The Madman's Reverie," "Be Kind to the Erring," and "All, All Alone." They are tinged with pious melancholy, abound in frightful visions, and their quality may be judged very fairly by these two

The Lesson of the Water-Mill

stanzas from "An O'er True Tale," which is
concerned with woman's inhumanity to woman:

See yon pale form, in garret high—
　Wearily stitching, on and on;
Oh! listen to the deep, low sigh!
　Ah! it should melt a heart of stone.

Her face—once fair, of Grecian mold—
　Now pale and wan with carking care;
Her eyes were bright, she once was told;
　What is she now? *a case not rare.*

The first stanza of the poem which gives the
book its title is as follows:

Oh! listen to the Water-Mill, through all the live-
　long day,
As the clicking of the wheel, wears hour by hour
　away;
How languidly the Autumn wind, doth stir the
　withered leaves,
As on the field the Reaper's sing, while binding up
　the sheaves,
A solemn proverb strikes my mind, and as a spell is
　cast,
"The mill will never grind, with water that is past."

Nobody seems to have doubted that this poem
was entirely original with General McCallum,
and the discovery that it was not came about
entirely by chance. Some years subsequently,

the late Irving Bishop, the thought-reader, while visiting in London, happened upon a little volume of poems by Sarah Doudney. Among them he found "The Water-Mill," and at once accused Miss Doudney of stealing General McCallum's poem. The matter was immediately taken up by a friend of Miss Doudney, Mr. William Isbister, of Isbister & Company, the publishers of *Good Words,* and a meeting was arranged at which Mr. Bishop and Miss Doudney were present.

"A copy of the *Churchman's Family Magazine,* containing 'The Lesson of the Water-Mill,' with an illustration, was shown to Mr. Bishop," Miss Doudney writes, "and he quite satisfied himself that I had written the poem before Mr. McCallum's lines appeared. But we could never explain the course which Mr. McCallum followed in appropriating and altering my poem.

"The *Churchman's Family Magazine* was edited by the Rev. Frederick Arnold," Miss Doudney continues. "The volume in which my poem appeared was kept by me for a long time, but was afterwards sold among other books. However the proofs of authorship are doubtless retained by Mr. Isbister.

"We have never been able to ascertain the origin of the proverb, but have heard that it is Italian. I saw it first in a child's scrap-book under a picture of a water-mill. The words were these: 'The mill cannot grind with the water that is past.'

"For a long time," Miss Doudney concludes, "I believed my claim was firmly established, but two or three years ago I had to defend myself against a spiteful attack in Mr. O'Connor's paper—the charge of being a deceiver was brought against me quite unexpectedly, in a most insulting manner. With respect to Mr. McCallum, I think it is likely that he did not intend the verses he wrote as an improved version of mine to appear in public. However, ii literary matters some people appear to have no conscience at all."

There is a legend that Miss Doudney, who was born in 1843, wrote the poem at the age of fifteen; however this is probably just an invention, since it was not until 1864 that the poem appeared in the *Churchman's Family Magazine.* The editor of that paper, Mr. J. A. Kensit, was asked if he could refer to the files and get the exact date, but answered that this was impossible. However, even in the absence of all other proof, the presumption would be altogether in favor of Miss Doudney. She passed the early years of her life in a remote village in Hampshire, England, to which it is altogether unlikely that any copy of General McCallum's privately printed volume would ever penetrate. On the other hand, her verses were printed in *The Sunday Magazine, Good Words,* and *The Churchman's Family Magazine,* and were widely read and copied in America as well as in England.

"The Lesson of the Water-Mill" was especially well-known for, besides being often reprinted, it was for many years a favorite recitation. Strangely enough, as a recitation it was usually given in German dialect, which was supposed to add to its pathos, and with a musical accompaniment (preferably on the 'cello) to enhance the general effect. It was so recited by George S. Knight in a comedy called "Fifth Avenue," produced at the old Booth Theatre in New York in the early 'seventies. Mr. Henry S. Blake, of Clinton, Conn., who has himself recited the poem hundreds of times during the past thirty-five years, possesses an old stage copy with the musical accompaniment used by Mel. B. Spurr, an English entertainer, published by Reynolds & Co., 13 Berners Street, London. This gives the author's name on the cover as Sarah Doudney, and at the foot of the first page is the line, "By permission, from *Psalms of Life,* by Miss Sarah Doudney."

Still further proof, if any were needed, is found in the poem itself. It is evident that Miss Doudney's version is the first one; it is simple and direct. What General McCallum tried to do was to elaborate and polish it up, to make it more flowing; but a comparison of his first stanza, as given above, with Miss Doudney's version will show that his changes were all for the worse. His punctuation, moreover, is that of a man who, if not exactly illiterate, was at least quite unskilled in writing. His "Reaper's sing" is a mistake which no one with any knowledge of grammar would make.

But he gave himself away still further, for he not only revised Miss Doudney's stanzas, but added one of his own, after his usual moralizing way. Here it is—it speaks for itself:

Oh! love thy God and fellow man, thyself consider
    last,
For come it will when thou must scan, dark errors
    of the past,
Soon will this fight of life be o'er, and earth recede
    from view,
And Heaven in all its glory shine, where all is pure
    and true,
Ah! then thou'lt see more clearly still, the proverb
    deep and vast,
"The mill will never grind with water that is past."

More than once, in the course of these papers, it has been shown what deadly peril the plagiarist runs when he attempts to add a stanza to the poem he has stolen. In General McCallum's case it is, as usual, fatal! Nobody who would write this sort of mush could, by any possibility, write a real poem.

Literary stealings of this sort have given rise to many controversies and to endless heartburnings. Many lives have been embittered by them, and they have often furnished a theme for the moralist. But few denunciations have been so vigorous as an editorial entitled "Literary Larcenies," published in the New York *Evening Gazette* of January 3, 1867. This polemic is so characteristic of the controversial style of that epoch, that it is worth quoting, in part at least:

There must be something in a literary reputation, or so many would not be striving to attain it by all sorts of means. There is a class of scribblers who wriggle themselves into momentary notoriety by puffery, and there is another class who impudently demand attention by claiming the authorship of productions which they could not under any circumstances have written. They generally fasten upon some striking poem which was published anonymously, or whose writer's name has been separated from it in its wanderings over land and sea, and make a manuscript copy which they read to their friends, who, of course, are ready afterwards to testify that they saw the piece in manuscript, fresh from the brain of the author, before it found its way into print, with other little fanciful additions which they very honestly believe.

288

The Lesson of the Water-Mill

Some of the most famous lyrics in the language have had their paternity disputed in this way. Among others, Wolfe's "Burial of Sir John Moore," upon which a number of imaginative Celts endeavored to father themselves, and Campbell's "Exile of Erin," which it is now pretended that he stole bodily, we believe from the traditional exile himself, McCann, if that was his name. They are very active here, and at this time—these barefaced purloiners of reputation—snapping up any little waif that may come under their observation.

Everybody remembers the young person of the softer sex, a Miss Peck, if we recall her name correctly, who said that 'twas she, and not Mr. William Butler, who wrote "Nothing to Wear," which, of course, she had no means of proving beyond her mere assertion, which nobody was gallant enough to accept. A second instance of disputed authorship was ventilated a few months since in the Round Table, the thing in dispute then being a copy of verses entitled "The Long Ago," and written by a Mr. Benjamin F. Taylor, of Chicago, who has had all sorts of hands grasping after his imaginary laurel, and rousing, through their friends, a mighty clamor for justice, which they richly deserved in the nearest literary pillory.

A third instance concerned the plaintive little lyric, "Rock Me to Sleep, Mother," which was written by Florence Percy, otherwise Mrs. Akers. We say that it was written by her since she has included it in the blue and gold edition of her poems which was published not long ago in Boston. This

289

fact proves nothing to those who dispute her claims in behalf of themselves or others, but it settles the question as regards the general reader. If an author of reputation says that he or she wrote such or such a poem, his or her word ought to end all controversy, particularly such controversies as are waged by persons of whom no one ever heard before or cares to hear again.

To which there is nothing to be added except Amen!

WHAT MY LOVER SAID

WHAT MY LOVER SAID

By the merest chance, in the twilight gloom,
  In the orchard path he met me;
In the tall, wet grass, with its faint perfume,
And I tried to pass, but he made no room,
  Oh, I tried, but he would not let me.
So I stood and blushed till the grass grew red,
  With my face bent down above it,
While he took my hand as he whispering said—
(How the clover lifted each pink, sweet head,
To listen to all that my lover said;
  Oh, the clover in bloom, I love it!)

In the high, wet grass went the path to hide,
  And the low, wet leaves hung over;
But I could not pass upon either side,
For I found myself, when I vainly tried,
  In the arms of my steadfast lover.
And he held me there and he raised my head,
  While he closed the path before me,
And he looked down into my eyes and said—
(How the leaves bent down from the boughs
    o'er head,
To listen to all that my lover said;
  Oh, the leaves hanging lowly o'er me!)

Had he moved aside but a little way,
　I could surely then have passed him;
And he knew I never could wish to stay,
And would not have heard what he had to say,
　Could I only aside have cast him.
It was almost dark, and the moments sped,
　And the searching night wind found us,
But he drew me nearer and softly said—
(How the pure, sweet wind grew still, instead,
To listen to all that my lover said;
　Oh, the whispering wind around us!)

I am sure that he knew when he held me fast,
　That I must be all unwilling;
For I tried to go, and I would have passed,
As the night was come with its dew, at last,
　And the sky with its stars was filling.
But he clasped me close when I would have fled,
　And he made me hear his story,
And his soul came out from his lips and said—
(How the stars crept out where the white moon
　　led,
To listen to all that my lover said;
　Oh, the moon and the stars in glory!)

I know that the grass and the leaves will not tell,
　And I'm sure that the wind, precious rover,
Will carry my secret so safely and well
　That no being shall ever discover

What My Lover Said

One word of the many that rapidly fell
  From the soul-speaking lips of my lover;
  And the moon and the stars that looked over
Shall never reveal what a fairy-like spell
They wove round about us that night in the dell,
  In the path through the dew-laden clover,
Nor echo the whispers that made my heart swell
  As they fell from the lips of my lover.

Homer Greene.

WHAT MY LOVER SAID

No theory is too far-fetched to find adherents.
Indeed, the more absurd it is the firmer seems
to be its hold on its disciples, who usually end
by exalting it into a cult. The Bacon-Shake-
speare controversy long ago passed into this
stage. Its apostles are few but devoted. Their
belief is founded not upon reason but upon
faith—the firmest of all foundations.

Fifty or sixty years ago, there were a great
many people who believed that the Waverley
novels were written not by Sir Walter Scott,
but by his brother Thomas, ably assisted by
Mrs. Thomas, who was alleged to be far the
brightest of the three arfd to be responsible for
such flashes of genius as the novels showed. Sir
Walter's part was merely to polish them up and
market them. There was something irresistibly
appealing in the idea of a talented woman being
exploited in this way, and an elaborate theory
was built up to prove that it had actually happened. The theory was founded principally
upon a letter Sir Walter had written to his
brother inviting him to send on a novel for
revision, and promising to advance a hundred

pounds on account as soon as the manuscript was received. Sir Walter himself refers to the controversy in the general preface to his works, saying that it had "some alliance to probability, and indeed might have proved in some degree true," only as it happened when brother Thomas tried to buckle down to the work of writing a novel, he found he could not do it.

Forster, in his life of Dickens, refers to "a wonderful story originally promulgated in America," to the effect that George Cruikshank and not Dickens was the real author of *Oliver Twist;* but, Mr. Forster adds, "the distinguished artist whom it calumniates, either not conscious of it or not caring to defend himself, has been left undefended from the slander." Whereupon, to the astonishment of every one, Cruikshank wrote a letter to the London *Times* stating that the story was true—that both the plot and the invention of the characters in *Oliver Twist* were his—and of course there were many people who believed it, although the truth was that his whole contribution had been to suggest the character of Fagin.

If Cruikshank had been a woman, as Mrs. Thomas Scott was, and posed as a shy and retiring creature, wronged by man's inhumanity but too diffident to fight for the laurels justly hers, there would have been no dearth of champions to espouse her cause and cast their gauntlets into the arena on her behalf. For such is the male protective instinct, craftily fostered through long centuries—frequently leading to absurdity and disillusionment, as in the instance about to be recorded.

On the 19th of November, 1875, the New York *Evening Post* published a poem entitled "What My Lover Said," signed only with the initials "H. G." The verses, which were concerned with love's young dream, were tenderly conceived and deftly written, with that sentimental appeal which finds an echo in so many bosoms. So they became popular at once and began a career in the newspapers which has endured to this day.

Before long, some over-zealous exchange editor, assuming that the initials "H. G." could stand only for Horace Greeley, affixed Greeley's name to the verses, and gradually a legend developed to the effect that the poem had been written by Greeley years before—perhaps was even the story of a youthful passion of his own —but had dropped from sight and had been resurrected only by accident.

Horace Greeley had been in his grave for three years at the time the poem appeared, so he was not there to affirm or deny the truth of this legend, but it was given a certain verisimilitude by the fact that as a young man he had written and published some fairly creditable verse. Nobody, apparently, thought of writing to the *Evening Post* to find out who the author really was, nor did any one on the *Post* think it worth while to relate the true history of the poem. So for five years, the fable went merrily on without effective contradiction.

But on Sunday, October 31, 1880, the Philadelphia *Times* published a story which was destined to be the starting point of a famous controversy. This story, which was in the shape of special correspondence from New York, gave an account of an informal gathering of actors and newspapermen in "the Palette Club beer-rooms on Twenty-second Street," in the course of which Barton Hill, the actor, had recited a lovely poem entitled "What My Lover Said," with such effect that "when he had finished, there seemed to be a finer sentiment pervading the crowd, and the next order for beer was in lower and less authoritative tones."

Questioned about the poem, Mr. Hill stated that it had been written by Horace Greeley, and had been given him by a friend who had clipped it from the New York *Evening Post* twenty-five years previously. Some surprise was expressed that Greeley should have written anything so exquisite, and Mr. Hill explained that all he knew about it was the *Post* had credited it to Greeley. He added that he had endeavored

299

to trace the history of the poem, but had been
unable to discover anything further.

A few days later, the Albany *Evening
Journal,* in an editorial under the caption
"H. G. and H. G.," announced that it could
give Mr. Hill the information he wanted, that
"What My Lover Said" had been written in
the fall of 1875 by Homer Greene, then a student at Union College, and that the fact that
it had been signed only with his initials had
caused it to be attributed to Greeley, the most
famous "H. G." in American history.

Both these articles were widely copied and
warmly debated, and on December 8, 1880,
fresh impetus was given the controversy by the
appearance of the following letter in the *Evening Post:*

I have noticed that some discussion has arisen of
late in the newspapers concerning the authorship of
the poem "What My Lover Said." The New York
correspondent of the Philadelphia *Times* writes that
the poem was recited the other evening to a select
company of actors and newspaper men by Mr.
Barton Hill, who said that the poem was cut from
the *Evening Post* some twenty-five years ago, and
ascribed by that journal to Horace Greeley. Will
the *Evening Post* kindly assist me now in an effort
—it is certainly a laudable one—to do justice to
Mr. Greeley's memory by relieving it from such a
burden of sentimentality, and allow me to confess,

300

hatchet in hand, that the cherry tree was chopped down by me?

I wrote the poem in the autumn of 1875—I was then in my senior year at Union College—and sent it to the New York *Evening Post* for publication, as your journal had already published several poems of mine. This poem appeared first in the daily issue of November 19, 1875, in the semi-weekly issue of November 23, and I believe in the weekly issue of that week. In the manuscript that I sent to the *Evening Post* I had written the title, "What Her Lover Said," and had signed my full name; but the editors, intent on preserving the sacred unities of title, poem and signature, and exercising, as one may say, a poetical license, changed the word "her" in the title to "my," and eliminated all of my name except the initial letters H. G. It can be readily seen that wherever the poem went—and it was widely copied in the press—its readers, well-informed as to the authorship of "What I Know About Farming," noting the rural character of each production, the similarity of titles, and above all the initial letters of the name, would jump easily to the conclusion that both were products of the same imagination.

Since the days when I neglected the study of "Differential and Integral Calculus" to write poor poetry, I have seldom been favored with the smiles of the Muses, and now, since entering into the active practice of the law, I fear that the tuneful Nine have entirely deserted me. But when I find my poetical children (pardon the figure, they are

301

the only children I have), wandering up and down
the land like "Japhet in Search of a Father," there
is still enough left of parental pride to acknowledge
them as mine, and enough left of poetic honor to
rescue others from the charge of their paternity.

HOMER GREENE.

Honesdale, Pa., November 26, 1880.

The *Evening Post,* strangely enough, did not
offer any comment upon this letter, but confirmation of Mr. Greene's statements was quick
in coming from another quarter. In 1875,
Mr. Francis E. Leupp had been a member of
the editorial staff of the *Evening Post,* but in
1880 he was connected with the Syracuse
Herald, and in the issue for December 12 published a statement to the effect that it was he
who had received the manuscript of "What
Her Lover Said," which Mr. Greene had mailed
to the *Evening Post,* that he "had dressed it up,
amending some trifling errors of word and
punctuation, put what he deemed a better title
to it, cut down the writer's name to a simple pair
of initials, H. G., and given it to the printer.

"The only reasons I have for bringing up
the matter here," Mr. Luepp concludes, "are to
suggest what is the possible origin of some of
the charges of plagiarism brought against modern literary men, to set the public right on a
matter in which I have unintentionally deceived
them, and to tender Mr. Homer Greene, of

302

Honesdale, Pa., my heartfelt congratulations and regrets."

It would seem that a statement so explicit as this would put an end to any controversy, but it takes a long time for the truth to overtake a lie (very often, indeed, it never does), and the verses continued to be printed as the work of Horace Greeley. Various papers even added editorial notes explaining that Mr. Greeley wrote the poem in 1842. Gradually, however, truth did prevail, Mr. Greeley's name was used less and less frequently, and Homer Greene's took its place. For a time it was rather the fashion to print the verses with the sub-title, "A charming poem attributed to Horace Greeley, but written in 1875 by Homer Greene of Honesdale, Pa."

However, the end was not yet. In the winter of 1886 the Philadelphia *News* published an article about the poem, asserting that it had been written neither by Horace Greeley nor by Homer Greene, but by Colonel Richard Realf, the author of "Indirection" and various other poems, who had committed suicide at Oakland, California, in 1879. Again the controversy was on. Now that they had been reminded of it, there were a number of persons who were quite certain that Colonel Realf was the author of the poem and who wrote to the papers to say so. One of his admirers stated positively that the verses had been written by Colonel Realf while he was city editor of the Pittsburgh *Commercial,* soon after being mustered out of the Union service at the close of the Civil War.

Fortunately an authoritative answer to this assertion was soon forthcoming from Colonel Richard J. Hinton, Realf's literary executor.

"It seems to me proper to state," Colonel Hinton wrote in a letter to the New York *Graphic* of October 20, 1888, "that Richard Realf was not the author of 'What My Lover Said,' either under that title or under that of 'My Lover and I,' " and he adds that the confusion probably arose from the fact that Colonel Realf did write a poem called "Sunbeam and I," but that while, in memory, one might suggest the other, there was really no resemblance between them. "There is nothing that I can find in Realf's poems," Colonel Hinton concludes, "and I believe that nearly all he has ever written are in my possession, many of them being in the original manuscript, which resembles the poem in dispute."

With this second claimant thus effectively placed *hors de combat,* Mr. Greene might well have supposed that his laurels were secure, but he had yet to cope with a feminine aspirant to his wreath—the most persistent of them all, and the one who proved most difficult to dispose of.

What My Lover Said

She entered the field with the following astonishing letter to the New York *Sun:*

Abbeville, Vermilion Parish, La.

To the Editor of the *New York Sun:*

About twenty-five years ago I sent the subjoined poem anonymously to the New York *Evening Post.* Since then I have seen it extensively copied, as originating from your paper, and attributed to Horace Greeley. Of course I felt much complimented; but as the true author is yet unknown to fame I think it would be but tardy justice to render honor to whom honor is due by republishing the poem under my signature.

Respectfully,

Mrs. O. C. Jones.

Accompanying the letter was a copy of "What My Lover Said," which the *Sun* obligingly republished, with Mrs. Jones's name attached. At about the same time she had written a similar letter to the New Orleans *Times-Democrat*, which had also printed the poem with her name signed to it, and from these two sources it started on its newspaper travels once again, this time credited to the Abbeville candidate.

Mrs. Jones soon discovered, no doubt considerably to her surprise, that her rival claimant was not the deceased Horace Greeley, who could say nothing, but a very much alive Homer Greene, whose friends quickly rallied to his defense. Such papers as were familiar with the evidence came at once to Mr. Greene's support, and a few of them treated Mrs. Jones with a disrespectful hilarity which, as appeared subsequently, was very galling to her proud Southern spirit. It was suggested, among other things, that if the people of Vermilion Parish had not been so busy painting the town red they would have known that this particular controversy had been settled long before, and that if Mrs. Jones wanted to claim something that was still in doubt she should have entered her name for "Beautiful Snow," or "Solitude," or "There Is No Death."

There were, however, a considerable number of romantic males who felt their chivalrous instincts stirred by this feminine appeal for justice, and who leaped, pen in hand, to the support of Mrs. Jones, though they must have deplored the fact that her name was not more picturesque. Among her most doughty champions was J. Andrew Boyd, who occupied an editorial position on the Wilkesbarre (Pa.) *News-Leader*. He started proceedings by writing Mrs. Jones "in the interest of justice alone and very pointedly asked her if she really was the author" of the poem in question, stating that "Mr. Homer Greene also claimed it as a child of his own brain."

"Most assuredly I wrote the poem," Mrs.

Jones replied promptly, "else I should never have had the audacity to claim it as my own. Passionately fond of poetry, I scribbled from my earliest recollection, publishing but little, as I wrote only for my own amusement, shyly concealing my penchant for verse and usually selecting a far-off paper for publication, and unfortunately, with the innocence and thoughtlessness of youth, sent the poetical waif to an anti-southern paper. Several northern sages having so long monopolized it of course will not admit that the true author was a little rebel lassie 'Way Down South in Dixie.' "

To any one familiar with the literature of such controversies, this letter would have been all-revealing, for it is the invariable boast of literary impostors that, scorning the commercial side of literature, they never write for publication, but only for their own amusement. Even to Mr. Boyd the letter left something to be desired, so he wrote again, asking for further details and enclosing a copy of a letter from Mr. Homer Greene telling when and where he had written and published the poem, and stating that this latest development of the controversy rather amused him. This brought forth a long reply from the southern song-bird, of which only a part need be quoted.

"Would that my fiery southern blood," she writes, "flowed as icily regularly as Mr.

307

Greene's, then I should only feel 'amused' instead of exceedingly annoyed by the cruel sarcasms allowed by the liberty of the press. The poem has been compared to 'a rose-bud fresh with morning dew-drops,' and my keenly sensitive nature is pricked and torn by its thorns. . . .

"I composed the verses just before the surrender of the conquered banner during a vacation spent at Port Barre, La. There was quite a romance connected with them; a vanished dream; for 'whom first we love, you know, we seldom wed.' I only told an actual occurrence in the simplest rhyme imaginable, for my lover was no myth, but an Apollo wearing a rebel uniform of gray.

"The poem itself will plead for me to every impartial critic for it is essentially a woman's poem and could only have emanated from a woman's soul, inspired by her first shy love. . . .

"The poem was really sent for publication immediately after the cessation of hostilities. I was a mere slip of a girl, shy as a fawn, and only ventured to show my verses to my brother and an old bachelor cousin, now dead, who advised me to send them to a northern paper. . . .

"In ante-bellum days there was no prouder name than mine, but I shared the financial wreck of the South. Frightened, widowed, and defenseless at having aroused such a hornet's nest by daring to assert that the true author of

What My Lover Said

'What My Lover Said' was an obscure lassie
'Away Down South in Dixie,' I appeal to the
chīvalry of my native land to shield me from
their stings."

The appeal was not in vain. "What more
can be said?" asks Mr. Boyd. "Does not Mrs.
Jones's statement touch every point at issue in
the controversy? Her letter is explicit, straightforward, and to my mind carries conviction
with it." The New York *Sun* was also convinced and said so editorially. So, no doubt,
were all the other chivalrous defenders of the
shy Southern lassie.

Mr. Greene, meanwhile, had offered to present his home at Honesdale, which he valued at
$15,000, to any one who could prove that the
poem had been published anywhere prior to its
appearance in the *Evening Post* in November,
1875. Mrs. Jones's partizans claimed that she
had won the prize, and that the house should
be turned over to her forthwith; but Mr.
Greene's friends asked for a little more evidence, and another Southern woman, living at
Raleigh, N. C., took her pen in hand to make
some caustic observations.

"Mrs. Jones brings no proof whatever into
court," she wrote in a letter to the *Sun,* which
was still warmly espousing Mrs. Jones's cause.
"Her unsubstantiated word, however excellent
her personal worth, can not outweigh facts and

dates. It may seem to her refined sensibilities somewhat narrow to have an equivocal auditor. Yet she should ask no more and no less consideration than is accorded other writers, even though doomed to live amid the fragrance of the magnolia and the melody of the mockingbird 'Away Down South in Dixie.' "

Mrs. Jones, however, had finally been pinned down to the definite statement that the poem had been sent by her to the New York *Evening Post* in 1865, and, under the direction of the indefatigable Mr. Boyd, a careful search was made of the files of the *Post* for 1864, 1865 and 1866. The result must have been a severe blow to him, for the poem could not be discovered. He laid this result before Mrs. Jones, who replied cheerfully that she "was under the impression that it was the *Evening Post*, but if the files for that year had been examined without success, possibly it was not published there."

And then she proceeded to recount another romance, previously unmentioned, with a "handsome young lieutenant" of the Union army, who had been detailed to guard her home. "I, being a hot-headed patriotic little rebel," she writes, "treated him with lofty disdain, withered him with a glance of scorn, for was he not wearing the blue? However, we gradually became more social, until quite a flirtation ensued; we read poetry together and

What My Lover Said

talked nonsense as young folks have from time immemorial. I even showed him some of my rhymes; he pretended to fancy 'What My Lover Said' so much that *he copied it as a keep-sake and carried it off.* [The italics are Mrs. Jones's.] I cannot even recall his name, but perhaps this may account for the mystery connected with the verses.

"I plead not guilty to the charge of plagiarism," she concludes, "and if my innocence is never proved, I implore, at least, the benefit of a doubt, if only that and nothing more. The sage of Highland Cottage may twine my laurel leaf with his proud chaplet, and as my own bread-winner I hope to retire once more into peaceful obscurity."

And as a final proof that she really wrote "What My Lover Said" she sent to Mr. Boyd a sequel, inspired by the same romance. This sequel is entitled "A Twilight Dream," and the first stanza is as follows:

Hand clasped in hand mid the clover we walked,
    In the gloaming long ago;
The moonbeams kissed the peach blooms pink,
    Coquettishly peeping to and fro.
How the stars blinked in the calm azure sky,
How the moon smiled down with inquisitive eye,
While the sweet south wind came prying by,
And the still hours of the night drew nigh,

Yet hands clasped in the orchard path we walked,
And—*zoe mou, sas agapo*—fondly talked
   In the gloaming long ago.

Poor Mrs. Jones! Driven to her last defense, with her back against the wall, she had fallen into the trap which has proved fatal to so many plagiarists—she had tried to prove that she had written something she didn't write by producing something she did write, with the usual result, which was merely to show her utter inability to distinguish poetry from doggerel. It was too much; her partizans, the New York *Sun* included, realized that the game was up, and most of them said so. As for Mrs. Jones, she slipped into that peaceful obscurity which she had craved and never afterwards emerged.

In a letter of recent date, Mr. Greene tells of an amusing experience when introduced to a prominent Boston man, some time ago, as the author of "What My Lover Said." The Boston man regarded him with open incredulity, and informed him that the Homer Greene who really wrote the poem was a well-known business man in New York, with whom a Mrs. Safford, a friend of his in Boston, had collaborated in the writing of the verses. He had this story from Mrs. Safford herself, who had given him complete details concerning the work of

What My Lover Said

collaboration and of her general friendly intimacy with Homer Greene.

"Up to that time," adds Mr. Greene, "I had never heard of Mrs. Safford, but I afterwards learned that she had done considerable journalistic and some literary work. A little later, Barton Hill, the actor, was my guest over-night, and he told me about his friendship with Mrs. Safford, and about their mutual fondness for the poem, but he said that Mrs. Safford had never claimed to him any part in its composition."

So perhaps the Boston man was mistaken, in spite of his circumstantial story.

"Barton Hill recited the poem to me that evening," Mr. Greene continues, "and he did it exquisitely. Later on, Kathryn Kidder (now Mrs. Louis K. Anspacher) recited the poem one evening to a little company of us at the house of a mutual friend in New York. She did it only indifferently well, and she told me afterward that the presence of the author had given her such an attack of stage fright that she simply went to pieces. And she a seasoned actress!

"I might add that the controversy over the authorship of the poem has not yet ended, and perhaps never will. The verses not infrequently appear, even now, accredited to some other known or unknown writer."

313

But that has long since ceased to bother their author!

Mr. Greene still lives in "Highland Cottage" at Honesdale, Pa.—the same cottage he once upon a time offered as a prize—and looking back from the summit of his threescore years and ten he can afford to smile at all that old trouble. The pleasantest part of it, perhaps, was that throughout it his rôle was merely that of interested spectator. His friends did the fighting for him.

DERELICT

DERELICT

A REMINISCENCE OF R. L. S.'s "TREASURE
ISLAND" AND CAP'N BILLY BONES,
HIS SONG

"Fifteen men on the Dead Man's Chest—
  Yo-ho-ho and a bottle of rum!
Drink and the devil had done for the rest—
  Yo-ho-ho and a bottle of rum!"
The mate was fixed by the bos'n's pike,
The bos'n brained with a marlinspike
And Cookey's throat was marked belike
      It had been gripped
      By fingers ten;
      And there they lay,
      All good dead men,
Like break-o'-day in a boozing-ken—
  Yo-ho-ho and a bottle of rum!

Fifteen men of a whole ship's list—
  Yo-ho-ho and a bottle of rum!
Dead and bedamned and the rest gone whist!—
  Yo-ho-ho and a bottle of rum!
The skipper lay with his nob in gore
Where the scullion's ax his cheek had shore—
And the scullion he was stabbed times four.

317

And there they lay
And the soggy skies
Dripped all day long
In up-staring eyes—
At murk sunset and at foul sunrise—
Yo-ho-ho and a bottle of rum!

Fifteen men of 'em stiff and stark—
Yo-ho-ho and a bottle of rum!
Ten of the crew had the Murder mark—
Yo-ho-ho and a bottle of rum!
'Twas a cutlass swipe, or an ounce of lead,
Or a yawing hole in a battered head—
And the scuppers glut with a rotting red.
And there they lay—
Aye, damn my eyes!—
All lookouts clapped
On paradise—
All souls bound just contrariwise—
Yo-ho-ho and a bottle of rum!

Fifteen men of 'em good and true—
Yo-ho-ho and a bottle of rum!
Every man jack could ha' sailed with Old Pew—
Yo-ho-ho and a bottle of rum!
There was chest on chest full of Spanish gold,
With a ton of plate in the middle hold,
And the cabins riot of stuff untold.

318

Derelict

And they lay there,
   That had took the plum,
  With sightless glare
   And their eyes struck dumb,
While we shared all by the rule of thumb—
Yo-ho-ho and a bottle of rum!

More was seen through the sternlight screen—
  Yo-ho-ho and a bottle of rum!
Chartings ondoubt where a woman had been!—
  Yo-ho-ho and a bottle of rum!
A flimsy shift on a bunker cot,
With a thin dirk slot through the bosom spot
And the lace stiff-dry in a purplish blot.
   Or was she wench . . .
    Or some shuddering maid . . . ?
   That dared the knife—
   And that took the blade!
By God! she was stuff for a plucky jade—
  Yo-ho-ho and a bottle of rum!

Fifteen men on the Dead Man's Chest—
  Yo-ho-ho and a bottle of rum!
Drink and the devil had done for the rest—
  Yo-ho-ho and a bottle of rum!
We wrapped 'em all in a mains'l tight,
With twice ten turns of a hawser's bight,
And we heaved 'em over and out of sight—

Famous Single Poems

With a yo-heave-ho!
　　And a fare-you-well!
And a sullen plunge
　　In the sullen swell
Ten fathoms deep on the road to hell!
Yo-ho-ho and a bottle of rum!
　　　　　　　Young E. Allison

DERELICT

"I AM now on another lay for the moment, purely owing to Lloyd, this one," wrote R. L. S. to Henley in August, 1881; "now, see here, 'The Sea-Cook, or Treasure Island: A Story for Boys.'

"If this doesn't fetch the kids, why, they have gone rotten since my day. Will you be surprised to learn it is about Buccaneers . . . and a map, and a treasure, and a mutiny, and a derelict ship, and a sea-cook with one leg, and a sea-song with the chorus, 'Yo-ho-ho and a bottle of rum' (at the last Ho you heave at the capstan bars), which is a real buccaneer's song, only known to the crew of the late Captain Flint."

And three years later, when the book was fetching not only the kids but their elders too, and R. L. S. was getting his first real taste of success, he wrote to Sidney Colvin, "Treasure Island came out of Kingsley's 'At Last,' where I got the Dead Man's Chest—and that was the seed."

"At Last" is an uninspired account of a trip to the West Indies and the only reference to the Dead Man's Chest is in the first chapter. "We were crawling slowly along," Kingsley writes, "looking out for Virgin Garda; the first of those numberless isles which Columbus, so goes the tale, discovered on St. Ursula's day, and named them after the saint and her eleven thousand mythical virgins. Unfortunately, English buccaneers have since given to most of them less poetic names. The Dutchman's Cap, Broken Jerusalem, The Dead Man's Chest, Rum Island, and so forth, mark a time and race more prosaic."

The English names will doubtless seem to many readers much more picturesque than the colorless virgins'; but however that may be, Kingsley's narrative identifies Dead Man's Chest as one of the Virgin Islands. Curiously enough, it may be doubted if it ever was really called "Dead Man's Chest." Present-day maps give its name as "Dead Chest Island," and that is the name it has been known by, on the maps at least, for a century and a half. It is so given on *Neptune Occidental, A Complete Pilot of the West Indies,* published by Thomas Jeffreys at London in 1782. Kingsley possibly made a mistake in the name, as he did in one of the others—for "Broken Jerusalem" should be "Fallen Jerusalem"—a most fortunate mistake, surely, since without it there would have been no "Fifteen men," and perhaps even no *Treasure Island!*

Derelict

A. Hyatt Verrill contends that it is the map-makers who are mistaken, all of them blindly following an error made by an early one, and says that during his residence in the West Indies he never heard the island called anything but "Dead Man's Chest," or "Duchess Island."

Whatever its name, legend has it that in the old days the pirates of those seas were in the habit of repairing thither to careen and scrape their ships, to stretch their legs, and to indulge in the boisterous pastimes peculiar to their profession. But this also rests on a very slender foundation. F. A. Fenger, who made a voyage through Sir Francis Drake Channel in a canoe in 1916, is one of the few men who have actually seen the island. He says in his account of the voyage in "Alone in the Caribbean" that he intended to land on it, but the surf was too high, and he had to give it up. He took a photograph of it, however, which shows that it is more of a rock than an island—about the poorest possible place to use as a harbor.

Of course the only thing that matters is not what the island really is, but what Stevenson transmuted it into. Doubtless most readers of his immortal tale have imagined, as Jim Hawkins did, a sailor's sea-chest with fifteen men heaped across it (although Stevenson was careful to use capitals as an indication of what it really meant):

323

" 'Suddenly,' says Jim, 'he—the captain—began to pipe up his eternal song,

"Fifteen men on the Dead Man's Chest—
 Yo-ho-ho, and a bottle of rum!
 Drink and the devil had done for the rest—
 Yo-ho-ho, and a bottle of rum!"

" 'At first I had supposed "the dead man's chest" to be that identical big box of his upstairs in the front room, and the thought had been mingled in my nightmares with that of the one-legged seafaring man.' "

There has been much speculation and discussion as to where Stevenson got this chantey, but, in the light of the evidence, there can be only one answer to that question. He got it out of his head.

In his letter to Henley he says explicitly that it was "only known to the crew of the late Captain Flint," which is surely plain enough, and Lloyd Osbourne testifies to the same effect.

"I am quite sure," he writes, "that the 'Fifteen Men' was wholly original to R. L. S.; and the most confirming fact of all to my mind is that he always considered the Dead Man's Chest not as a literal chest, but as a small rock that had thus been fancifully named by the buccaneers. Though I remember his often speaking of this, it is strange that no explanation

324

of the kind appears in *Treasure Island.*"
Probably Stevenson thought such an explanation
unnecessary in view of his having capitalized
the words. In discussing the story he may have
mentioned the fact that the Dead Man's Chest
was one of the Virgins, and this has simply
slipped from Mr. Osbourne's memory—he was
only thirteen years old when *Treasure Island*
was written. It was "purely owing to Lloyd,"
by the way, who had complained that R. L. S.
never wrote anything exciting, that *Treasure
Island* was begun; it was his enthusiasm for it
which helped carry it to a triumphant finish;
and to him, very fittingly, the book is dedicated.

The Manchester *Guardian,* in a solemn article, recently asserted that on the Chilean coast
there is a little church obviously constructed of
timber taken from a ship, and that round the
edge of its bell, which was presumably once a
ship's bell, run the words, "Fifteen men on the
Dead Man's Chest." The priest in charge of
the church assured an inquirer, whom the
Guardian does not name, that the building
dated from early in the eighteenth century.
"Considering that it is not to be found in the
printed page," adds the *Guardian* gravely, "it
is an interesting sidelight on the strange nooks
and corners from which Stevenson collected the
material for his books," the inference being that
at some period of his career Stevenson visited

this church, climbed up into the steeple and perused the legend on the bell!

It is a fact, however, that, outside of *Treasure Island,* the chantey has never been found anywhere in print, and it has always been one of the tragedies of literature that the Captain never got any further than the first four lines. The beginning is so admirable! Though, of course, as a chantey four lines are enough; many chanteys consist of no more than that. For a chantey is made to be sung as a gang of sailors heave on a rope, or do some other work in concert, one voice carrying the lines and all of them coming in on the chorus. It is like a marching-song: the simpler and more repetitious it is the better.

Mr. E. B. Osborn, the literary editor of the London *Morning Post* and the author of a collection of charming essays, *Literature and Life,* has the audacity to assert that even these four lines would not have been tolerated aboard the *Hispaniola,* for Flint's cutthroats would have preferred such jocund stuff as "Haul Away, Joe," or "Hog's-Eye Man," and adds that "it is highly improbable that there ever was an authentic chantey of the Dead Man's Chest. If there had been, it would have been found in one of the standard collections, such as Captain W. B. Whall's or that published by Dr. R. R.

Terry, whose qualifications for collecting and editing a book of chanteys are exceptional."

It may be taken for granted, then, that when *Treasure Island* was published, this chantey consisted of four lines only, and that they had originated with R. L. S. One can imagine him smacking his lips over them, like Sentimental Tommy! And consider the cunning of the man—and his self-restraint—in writing only four!

But these lines were to waken an echoing chord in an American brain, and the result was to be—not a chantey, to be sure!—but one of the most truly piratical, bloodthirsty songs ever written.

In the city of Louisville, Kentucky, there lives a quiet and retiring man by the name of Young Ewing Allison. He is slightly built, not in any way piratical in appearance, somewhat deaf, with an eye full of humor, and a reputation for kindly satire. At the time *Treasure Island* appeared, he was twenty-eight years old, and was city editor of the Louisville *Courier-Journal*. He had started his wage-earning career as a printer's devil at the age of thirteen, and had been scented with printer's ink ever since. History does not record when he first read Stevenson's romance, but in 1891, three years after he had left daily newspaper

327

work to start an insurance paper, he fell in with Henry Waller at Louisville, and one result was his first elaboration of Stevenson's quatrain.

Waller was the adopted son of Mary Francis Scott-Siddons, the famous English actress. He had been an infant prodigy as a pianist, but his father had overdriven him and he was on the verge of complete breakdown, when Mrs. Siddons intervened and bought his freedom. She sent him to study with Liszt, and he remained there three years, but, like most infant prodigies, his development was soon arrested, and he never became a great pianist. But he had acquired a thorough knowledge of music, which he put to use as a teacher and composer. He drifted to America and settled at Louisville, where Mr. Allison, who was also a music enthusiast, met him. The two became fast friends, and the idea of an American opera germinated between them. They went to work, Allison writing the lyrics and libretto and Waller the music—and, wonder of wonders, they *did* produce an opera, which they named "The Ogallallas," which was accepted by the Bostonians, and which was actually produced at the Columbia Theater, Chicago, February 16, 1893. It had a regular dime novel plot—heroic scout, beautiful maiden, bloodthirsty redskins—and it was a failure. Americans weren't interested in scouts and redskins, at least on the stage. They preferred picturesque Spanish bandits or tragic Italian clowns.

But meanwhile their friendship had had another result. It was one evening in 1891, that Mr. Allison happened to mention *Treasure Island,* and the famous and haunting quatrain of old Billy Bones. They bewailed the parsimony of Stevenson in revealing so little of a song which had such tremendous possibilities; and finally Waller remarked that if Allison would write two or three stanzas around the theme, he would set them to music, and maybe they could make some money out of it. The suggestion appealed to Allison, and he composed three ragged but promising stanzas, which Waller set to music next day. They called it "A Piratical Ballad," and sent it to William A. Pond & Co. It was accepted and published—but while it was a good song, it never made anybody's fortune.

But Mr. Allison had found what was to become his avocation for many years—to devise fitting and adequate expression for an entrancing theme:

Fifteen men on the Dead Man's Chest—
Yo-ho-ho and a bottle of rum!

He himself has applied the adjective "ragged" to the three stanzas which he wrote for Waller's song; they were far from satisfying

him, and he went to work to improve them.
He pondered, he polished, he expanded. Stray
phrases, as they came into his head, were jotted
down on scraps of paper and stuck away in odd
corners of his desk. That theme was always at
the back of his mind, and his brain was inces-
santly at work upon it. It was the "labor of
the file" so dear to Gautier—changing a phrase
here, a word there; rejoicing over the discovery
of the word "yawing" to describe a gaping hole
in a battered head; tasting the joy of the true
artist in winning closer and closer to perfection.

At last he had five stanzas which suited him
fairly well, and he sent them to the *Century
Magazine*. The editor accepted them in a flush
of enthusiasm when he first read them; but
when, some time later, he got them out of his
manuscript safe and looked them over, he perceived that they were rather strong meat for his
clientele, and he wrote to Mr. Allison suggest-
ing that they be toned down a little, especially
in the closing lines. This Mr. Allison refused
to do, and the poem came back to him. So it
was printed in the Louisville *Courier-Journal*,
and started on its travels through the press. As
is almost always the case, some exchange editor
soon clipped off the author's name, and from
that time on it was usually credited to that prolific writer, "Anon."

But the theme was still stirring around in

Derelict

Mr. Allison's mind, and he began to wonder if it would be permissible to introduce the trace of a woman on board the *Derelict*. Up to this point he had tried to develop his theme strictly in accordance with the Stevensonian spirit—and there was no woman in *Treasure Island*. But after all Billy Bones's song had nothing to do with the *Hispaniola*—it was a reminiscence of his own past, in which doubtless more than one woman had played a part! So why not? And Mr. Allison went to work in his usual careful fashion on what was to become one of the most striking stanzas of the poem. He even consulted a girl as to whether it should be a "flimsy shift" or a "filmy shift"—a perilous thing to do, but by good luck the girl preferred flimsy. And he decided that this stanza should be set in italics to show that it was, in a way, an interpolation.

In 1901, the editors of the *Rubric*, a magazine published in Chicago, having happened upon the poem somewhere, and also having learned by some strange chance that Mr. Allison was its author, wrote him asking his permission to use it. He not only consented, but sent them the revised version with the new stanza about the woman, and the poem was published very happily illustrated in two colors and occupying eight pages of the magazine. It was called "On Board the Derelict," and the issue of the magazine containing it is a prized possession of a few fortunate collectors.

This publication gave a new impetus to the poem, which by this time was coming to be recognized by the discriminating as something of a classic. But very few people outside of Louisville had ever heard of Young E. Allison, the name meant nothing to the exchange editor, and before long it was again dropped and old "Anon." was brought back into service. It had such an air of verisimilitude that most people assumed that it was a real pirate song, dating from the days of the Spanish Main. It was this assumption which caused one of the editors of the New York *Times* to get tangled up in a controversy which served to lighten the sky a little during the first dark days of the European war.

On July 26, 1914, the *Times* published a letter from Mr. Edward Alden asking if there was any more to Billy Bones His Song than the four lines given in *Treasure Island*.

On the September 20 following, an answer signed "W. L." was published, to the effect that the verse "is the opening stanza of an old song or chantey of West Indian piracy, which is believed to have originated from the wreck of an English buccaneer on a cay in the Caribbean Sea known as 'The Dead Man's Chest.' The cay was so named from its fancied resemblance to the old sailor's sea-chest which held his scanty belongings. The song or chantey was familiar to deep-sea sailors many years ago. The song is copied from a very old scrap-book in which the author's name was not given." And a garbled version of Mr. Allison's poem followed in its six-stanza form.

On the same day, the *Times,* never suspecting that this story was woven of the fabric of which dreams are made, published an editorial calling attention to the chantey and adding that "while it can hardly be recommended as a delectable piece of literature, in any sense, it is interesting as a bit of rough, unstudied sailor's jingle, the very authorship of which is long since forgotten."

On October 4, this bubble was pricked by Walt Mason, who wrote to the *Times* stating that "the fine old sea poem, 'Fifteen Men on the Dead Man's Chest,' recently quoted in your columns, was written by Young E. Allison. I have raked through various biographical dictionaries trying to discover who Young E. Allison was, but without result." (Mr. Mason was also evidently under the impression that it was an old poem, and that its author had long since passed to his reward.)

"The man who wrote such a poem," Mr. Mason continued, "should not be unknelled, unhonored, and unsung. In your editorial touch-

ing the rhyme I don't think you do it justice.
You describe it as a rough, unstudied sailor's
jingle, whereas it is a work of art. Some of
the lines are tremendous, and the whole poem
has a haunting quality that never yet distinguished a mere jingle."

But the *Times* was not convinced. It followed Mr. Mason's letter with the following
condescending editorial note:

We have received several other letters in which
the authorship of the lines is credited to Mr. Allison, who is a resident of Louisville, Ky., and the
editor of the *Insurance Field*. It is not likely,
however, that he wrote the famous old chantey.
Our correspondent, "W. L.," says that he copied
the verses from a manuscript written into a book
. . . published in 1843. This book belonged to
his grandfather, who died in 1874.

Thereupon Mr. Champion I. Hitchcock, a
close friend of Mr. Allison and his associate
on the *Insurance Field*, took up the cudgels and
wrote the *Times* a letter setting forth the history of the inception and development of the
poem from the first three-stanza version published as a song in 1891, to the final six-stanza
version published in the *Rubric* in 1901; and
pointing out that, no matter how old a scrap-
book might be, additions to it could be made at
any time, and that this poem had certainly been

Derelict

written into this one subsequent to 1901, which
was the first time that the six-stanza version
had ever been published anywhere.

But the *Times,* apparently, had had enough
of the controversy, for it refused to publish Mr.
Hitchcock's letter. Whereupon that gentleman,
his fighting blood thoroughly aroused, wrote a
monograph on the subject, complete and convincing, and published it himself. This book,
it may be added, is not only one of the rarest in
existence, but is one of the finest expressions of
friendship to be found anywhere, and is a
credit alike to its author and to the man whose
qualities and achievements it celebrates.

Now of course Walt Mason was entirely
right. "Derelict" is not a rough, unstudied
jingle; it is a piece of polished artistry. No
sailor could have composed it unless he was
also a scholar and a poet. But it is art that
conceals art. "Taking Stevenson's quatrain as
a starting-point, Allison succeeded in writing a
wholly modern versification in words and meter
so skilfully used as to create not only a vivid
atmosphere of piracy and antiquity, but of un-
skilfulness and coarseness."

Also it is not a chantey. It could not possibly
have been used, as chanteys were used in the
days of sailing-ships, to get a gang of men to
heaving or pulling together. True chanteys
consist of one line only, used as a chorus, the

rest depending on the imagination of the man who sang the solo part, and usually this imagination was of the most limited description. The pull was always on the accent of the chorus, as, for example:

> Rendso was no sailor—
> Rendso, boys, Rendso;
> He shipped on board a whaler—
> Rendso, boys, Rendso.

And finally the nautical references in the poem leave much to be desired. As a sailorman pointed out in the *Scoop* of Chicago, it would be about as easy to wrap a man in sheet-iron as in a piece of the mainsail, which is of canvas heavy and stiff enough to stand alone; and as for tying him up "with twice ten turns of a hawser's bight"—well, a hawser is the largest rope on board a ship, and to make a bight or loop in it would require a Samson or a Hercules.

"We of the sea," continued this old salt, "locate the scene of the verse at Dead Chest Island, half-way between the S.W. and S.E. points of Porto Rico, four and a half miles off-shore, which was used as a pirate rendezvous and later as the haven of wreckers and smugglers. It was first named by the Spanish 'Casa de Muertos'—the coffin."

Mr. Allison acknowledged cheerfully that

the points about the mainsail and hawser were beyond reproach. "My own education as an able seaman," he explained, "was gained from years of youthful study of dime-novel sea yarns by Ned Buntline, Sylvanus Cobb, jr., Billy Bowline, and other masters of the sea in libraries. I feel stronger in my piracy than in my seamanship. If there is a single verse, or, mayhap, one line of 'Derelict' that will hold, without leaking, anything of a specific gravity heavier than moonshine, it would surprise me. But it *seems* to, when it is adopted as a 'real chantey'—and that's the test, that it 'seems.' "

Which is absolutely true—seeming is all that is necessary.

It is an amusing coincidence that R. L. S. made practically the same answer when some aspersions were cast upon the seamanship of his story.

"Of course," he wrote in a letter to W. E. Henley, "my seamanship is jimmy. But I have known and sailed with seamen too, and lived and eaten with them; and I made my put-up shot in no great ignorance, but as a put-up thing has to be made, *i.e.*, to be coherent and picturesque, and damn the expense. Are they fairly lively on the wires? Then, favor me with your tongues. Are they wooden, and dim, and no sport? Then it is I that am silent, otherwise not."

Famous Single Poems

For the benefit of future biographers, the
following facts are here set down about Young
E. Allison: born at Henderson, Ky., December
23, 1853; printer's devil at 13; "local
editor" at 15; city reporter on a daily at 17;
city editor Louisville *Courier-Journal;* managing
editor Louisville *Commercial;* founded
The Insurance Herald, 1888; sold it and established
The Insurance Field, 1899; editor-in-chief
Louisville *Daily Herald,* 1902; chose
Champion I. Hitchcock to carry on *The Insurance
Field,* 1903; resumed editorial management
of *The Insurance Field* in association with
Mr. Hitchcock, 1905; died at Louisville, Ky.,
July 7, 1932. Author of two tales, "The Longworth
Mystery," and "The Passing of Major
Kilgore," and of various poems, the best known
of which after "Derelict" is "The Ballad of
Whisky Straight." But it is a long way after!

"I do not pretend to be a poet," wrote Mr.
Allison in a letter to the compiler. "Since boyhood,
indeed, I have not had the habit of reading
much poetry. I have written a lot of verse, but
mere 'mood satisfiers,' not put out as literature.
Among this lot were lyrics for four operas, the
librettos of which I prepared for music composed
by Henry Waller. One of them, 'The
Ogallallas,' was produced by the Bostonians
thirty years ago. Another, a tragic grand opera
called 'Father Francesco,' was brought out at

338

the Royal Opera at Berlin in 1895. The others did not come up for breath.

" 'Derelict' was first smudged in in 1891, when Mr. Waller and I were friends and not collaborators. He had not read *Treasure Island,* whereupon I loaned him the book. The refrain of Long John Silver struck him—as it has countless others—as containing endless lure. He said it called for music and if I would make a song around it he would set it. Next morning I gave him three hazy but singable verses and before night it was set musically and the manuscript was sent off to Pond & Co., and met immediate acceptance and publication. It was fine, grisly music, but I recognized that the words were inadequate and so began the work of polishing and constructing. It took about six years to get it to suit me. I was after an atmosphere of the perfect silence of dead life filled with horror by the refrain. There came other verses which did not 'belong,' and all that, and they never got in."

But there is still one other which he has in mind—a stanza celebrating Captain Flint's green parrot with its "Pieces of eight! Pieces of eight!" It is awaited with the most pleasurable anticipations!

There have been various extensions of Stevenson's quatrain by other hands, and some of them have been set to music, but none of them succeeds in achieving the atmosphere of horror which Mr. Allison maintains so successfully. James Whitcomb Riley, who knew a good poem when he saw it, not long before his death sent to Mr. Allison the following stanza, which expresses perfectly the feelings of that gentleman's admirers:

Fifteen men on the Dead Man's Chest—
  Yo-ho-ho and a bottle of rum!
Young E. Allison done all the rest—
  Yo-ho-ho and a bottle of rum!
He's sung this song for you and me,
Jest as it wuz—or ort to be—
Clean through time and eternity,
  Yo-ho-ho and a bottle of rum!

THE MOUSE-TRAP

THE MOUSE-TRAP [1]

ABOUT the middle of December, 1889, there was published at Oakland, California, a little volume called *Borrowings*, which was destined to become famous by one of the queerest freaks of chance that ever saved a book from oblivion. *Borrowings* was a collection of short quotations from various writers, and had been compiled, as its title page announced, by "Ladies of the First Unitarian Church of Oakland, California," presumably for the purpose of raising some money to meet the church expenses. The first edition was printed by C. A. Murdock & Co., of San Francisco, and has become a rarity.

The book was so successful that early in 1891, William Doxey, of San Francisco, printed a second edition, a copy of which was sent to the Library of Congress to be registered for copyright. This copy bears the date May 18, 1891, stamped on the title-page by the Library of Congress, so it may be assumed that that was approximately the date of publication. There was another edition of *Borrowings* printed from the same plates in 1893, and still another in 1894,

[1] Reprinted by permission from *The Colophon.*

343

so that the venture seems to have been a successful one financially, but there was nothing remarkable about the book, which was, in fact,
merely a hodge-podge of quotations put together
without much regard for accuracy, and it would
have been forgotten long since but for the following quotation which appeared near the bottom of
page 38:

> If a man can write a better book, preach a better
> sermon, or make a better mouse-trap, than his neigh-
> bor, though he builds his house in the woods, the
> world will make a beaten path to his door.
> —EMERSON.

There was something about this apothegm
which caught the public fancy—somewhere within it lurks that mysterious spark which makes for
immortality. Probably it is in the single word
"mouse-trap," which arrests attention and forces
itself upon the memory by its very singularity.
At any rate, the sentence began to be quoted here
and there, newspapers copied it, an advertising
writer used it, and of course Emerson devotees
began to search his works in an effort to place
it exactly. But it could not be found. The
nearest approach to it was the following entry in
his *Journals* (Vol. viii, p. 528) for 1855, headed
Common Fame:

> I trust a good deal to common fame, as we all
> must. If a man has good corn, or wood, or boards,

344

or pigs, to sell, or can make better chairs or knives, crucibles, or church organs than anybody else, you will find a broad, hard-beaten road to his house, though it be in the woods.

And the editors of his *Journals,* Edward Waldo Emerson and Waldo Emerson Forbes, added the following footnote:

There has been much inquiry in the newspapers, recently [1912], as to whether Mr. Emerson wrote a sentence very like the above, which has been attributed to him in print. The Editors do not find the latter in his works; but there can be little doubt that it was a memory-quotation by some hearer, or, quite probably, correctly quoted from one of his lectures, the same image in different words.

It was an advertising writer in the employ of the West Publishing Company, of St. Paul, Minnesota, who seems to have given the quotation its first fillip. Where he picked it up has never been disclosed, but he inserted it in an advertisement, crediting it to Emerson, and thereby brought down such a storm upon his head that his employers, in the West Company's house-organ, *The Docket,* for February, 1911 (p. 405), explained that this employee "undertook to add a literary flavor to a commercial announcement which he was constructing by inserting a quotation which his memory gave to him in the following form: [as given in *Borrow-*

ings]. He thought it sounded Emersonian and so gave Emerson the credit for it." Edward Waldo Emerson, in a letter to Dr. John H. Woods, of Cambridge, Massachusetts, refers to this incident when he writes:

I do not think the quotation you ask about can be found in any of my father's works. I presume it may have been used in a lecture and reported in some paper, and someone who heard of it used it, I am told as an advertisement.

This, as will presently be seen, was a remarkably good guess.

The woods are always full of literary hyenas ready to pounce upon any unappropriated piece of literary property, as has already been made abundantly clear in the preceding chapters, and as soon as word got about that the "mouse-trap," by this time famous, could not be found in Emerson's writings, a number of people came forward to claim it for their own. One of these was a Presbyterian minister named John Randolph Paxton—or perhaps it would be more correct to say that the authorship was wished upon him by admiring friends, just as had happened thirty years earlier when a respected harness-maker of Elizabeth, New Jersey, named Alexander M. W. Ball, was compelled to attempt to prove that he was the author of Elizabeth Akers Allen's poem, "Rock Me to Sleep," because some of his

misguided acquaintances insisted that he do so—
a story which has been told in detail elsewhere in
this book. There is no record that Dr. Paxton
ever made any claim in his own behalf—in fact,
he neglected to make a direct reply to an inquiry
about it—but his friends did so quite vigorously,
basing the claim upon a sermon, sometimes called
"The Unhidden Christ," and sometimes "He
Could Not Be Hid," which he preached on a
number of occasions. On August 25, 1889, he
preached it at Chautauqua, and the following
day the New York *Sun* published the following
extract from it:

A man can't be hid. He may be a peddler in the
mountains, but the world will find him out and
make him a king of finance. He may be carrying
cabbages from Long Island, when the world will demand that he shall run the railways of a continent.
He may be a groceryman on a canal, when the country shall come to find him and put him in his
career of usefulness. So that there comes a time
finally when all the great barrels of petroleum in
the land suggest but two names and one great company.

This is a long way from the "mouse-trap,"
but there can be little doubt that Dr. Paxton had
been reading Emerson before he wrote it, for in
that same entry in his *Journals* for 1855, headed
Common Fame, Emerson had continued as follows:

347

Famous Single Poems

If a man knows the law, people find it out, tho'
he live in a pine shanty, and resort to him. And
if a man can pipe or sing, so as to wrap the prisoned
soul in an elysium; or can paint landscape, and con-
vey into oils and ochres all enchantments of Spring
and Autumn; or can liberate and intoxicate all people who hear him with delicious songs and verses,
it is certain that the secret cannot be kept; the first
witness tells it to a second, and men go by fives and
tens and fifties to his door.

There are probably a good many artists and
poets who would disagree with this, but its resemblance to Dr. Paxton's outgiving is obvious.

By far the most famous and most self-assertive
claimant to the "mouse-trap" was Elbert Hubbard. The first time he had cited the quotation
in *The Philistine,* he had attributed it to Emerson, but in 1911 the Roycrofters published a
little book called *A Thousand and One Epigrams by Elbert Hubbard,* and on page 167 appeared the following:

If a man can write a better book, preach a better
sermon or make a better mouse-trap than his neighbor, though he build his house in the woods, the
world will make a beaten path to his door.

It will be noted that this is identical with the
version in *Borrowings* except that Hubbard has
taken out a couple of commas and changed
"builds" to "build"—an improvement in gram-

mar which was stressed by Dr. Frank H. Vize-
telly in an article in the *Literary Digest* (15
May, 1915, p. 1196), written in support of his
previous assertion (*Literary Digest*, 6 March,
1915), that Hubbard was the author of the epigram.

It would be interesting to analyze *A Thousand and One Epigrams* with care. A cursory
examination of it discloses on page 73, "Home is
where the heart is," which is usually attributed
to Livy; on page 136, "Life is just one damn
thing after another," which has been claimed for
Frank Ward O'Malley; and on page 82, "The
reward of a good deed is to have done it," which
is certainly a close echo of Emerson's "The reward of a thing well done is to have done it,"
(*Essays, Second Series: New England Reform-
ers*), which, of course, derives directly from
Seneca's "Recte facti fecisse merces est."
(*Epistulæ ad Lucilium.* Epis. 81, sec. 20.)

To confuse the matter further, the following
appeared on the back cover of *The Philistine* for
August, 1912:

> If a man
> write a bet-
> ter book or
> preach a better
> sermon than
> his neighbor,
> the world will

349

bring rat-traps
to his door, tho'
he live in a
forest.

(Ralph Waldo Emerson)

Hubbard probably intended this as a joke, but undoubtedly Emerson, though thirty years dead, turned over in his grave when his name was attached to such tommyrot.

Naturally there was a lot of inquiry as to why Mr. Hubbard should first attribute the quotation to Emerson, and then claim it for himself, and in *The Fra* for May, 1911, he gave the following explanation of this seeming inconsistency:

Mr. Hubbard, like all writers of epigrams, has attributed some of his good Class A product to other writers. For instance, he was once writing about the Roycrofters, and, having in mind the number of visitors who came to see us, he wrote: "If a man can write a better book," etc. . . . It was a little strain of his ego to let this thing go under his own stamp, so he saved his modesty and at the same time gave his epigram specific gravity, by attributing it to one Ralph Waldo Emerson.

A somewhat similar explanation was given in *The Philistine* for July, 1912, and in answer to an inquiry from the editor of *The Docket*, Mr. John T. Hoyle, assistant superintendent of the Roycrofters, writing in Hubbard's absence, said:

The Mouse-Trap

Elbert Hubbard evolved that Emersonian Dictum from the depths of his own cosmic consciousness, and put the credit where he believed it belonged. (*The Docket*, April, 1911, p. 454)

Finally, in July, 1930, Mr. Elbert Hubbard II, writing to Mr. Edward W. Putnam, of New York, said:

Perhaps you know that he [Hubbard] accredited it [the mouse-trap quotation] to Emerson in the first place, but later on, *after Emerson students failed to find it in his writings*, Hubbard finally admitted that he wrote it himself. [Italics mine.]

Now it is quite possible that, with the passage of the years, Elbert Hubbard came to believe that he had really evolved the epigram "from the depths of his own cosmic consciousness," but it is certain that he did not. If he evolved it from anywhere, it was from his memory, for the first issue of *The Philistine* did not appear until June, 1895, whereas, beyond the possibility of question, the epigram had appeared in a book published in 1889, and there is every reason to believe that it was coined in 1871, when Hubbard was only eleven years old. It may be added that there is a certain lack of verisimilitude in his assertion that he had not originally claimed it because to have done so would have involved "a little strain of his ego."

351

Famous Single Poems

The question of authorship, then, simmers down to this: Where did the editors of *Borrowings* find the quotation?

Borrowings had been compiled by Mrs. Sarah S. B. Yule and Miss Mary S. Keene, with perhaps some minor contributors, and it was these two who copyrighted a later volume, *More Borrowings,* published apparently just before Christmas, 1891. Inquiry developed that the mouse-trap quotation had been contributed by Mrs. Yule. She was not a native of Oakland, but had been born in Wisconsin and taken to California by her parents, Mr. and Mrs. Tyler E. Beach, when she was about ten years of age. She subsequently married Judge John Yule, of Oakland, and died there November 1, 1916, at the age of sixty. The West Publishing Company, in tracing to its source the inspiration which had moved their advertising writer to use the mouse-trap quotation, had in some way arrived at Mrs. Yule, and in *The Docket* for February, 1912 (p. 651), published the following statement from her:

To the best of my knowledge and belief, I copied it [the mouse-trap quotation] in my handbook from an address delivered long ago, it being my custom to write everything there that I thought particularly good, if expressed in concise form; and when we were compiling *Borrowings*, I drew from this old book freely.

The Mouse-Trap

There is no reason to doubt that Mrs. Yule was telling the exact truth, but unfortunately the question is still left a little misty. If she were a precise user of English, "copied" would seem to mean that she had taken the quotation from some printed report of the address; but it is also possible that she may have heard it from Emerson's own lips, for he visited San Francisco in 1871, when Mrs. Yule was a girl of sixteen, and not only delivered five lectures there, but also delivered one in Oakland itself. The San Francisco lectures were as follows:

Sunday, April 23, 1871, "Immortality of the Soul."
Wednesday, April 26, "Society in America."
Saturday, April 29, "Resources."
Monday, May 1, "Character."
Wednesday, May 17, "Chivalry."

On the next day, Thursday, May 18, he crossed the bay to Oakland, which, in a letter written a few days later to his wife, he called "the Brooklyn of San Francisco," and that evening, at Brayton Hall, lectured on "Hospitality and How to Make Homes Happy." He started back to Concord the following day.

As good Unitarians, it is exceedingly probable that Mr. and Mrs. Beach would not only go to hear Emerson themselves, but would also take their sixteen-year-old daughter, who was already proving her devotion to literature by

353

keeping a "handbook," and it is possible that she may have heard the word "mouse-trap" fall from Emerson's lips during that lecture in Oakland. But it is the guess of the present writer that she used the word "copied" correctly, and actually did copy the sentence into her handbook from a report either of the Oakland lecture or of one of the San Francisco ones.[1]

Unfortunately he is unable to offer any proof of this. At his request, the Library of Congress, the San Francisco Public Library, the Oakland Public Library, and the Bancroft Library have been good enough to make a search of such files of the San Francisco and Oakland papers as they possess covering the dates of the lectures, and have been unable to find the "mouse-trap." The files are incomplete, and such reports of the lectures as have been found are very short and perfunctory, San Francisco, apparently, having more important things to think about than the outgivings of the Concord Platonist. But whether she copied it, or whether she heard it, there can be no reasonable doubt that it was actually used by Emerson in one of these lectures—a happy thought, perhaps, which came to him at the moment of delivery, for there is no record of his ever having used it anywhere else.

[1] See the following article for partial confirmation.

MORE ABOUT THE MOUSE-TRAP

MORE ABOUT THE MOUSE-TRAP [1]

If a man has good corn, or wood, or boards, or pigs, to sell, or can make better chairs or knives, crucibles, or church organs than anybody else, you will find a broad, hard-beaten road to his house, though it be in the woods.—RALPH WALDO EMERSON, *Journals*, 1855. Vol. viii, p. 528.

If a man can write a better book, preach a better sermon, or make a better mouse-trap, than his neighbor, though he builds his house in the woods, the world will make a beaten path to his door.—EMERSON. As quoted by Mrs. Sarah S. B. Yule in *Borrowings*, 1889.

INTEREST in the "mouse-trap" quotation, which has been a subject of controversy for more than a quarter of a century, seems to increase rather than diminish, and since the publication of the preceding article in *The Colophon*, a mass of additional material concerning it has come into the hands of the writer. Let it be said at once that nothing in this new material invalidates, or even weakens, the conclusion already arrived at: that Ralph Waldo Emerson is the author of the quo-

[1] Reprinted by permission from *The Colophon*.

tation; that it derives from a very similar entry in his *Journals* for 1855; that it was probably spoken by him in its commonly-quoted form during one of his lectures in San Francisco in the spring of 1871; and that it was copied from a newspaper account of the lecture by Mrs. Sarah S. B. Yule, then a girl of sixteen, into her commonplace book, and used by her when she was assisting to compile a book called *Borrowings*, first published in December, 1889, which was also the first appearance in print of this famous apothegm. But a number of new details have come to light which are both interesting and amusing, and which are worth discussing.

The principal items of this new material are a bibliography of publications relating to the quotation, compiled by Mr. David C. Mearns, of the Library of Congress, and a file of the issues of *The Docket* containing articles referring to it. The bibliography will be dealt with first. It is dated January 22, 1935, is very complete—a remarkable piece of work, in fact—and has been drawn upon freely in the following pages.

"BORROWINGS" AND MRS. YULE

1889. *Borrowings.* Compiled by Ladies of the First Unitarian Church of Oakland, California. San Francisco, C. A. Murdock & Co., Printers, 1889. [The first edition, no copy of which was deposited with the Li-

brary of Congress for copyright registration.
The mouse-trap quotation appears for the
first time in literature near the bottom of
page 38, credited simply, "Emerson."]

1891. *Borrowings.* Compiled by Ladies of the
First Unitarian Church of Oakland, California. San Francisco, William Doxey, Publisher, 1891. [The second edition, with the
mouse-trap quotation on page 38 as before.
Copies received by the Library of Congress,
May 18, 1891.]

1891. *More Borrowings.* Compiled by Ladies of
the First Unitarian Church of Oakland,
California. San Francisco, C. A. Murdock
& Co., Printers, 1891. [Copies received at
the Library of Congress, December 16, 1891.
The page following the title-page contains
the following note: " 'Borrowings,' a small
volume issued Christmas '89, having met with
so large a measure of favor, the compilers
have been encouraged to offer a second volume, 'More Borrowings,' trusting that it will
prove equally acceptable." The mouse-trap
quotation does not appear in this book.]

1894. *Borrowings, a compilation of helpful
thoughts from great authors.* Fourth edition. San Francisco, C. A. Murdock &
Company, 1894. [Registered, as "authors
and proprietors," by Sarah S. B. Yule and
Mary S. Keene, December 8, 1893. Copies
deposited in the Library of Congress, January 9, 1894. The mouse-trap quotation appears as usual on p. 38. It will be noted that

359

this is said to be the fourth edition. A
third edition was probably printed in 1893,
but no copy of it has come to light.]

1901. *Thoughts.* Selected and Compiled by Ladies
of Fabiola Hospital Association, Oakland,
California. New York, Dodge Publishing
Company. [Verso of title-page bears claim:
Copyrighted, 1901, by Jessie K. Freeman and
Sarah S. B. Yule. Copies were received at
the Library of Congress, March 11, 1901.
The mouse-trap quotation appears on page
115, identical in form with its first appear-
ance in *Borrowings.*]

1902. *Strength for Every Day. A compilation of
beautiful thoughts for my friend.* New
York, Dodge Publishing Company, 40 West
13th Street. [Copies registered at the Library of Congress, September 3, 1902.
Verso of third preliminary leaf contains an
advertisement for "Four Beautiful Books of
Ideal Thoughts By the Compiler of 'Borrowings' Thirty Thousand Copies Sold."]

1903. *For Thy Good Cheer: A Collection of Helpful and Beautiful Thoughts.* Selected and
Compiled by the Ladies of the Fabiola Hospital Association, Oakland, California. New
York, The Dodge Publishing Company.
[Copies received at the Library of Congress,
March 18, 1903. The verso of the title-
page bears a copyright notice: "Copyrighted,
1903, by Jessie K. Freeman, Evelyn Stevens
Wilson and Sarah S. B. Yule." A second
edition was published in 1904.]

More About the Mouse-Trap

From all this it will be seen that Mrs. Yule, encouraged by her first success, had become a fairly industrious compiler: But she had never been a very careful one, and she does not seem to have grown more meticulous as time went on, for in both editions of *For Thy Good Cheer* (p. 78) the last stanza of William Ernest Henley's "Invictus" is quoted, and attributed to Elbert Hubbard—for a reason which will presently be made clear.

Mrs. Yule died at Oakland, November 1, 1916, at the age of sixty, and on the following day the San Francisco *Chronicle* printed an obituary (vol. v, p. 6), which gives a little additional information about her. She was, as stated in the preceding article, a native of Wisconsin, and when she was ten years old, that is, about 1856, was taken to California by her parents, Mr. and Mrs. Tyler E. Beach. They settled in the Santa Clara Valley, where Beach became one of early California's largest landowners. The *History of Alameda County, California* (Oakland, 1883), states (p. 999) that John Yule "married Miss Sarah S. Beach, a sister of C. W. Beach, of San Francisco, in 1882." Yule was a prominent young attorney, and took his wife to Oakland to live.

The discovery of this detail necessitates a slight revision of the theory outlined in the preceding article, for evidently the Beaches were not living at Oakland when Emerson lectured there in 1871, and so it is improbable that Sarah Beach actually heard him. But this fact makes even more probable the writer's guess that when she stated she had "copied" the quotation into her "handbook," she meant that she actually *had* copied it from some newspaper report of one of Emerson's lectures.

Some slight information concerning these lectures is given in a little book called *A Western Journey with Mr. Emerson*, written by James Bradley Thayer, and published by Little, Brown & Company, of Boston, in 1884. Says Mr. Thayer (p. 49): "The next evening, Sunday, the twenty-third [of April, 1871], Mr. Emerson read his address on 'Immortality' at Dr. Stebbins's Church." This was the distinguished Dr. Horatio Stebbins, who succeeded Dr. Starr King in the pastorate of the Unitarian Church of San Francisco, and with whom Emerson spent a large part of his time while he was in the city. On April 29, he delivered his lecture on "Resources," and "at the end of that [again quoting Mr. Thayer, p. 87] crowded some things he had said at Cambridge in a lecture on 'Inspiration.'" On May 17, he lectured on "Chivalry," and Mr. Thayer (p. 121) calls it "a disappointing address which he extemporized from certain fragments—having failed to find one of his best lectures that had been brought along, but lay hidden somewhere in his trunk."

It is impossible to resist suspecting that it was during this lecture, "extemporized from fragments," the "mouse-trap" had its birth!

"THE UNHIDDEN CHRIST" AND
JOHN R. PAXTON

In its issue for March, 1889, *The Treasury*, "an evangelical monthly," as its sub-title announced, published a sermon entitled "The Unhidden Christ" by the Rev. John R. Paxton, D.D., then pastor of the West Presbyterian Church, on West Forty-second Street, New York City. The sermon had been delivered at the John Street Methodist Episcopal Church in New York, during a series of evangelical meetings conducted by clergymen of different denominations, and it forms the basis of the claim made insistently by many of Dr. Paxton's admirers that he is the author of the mouse-trap quotation. These particular sentences are supposed to blaze the way:

When you have something the world wants, the world will find you out. . . . When you have something the world wants, you'll be found even if you are behind stone walls and prison bars. There is no privacy when you have what the world wants. . . . You may begin business in an obscure place, but if there is ability, power and a mastery of affairs in

you, then all the steamboats in the river will whistle
for you and the railroads say, Come over and man-
age us. . . . The world will not let any man be
long out of sight who has something the world wants
or needs.

The following August, Dr. Paxton was at
Chautauqua, where he delivered the same sermon, and the New York *Sun* for August 26,
1889 (p. 2, col. 1), under the caption, "Sunday
in Chautauqua," published a brief extract from
it, which contained the following:

A man can't be hid. He may be a peddler in
the mountains, but the world will find him out and
make him a king of finance. He may be carrying
cabbages from Long Island, when the world will
demand that he shall run the railways of a continent.
He may be a groceryman on the canal, when the
country shall come to find him and put him in his
career of usefulness.

Evidently Dr. Paxton had been giving his
sermon a thorough revision, for not one of the
extracts which the *Sun* published as having been
delivered at Chautauqua agrees with the text of
the sermon as given in *The Treasury*, but, as
noted in the preceding article, it does agree quite
closely with an entry in Emerson's *Journals* for
1855 (vol. viii, p. 528) headed "Common
Fame." It has already been quoted, but the
first sentence will indicate the resemblance:

More About the Mouse-Trap

If a man knows the law, people find it out, tho'
he live in a pine shanty, and resort to him.[1]

Nothing more was heard of this sermon for
nearly twenty-five years, though Dr. Paxton
probably went on preaching it, and then, suddenly, in 1913, Mr. Calvin Dill Wilson, of
Glendale, Ohio, discovered that it contained
the mouse-trap quotation, and announced his
discovery to the world. Correspondence developed the fact that Mr. Wilson did not actually have a copy of the sermon, but he had
read it in *The Treasury* in 1889, and he was
certain that it contained the mouse-trap allusion.
As has been shown, it did not contain it, but
that made no difference, for now came Rev.
William E. Barton, of Oak Park, Illinois, in a
statement to the Chicago *Tribune* to the effect
that the quotation was part of a sermon delivered

---

[1] Mr. Mearns has recently discovered in *The
Saturday Evening Post*, for March 20, 1852, an
abstract of Emerson's lecture on "Wealth," in which
occurs the following: "Every man must be bought
at his own price in his own place. Lawyers agree
that if a man understand the law he may open his
office in a pine barrel, and people will come to him
when they want law." This points straight at the
mouse-trap three years earlier than the famous entry
in the *Journals*. There is nothing like it, however,
in the essay as printed in Emerson's works. The
nearest approach to it is in the ninth paragraph, but
the resemblance is very faint.

by Dr. Paxton many years before, and *Unity*, a
church paper published in New York, announced
with great positiveness that "the author of the
sentence was Dr. John Paxton. . . . It occurred
in a sermon on the text, 'He could not be hid,'
which was preached first in his own pulpit, and
afterwards repeated at the New York Chautauqua. If any reader of *Unity* has suffered brain-
fag in hunting for the writer of this famous
sentence, he may now rest." This statement
was copied by papers all over the country, usually
under the caption, "That Emerson Quotation
Located at Last," and a great many people, of
course, supposed the matter settled.

Finally it occurred to the editor of a pamphlet
entitled *What Emerson Might Have Said,* published by the New York *American* in 1920, to
ask Dr. Paxton himself about it. So Dr. Paxton
was written to, and took the extraordinary
course of turning the letter over to a friend to
answer. This friend was Mr. J. M. Mealy, of
Sewickley, Pa., a suburb of Pittsburgh, where
Dr. Paxton had lived in 1894, and he wrote as
follows, under date of December 16, 1913:

My friend of fifty years, the Rev. John Paxton,
of New York City, sent me your letter of November
18th, with the request that I answer it for him.

There is no doubt about Dr. Paxton's authorship
of the lines of which the quotation in question was
taken. I heard the sermon in which it was written,

delivered over thirty years ago, at Chautauqua, N. Y.

It ran in this way: "If a man write a better book, preach a better sermon, or a woman sing a more beautiful song, than his or her neighbor, then, though the man preaches way off in an obscure parish, or the woman sings in the Aroostook wilderness of Maine, in a country schoolhouse, the world will have that sermon, that song, and make a road to find him or her.

Mr. Mealy added that it was Dr. Paxton's custom to vary from his manuscript in preaching, "leaving out and adding to," and the author of the pamphlet was so impressed by Mr. Mealy's assurances that he declared:

Assuming even that the Reverend Paxton got the inspiration of his lines from Emerson, the Paxton version is certainly closest to that which is current to-day.

Further reference will be made to this pamphlet later on, but it need only be pointed out here that even in Mr. Mealy's inspired version (which is pretty poor stuff!) the word "mouse-trap" does not occur, and that Emerson's entry in his *Journals*, given at the beginning of this article, is far nearer Mrs. Yule's version than is this outgiving by Dr. Paxton.

But the curious thing is that, instead of answering the letter himself directly and un-equivocally, he should have turned it over to Mr. Mealy. It was certainly as much trouble

367

to write to Mr. Mealy as it would have been
to write to the author of the letter, and the only
inference the present writer can draw is that,
while Dr. Paxton was unwilling to claim the
quotation himself, he *was* willing that it should
be claimed for him.

So the Paxton legend went on its way, and
in 1927, four years after his death, *Printer's Ink,*
in its issue for June 9 (Vol. 139, No. 10),
printed two letters upholding it. One was
signed W. G. Bryan, and was in part as follows:

Emerson was not the author of the quotation.
Neither was Elbert Hubbard. Credit for it should
really go to the Rev. John Paxton, a Presbyterian
minister. He died in New York a year or so ago.
At that time the newspapers estimated his estate to
be worth about a million dollars, so evidently the
world did make a beaten path to his door.

Hubbard never gave Emerson credit for the idea.
That was done by Harry Bishop, formerly the head
of the copy department of the Bryan Organization
and now high in the productive counsels of the
McManus advertising agency in Detroit.

I have spent about fifteen years trying to correct
the mistake I made in first putting Emerson's name
after the mouse-trap quotation. To my knowledge
Harry Bishop has been writing on this subject for
the last ten years and I trust that in the future
Printer's Ink will throw its weight toward the right
conclusion so that the Emerson quotation will not
continue as a matter of controversy.

More About the Mouse-Trap

The first sentence of the last paragraph is a little cryptic, unless Mr. Bryan means that he was the employee of the West Publishing Company who some years before 1911 used the quotation in an advertisement and put Emerson's name to it, as related further on. It is interesting to note that in his bibliography Mr. Mearns states that he was permitted to examine the pamphlet, *What Emerson Might Have Said,* "through the courtesy of Mr. Walter G. Bryan, of New York City," and since its conclusion with regard to Dr. Paxton's claim agrees with that of Mr. Bryan, it seems safe to infer that Mr. Bryan was the author of the pamphlet.

But Mr. Bryan's letter did not change the opinion of the editor of *Printer's Ink,* who had already expressed his belief that credit for the quotation should go to Emerson. After printing the letter, he adds:

> In spite of letters to the contrary, we still insist that credit for the authorship of this idea should go to Ralph Waldo Emerson. None of the claims which we have ever seen antedates what Emerson wrote and what is to be found in the eighth volume of "Emerson's Journal" on page 528. . . . Until we can be shown that someone else recorded this idea before the Sage of Concord got on the job we shall continue to insist on giving him the credit.

Let us consider Dr. Paxton for a moment. John Randolph Paxton was born at Canonsburg,

Pa., September 18, 1843. He was a student at Jefferson College (now Washington and Jefferson) when the Civil War broke out, and left college to enlist as a private in the 140th Pennsylvania Regiment, rising to the rank of second lieutenant. When the war was over, he re-entered college and graduated in 1866. Three years later he was graduated from the Western Theological Seminary, at Allegheny, Pa., and in 1871 was ordained to the Presbyterian ministry. He held pastorates at Churchville, Md., Harrisburg, Pa., Washington, D. C., and New York City, retiring from the ministry in 1893, and devoting himself to evangelistic work until his death, April 11, 1923, in New York.

Now, while it has never been shown that Dr. Paxton ever used the word "mouse-trap" in any public utterance, Mr. Mearns has dug up an interesting detail. In the "Conclusions" with which he ends his bibliography, he speculates as to the identity of the persons Dr. Paxton had in mind when he was writing his sermon: the preacher in an obscure parish, the woman singing in the Aroostook wilderness, and the peddler who becomes a king of finance. He believes the preacher to have been Henry Ward Beecher, who began his ministry in a frontier pulpit at Lawrenceburg, Ind., and that the singer "could almost certainly be identified with Emma Eames, whose girlhood had been spent at Bath, Maine,

370

and whose début in opera had been made in Paris, March 13, 1889. Had any railroad executive begun his career with an ingenious mouse-trap?" Mr. Mearns inquires. And adds, "What about Jay Gould?" He then quotes the following from J. S. Ogilvie's *Life and Death of Jay Gould* (pp. 25-26), published in 1892, ten days after Gould's death:

> It was in 1853, when the World's Exhibition was held in this city [New York], that young Gould, then about seventeen years old, is said to have made his first visit to the metropolis, in which he was to become such a power. He carried with him a showy mahogany case, containing an invention which the boy hoped would bring him fame and fortune. The invention was a mouse-trap.[1]

Ogilvie goes on to explain something of Gould's connection with Dr. Paxton. In February, 1892, Gould had invited the members of the Church Extension Society of the Presbyterian Church to his house and given $10,000 to its fund. The gift was announced on his behalf by Dr. Paxton. He was a pewholder, but not a communicant, in Dr. Paxton's church, and a fairly regular attendant. It was Dr. Paxton who presided at his funeral. Says Mr. Ogilvie:

[1] This story is repeated with some imaginative embellishments by Robert Irving Warshow, in his *Jay Gould, The Story of a Fortune*, published in 1928.

The choir of Dr. Paxton's West Presbyterian Church had seats at the foot of the staircase. . . . Just as the clock on the mantel chimed the hour of 4, Dr. Paxton arose from his seat in the hallway and, stepping to the doorway that opened into the rear parlor, followed with an invocation.

Mr. Ogilvie, perhaps, got these graphic details from the New York *Tribune* of December 2, 1892 (p. 2, cols. 1-2), where the funeral is described at great length.

Considering all these facts, Mr. Mearns suggests that, while credit for the basic idea must be accorded Emerson, "it seems not unlikely that Dr. Paxton, who so closely paraphrased the quotation in 1889, introduced the reference to 'the better mouse-trap.' But," he adds, "if he did, it would be interesting to know how Mrs. Yule got track of it. Dr. Paxton's sermon at Chatauqua was delivered seven months [really less than four months] before the publication of *Borrowings*, but it would not explain how the quotation found its way into a commonplace book on the other side of the continent."

But neither in the sermon as published in *The Treasury* nor as reported in the *Sun* is there any reference to a mouse-trap, and so it was impossible for Mrs. Yule to get hold of the word from either of those sources. If any other source exists, it has not yet been discovered. In any event, it is impossible to explain why she should attribute to Emerson a quotation which she had taken from a sermon delivered by Dr. Paxton. The fact that Jay Gould invented a mouse-trap and that Dr. Paxton was his pastor is a most amusing coincidence, but it scarcely justifies the inference that therefore Dr. Paxton was the author of the mouse-trap quotation—more especially since the invention brought Gould neither fame nor fortune, nor a hard-beaten path to his door!

Now for *The Docket* file.

The Docket, it will be remembered, is the house-organ of the West Publishing Company, for many years an important publisher of law books. The first reference to the mouse-trap quotation occurs in the issue for February, 1911 (p. 405-6). The article, which is unsigned, carries the heading "A Trap—-for Mice and Men," and begins as follows:

> Some years ago an attaché of the advertising department of the West Publishing Company, who in his youth had read Emerson and one or two other authors, undertook to add a literary flavor to a commercial announcement which he was constructing by inserting a quotation which his memory gave to him in the following form: [As printed in *Borrowings*.]
> He thought it sounded Emersonian and so gave Emerson credit for it. . . . His mind was disturbed by no qualms until he received a letter from Mr.

J. S. Dewell, of Missouri Valley, Iowa, asking him to verify his citation.

Mr. Dewell had ventured to wager five dollars that *The Docket's* attribution was correct, so the young man (whose identity with Walter G. Bryan, of New York City, has already been suggested) went to work to verify his reference. The article tells of his fruitless search and of his unanswered query in the "Appeals to Readers" column of the New York *Saturday Review*. An article by George W. Sackett was discovered in *Munsey's Magazine* with the quotation at its head, but Mr. Sackett did not reply to a query as to its source.

The matter rested there until last month [the article continues], when the office interest was revived by a report in the newspapers to the effect that, when Senator La Follette was coming out from the influence of ether in a recent operation, he quoted a famous statement from Emerson:
"If a man build a better mouse-trap or preach a better sermon than his neighbor, though his house be built in the woods, the world will find him out and wear a beaten path to his door." . . .
Who can help us, and help Mr. Dewell win his five?

In the April, 1911, issue (p. 454), there is another article. Several people, it says, had attributed the quotation to Thoreau's *Walden*,

but an examination of *Walden* failed to find it.
It had been credited to Emerson by Dr. O. S.
Marden, in his book, *Pushing to the Front*, published in 1894, and in a contribution to *Everybody's Magazine* in 1905. Then somebody suggested,

Unless you fear that he might claim it as his very
own, you might submit the Emersonian quotation
to Elbert Hubbard. I seem to recall that he used
it in one of his disquisitions.

So to Mr. Hubbard it was referred, and in
due time the famous answer came from John T.
Hoyle, assistant superintendent, writing in Mr.
Hubbard's absence:

We believe you are the forty-eleventh good soul
to ask us about that Emersonian teaser.

Now, if Emerson did not pen those momentous
words, we believe he certainly intended to; and
after he had passed on, he had a realizing sense of
his remissness, and endeavored to make good by
sending a psychic vibe [1] to some present-day scribe.

We, too, have spent several sleepless nights por-
ing over our Emerson, our Thoreau, and even Robert Louis the Beloved; but all to no avail—nary a
sign of a mouse-trap.

Suddenly, it occurred to us to ask Mr. Hubbard

[1] This is not a misprint; it is apparently Roy-
croftese for vibration.

375

himself, since we had seen it used by him several years ago.

The good Fra is supersaturated with Emerson, and knows him as well as did Jonathan Edwards his Bible; in fact, he oozes Emersonianisms at every pore. But when we tackled him regarding that mouse-trap, and urged him to designate chapter and verse, he smiled a far-away quizzical smile—and said nothing. Noting, however, the strained, expectant look on our cherubic countenance, he gave vent to the following, which seemed so good that we have set it down as a classic:

"I have given as much to Emerson, Schopenhauer, Nietzsche, and Whitman as I ever took from them. That they are dead and cannot receive my gifts in exchange for theirs, is not my fault."

So there you are!

Elbert Hubbard evolved that Emersonian Dictum from the depths of his own cosmic consciousness, and put the credit where he believed it belonged. That his actions should have caused us fellers, metaphorically, to sweat drops of blood, evidently appeared to him as nothing so very serious, you know. Perhaps, after all, we should be grateful to him, rather than otherwise; for, speaking for one, I know my Emerson better than I ever did before.

Hoping that the ghost is now down, we remain, with kind regards and all good wishes ever,

Cordially yours,
THE ROYCROFTERS.
Per JOHN T. HOYLE,
Assistant Superintendent.

376

More About the Mouse-Trap

Upon which the editor of *The Docket* comments as follows:

This will be enough to convince some people that Mr. Hubbard is the only and original author of the quotation in question. Others will be reminded of that old, old story, told of Ben Butler when he was Governor of Massachusetts.

Noticing two lawyers in private disputation on the Capitol steps, he inquired the point at issue.

"We'll leave the question to you," they both exclaimed. "We were disputing as to who is the greatest lawyer in Massachusetts."

"I am," said Ben Butler.

The lawyers looked nonplussed for a moment, and then one ventured to ask, "But how can you prove it, Governor?"

The Governor fell back upon his knowledge of the law.

"I don't have to prove it," he said with dignity. "I admit it."

In the February, 1912, issue (p. 651), *The Docket* prints the most important contribution of all, for it contains the letter from Mrs. Yule in which she stated that she had "copied the quotation in my handbook from an address delivered long ago" (already quoted in full in the preceding article in this book). The final reference to the matter in *The Docket* is in the issue for June, 1913 (p. 991), where the history of the controversy is recounted, and the claim made by

Mr. Wilson in behalf of Dr. Paxton is commented upon with skepticism. The outstanding feature of all these articles is, of course, the letter from Mrs. Yule, which is a really important piece of first-hand evidence.

The controversy has raged through many other papers, and every "Queries and Answers" editor in the country has taken a whack at it. One of the most curious contributions was the pamphlet already mentioned, *What Emerson Might Have Said,* published in 1920 by the New York *American.* It begins with a story of how two young newspapermen of Kansas City had, years before, attributed the quotation to Emerson when using it in connection with some advertising matter (evidently the West Publishing Company episode), and then continues with a very detailed account of the ensuing controversy, and finally prints the letter from Dr. Paxton's friend, Mr. J. M. Mealy, which has already been quoted. How much more interesting it would have been had the editor succeeded in getting an answer from Dr. Paxton himself!

And now for Mr. Hubbard.

ELBERT HUBBARD AND "THE PHILISTINE"

As *The Docket* once remarked, the story of Elbert Hubbard's connection with the mousetrap quotation would make a book by itself, but so much has already been said about him, both in this article and the preceding one, that little need be added.

It will be remembered that the quotation was originally published in *Borrowings* in 1889. According to the biographical sketch of Mr. Hubbard in the *Dictionary of American Biography*, his first published writing appeared in the *Arena* in 1893, and *The Philistine* was not started until two years later. When this discrepancy was pointed out to the Sage of East Aurora by the author of *What Emerson Might Have Said*, he promptly replied:

The fact that *The Philistine* was started in 1895 has nothing to do with the mouse-trap quotation. I was born in 1856 and began writing hot stuff when four years old.

Which shows, of course, that Mr. Hubbard was not easily disconcerted; but one can only wonder what happened to all the stuff he wrote between 1860 and 1893. Perhaps he kept it in a barrel and drew upon it during his later years.

The Docket, in its issue of January, 1912, traced the steps of the development of Mr. Hubbard's claim to the quotation. (1) When there was a possibility that it might be found in Emerson, he left the answering of inquiries to his assistant superintendent. (2) When the inquiry

379

had been pending for some months and the possibilities in Emerson's favor grew more dubious, the Roycrofters, "per. E. R. S.," wrote more definitely, "It was written by Mr. Hubbard, but inspired by Ralph Waldo Emerson." (3) Finally all hedging is cast aside and in an advertisement in *The Fra*, for May, 1911, the assertion is made that Mr. Hubbard wrote the quotation but attributed it to Emerson "to save his modesty" [!], and adds:

Mr. Hubbard may have found a few mental mavericks in Emerson, which in moments of aberration he has branded as his own; but if so, the debt is more than offset by things which he has attributed to Emerson that Emerson never wrote.

Mr. Hubbard had a habit of running in *The Philistine* unsigned epigrams and verses from the work of other writers, and his uninformed readers naturally supposed that he had evolved them from the depths of his own cosmic consciousness. This sometimes led to embarrassing consequences. For example on the back cover of the issue for December, 1901, he printed, unsigned, the following lines:

It matters not how strait the gate,
　　How charged with punishments the scroll,
I am the master of my fate:
　　I am the captain of my soul.

380

More About the Mouse-Trap

He thought them so admirable that he repeated them, still unsigned, on the cover of the February, 1902, issue. The unwary Mrs. Yule saw them, and appropriated them for the compilation she was then working on, *For Thy Good Cheer*, where, on page 78, they duly appeared, credited to Elbert Hubbard!

As to Mr. Hubbard's predatory habits in the realm of letters there is abundant evidence. He himself, in fact, did not deny them. The Christmas number of Brentano's *Book Chat* (vol. iii, No. 1), published a letter from Edwin O. Grover, of Chicago, reviewing the history of the mouse-trap quotation, and continuing as follows:

It has been proven repeatedly that Mr. Hubbard was an adaptor and user of other people's ideas and material, and did not hesitate to appropriate matter verbatim and sign his name to it. I have in my own possession a letter from Mr. Hubbard in which he acknowledges the appropriation and use of certain matter and invites the writer "to come up to East Aurora and spend a week-end at his own expense and have a good laugh over it"; signed "Lovingly, Elbert."

And there the matter rests.

NOTES ON SOME FAMILIAR QUOTATIONS

.

NOTES ON SOME FAMILIAR
QUOTATIONS

I

ON the evening of December 28, 1871, a dinner for the alumni of Williams College was given at the famous Delmonico restaurant in New York City, and the newspapers of the following day noted that there was a large attendance. The Honorable Erastus C. Benedict, who had formerly been a member of the teaching staff, was toastmaster, and among those present were William Cullen Bryant, Washington Gladden and James Abram Garfield. Mr. Benedict started the speechmaking in the usual way with some mellifluous phrases about dear Alma Mater and how proud they all should be of her, and then called upon the "Rev. Dr. Adams," as the papers put it, who spoke admiringly of the splendid work done by the colleges in America founded and administered by the clergy, and contrasted this happy state of affairs with the deplorable situation in Europe, where a deep schism existed between men of the church and men of science. Mr. Bryant, the lion of the evening, chose to comment humorously on the

Darwinian theory, and brought down the house (so the papers said) by hoping that no analogy would ever be found between professors and baboons.

Then came Mr. John Bascom, professor of rhetoric and oratory on the college faculty, who, instead of giving his hearers an example of his art—to which, as a matter of fact, he was only moderately devoted—considerably mitigated the joy of the occasion by painting a gloomy picture of the condition of the college, whose students, he said, were steadily diminishing in number because of a lack of executive enterprise in college affairs. Many of the alumni, he added, felt that better buildings and equipment must soon be provided to stop this disintegration, and most of those present, apparently, agreed with him. But one of them, Mr. Garfield, did not. In the *Times* and the *Post* he is referred to as having spoken, but no part of his address is given; in the *Tribune* he is not even mentioned—and yet it is only because of his address that the dinner is remembered at all.

Garfield was then a Congressman from Ohio, and was to become the last of that long line of log-cabin presidents which began with Andrew Jackson. His boyhood had been one of biting poverty, but he had managed to work his way to Hiram College and then to Williams, where he graduated with the class of 1856, at the age of twenty-five. Mark Hopkins had been president of the college since 1836—a post he was to hold for thirty-six years—was also Professor of Moral Science, and was the dominant spirit in college affairs. Professor Bascom's statement was, therefore, a direct criticism of Hopkins's administration, and was no doubt deserved, for Hopkins was a very different type from the modern college president—a great teacher, but uninterested in, and, indeed, a little contemptuous of, such physical properties as new buildings, new equipment, or even new books. He stated this clearly enough more than once—for example, in his *Lectures on Moral Philosophy* (p. 39), where he said that, for this subject, at least, "no learning is needed, no science, no apparatus, no information from distant countries." Perhaps Garfield had heard Hopkins speak these very words in one of his lectures—at any rate, he sprang to the defense of his revered teacher.

He took exception to the idea that buildings and apparatus were of the first importance. The essential thing was a distinguished and well-paid faculty, for great teachers and not great buildings make a great college; and then he coined the epigram which made the dinner famous. Or perhaps he did not coin it; perhaps it was coined by somebody else long afterwards; but it is based upon his words. What the exact words

were nobody knows, for no stenographic record
was made of them, and they survived only in
rough notes, or in the memories of his hearers,
which naturally differed widely.

The most nearly contemporary version thus
far discovered appeared in the Williams *Vidette*
for January 27, 1872 (p. 93), and is as follows:

> Offer him the finest college buildings, the largest
> library and the most complete physical appliances,
> and he would rather have Dr. Hopkins in a brick
> shanty than them all.

Ten days later, the Williams *Review* for
February 5, 1872 (p. 85), put it this way:

> Give me Mark, with a piece of birch bark to write
> upon, and I'll defy all the colleges in the country.

And in Burke A. Hinsdale's *President Garfield and Education*, published at Boston in 1882,
the following was put in quotation marks, without giving its source:

> Give me a log hut with only a single bench, Mark
> Hopkins on one end and I on the other, and you
> may have all the buildings, apparatus and libraries
> without him.

Finally, nearly forty years after the event,
when Washington Gladden wrote his *Reminiscences* (Boston, 1909), he referred to the dinner at page 73, and quoted Garfield thus:

Notes on Familiar Quotations

A pine bench, with Mark Hopkins at one end of it and me at the other, is a good enough college for me!

Mr. T. C. Smith, in his *Life and Times of James Abram Garfield,* sums up these varying versions with the remark that contemporary evidence seems to indicate that Garfield "used a less pungent figure" than that of the log, and that, very probably, his remark was much less epigrammatic than the form in which it is usually quoted, "A university is a student on one end of a log and Mark Hopkins on the other."

Abraham Flexner in his *Universities* (p. 151), cites as "a dictum of Mark Hopkins" the statement that "the ideal college consists of a log of wood with an instructor at one end and a student at the other," but he gives no source for the quotation and it is extremely improbable that Hopkins ever expressed the idea in those words. A search through his writings has failed to disclose it, and it undoubtedly derives from Garfield.

It is worth noting that Garfield's assassination occurred in the railway station at Washington as he was starting for Williams to attend the twenty-fifth reunion of his class. "The last time I saw him alive," said Senator John J. Ingalls (*Writings and Orations,* p. 405), "—it was in the early summer of 1881—he alluded to the pleasure with which he anticipated his visit to Williamstown and repeated in substance the declaration of 1872." The date is, of course, an error—repeated by Balch in his *Life of President Garfield,* where the date of the dinner is given as January 18, 1872—but the reference shows that Garfield took pride in the utterance up to the very end of his life, and wished it to be remembered. It had endeared him to Williams, just as Daniel Webster had been endeared to Dartmouth when he said, in an argument before the Supreme Court, "It is a small college, and yet there are those that love it."

II

Everyone is familiar with the naïve astonishment of Monsieur Jourdain[1] when he discovered that he had been speaking prose all his life without knowing it, but it was no greater than the chagrin of a staid professor of moral philosophy and casuistical divinity when he learned that, all unwittingly, he had inserted a sort of nursery jingle into one of his most learned books. The professor in question was William Whewell, scientist and philosopher, whose whole life had been bound up with Trinity College,

[1] Par ma foi! il y a plus de quarante ans que je dis de la prose sans que j'en susse rien, et je vous suis le plus obligé du monde de m'avoir appris cela. —MOLIÈRE, *Le Bourgeois Gentilhomme.* Act ii, sc. 4, l. 179.

Cambridge; the occasion was a dinner of the fellows of the college; and the man who sprang the surprise was Adam Sedgwick, the famous geologist, whose learning had not diminished his fondness for practical jokes.

Whewell started at the bottom, but he climbed to the top. He was born at Lancaster, England, in 1794, the son of a carpenter who intended to apprentice him to the same trade, but fate intervened in the person of Joseph Rowley, master of the local grammar-school, who, happening one day to talk to the boy, was so impressed by him that he offered to teach him free of charge. His father hesitated for a time, but finally consented, and young William entered the grammar-school, where he forged ahead so rapidly that the other boys decided to take forcible measures to persuade him to a reasonable amount of idleness. So, two at a time, they attempted to "wallop" him, only to meet humiliating defeat, for it was William who did the walloping. He was a young giant, and years later, a prizefighter, contemplating his Herculean physique, is said to have remarked, "What a man was lost when they made you a parson!"

Whewell had been ordained in 1825, and after that his career was continuously onward and upward, until in 1841 he was appointed Master of Trinity College, a position he was to hold for twenty-five years, during which he

enlarged the college buildings, founded professor-
ships, fought some valiant battles for academic
freedom, and even secured the election of Albert
the Good, Consort to Queen Victoria, as chancellor of the University. A scholarly, earnest
and serious-minded man, who, apparently, had
never done anything to blush for—but there was
a skeleton in the cupboard, rattling to be re-
leased.

The cupboard in question was his first important book, *An Elementary Treatise on Me-
chanics*, which had been published in 1819, and
the skeleton was rattling away in the chapter
called "The Equilibrium of Forces on a Point."
Professor Whewell was serenely unaware of its
existence, but some unknown Cambridge wag
discovered it, and communicated the news to
Henry Malden, then a student at Cambridge
and afterwards a famous classical scholar, who
in turn carried it to Thomas Babington Macaulay, who passed it on to Adam Sedgwick, professor of geology at the University—and Sedgwick bided his time to drag it forth to public
view. Since Whewell's temper had grown
more fiery with the years and his strength had
remained unabated, certain precautions were
no doubt considered advisable; but the opportunity came one evening when the fellows of the
college were dining in hall, with Whewell at
the head of the table.

Notes on Familiar Quotations

The meal had progressed as usual until they reached the wine and walnuts. Then Sedgwick began pulling at the tablecloth to attract attention, and inquired if anyone present happened to know the author of the following lines:

> And hence no force, however great,
> Can stretch a cord, however fine,
> Into a horizontal line
> That shall be absolutely straight.

The stanza-form, it will be noted, is that afterwards made famous by Tennyson in "In Memoriam," but no one present at the dinner had ever heard the lines before. Whereupon Sedgwick announced that their author was none other than their revered colleague, William Whewell.

Whewell indignantly denied the accusation, but Sedgwick triumphantly produced a copy of the first volume of the *Treatise,* opened it to page 44, and pointed to the following sentence:

> Hence no force however great can stretch a cord however fine into a horizontal line which is accurately straight.

The last phrase had been touched up a little to make it flow more smoothly, but there the rhyme unquestionably was, and Whewell was so vexed that he deleted the sentence from all subsequent editions of his book.

The details of this story have recently been

brought to light by the discovery in London of the copy of the first edition of Whewell's book which had belonged to the Cambridge wag who discovered the accidental jingle, and passed the news of it on to Mr. Malden. On the flyleaf of the book he wrote a short account of the incident. He speaks of Mr. Malden as "my pupil," so he was no doubt one of the fellows of the college, but his name has not been divulged.

It is worth noting that Whewell had occasionally written poetry with full knowledge of what he was doing, for in 1814 he won the Chancellor's English medal with a poem on Boadicea, and in 1847 he published two volumes of verse, one of translations from the German, and the other of original poetry. It was entitled *Sunday Thoughts and Other Verses,* but none of them is remembered to-day. The only thing that survives is the jingle which crept into a very prosy book—a fate not unlike that of Clement Clarke Moore, that once-eminent professor of Oriental literature, whose name has been kept alive by a nursery rhyme.

III

"One lyric is enough," says the Old Master, in *The Poet at the Breakfast-Table* (p. 129). "It will carry your name down to posterity like the ring of Thothmes, like the coin of Alexander." And he is right, for fame has often been won by a single snatch of song which somehow defied oblivion. But for a single phrase to win it has not happened very often, and yet that is what befell an officer of the American Revolution, who never wrote another really memorable word, but who, under the stress of deep emotion for the loss of a life-long friend, struck out a sentence which has engraved itself on the memory of every American as the consummate characterization of the First American,

First in war, first in peace, and first in the hearts of his countrymen.

Something of the same sort happened, twenty years later, to Fitz-Greene Halleck when, under somewhat similar circumstances, he wrote of Joseph Rodman Drake,

None knew thee but to love thee,
Nor named thee but to praise,

in a little lyric which is Halleck's principal claim to remembrance; but, famous as it is, it never attained the nation-wide celebrity of the phrase coined by "Light-Horse Harry" Lee, in the seclusion of his room at Philadelphia, on the afternoon of Wednesday, the eighteenth of December, 1799.

Henry Lee had been one of Washington's most trusted lieutenants throughout the Revolution. There is a legend that his mother, Lucy Grimes, was one of Washington's boyhood loves, but Lee won his regard through merit, not through sentiment. In 1773, at the age of seventeen, Lee had graduated from the College of New Jersey, now Princeton University, and was preparing to go to England to study law, when the on-coming of the Revolution changed his plans. In 1776 he was appointed a captain in Theodoric Bland's regiment of Virginia cavalry, and a year later his company joined the Continental army. From the first, he was admitted to Washington's friendship and confidence, and performed notable service during the whole period of the war, developing into one of the most dashing cavalry leaders the American army ever had, second, perhaps, only to Stonewall Jackson. In 1785 he was sent to Congress.

Such a life, one would think, must have a brilliant close, but it ended in disaster, for after his retirement to civil life, Lee, like so many others, became involved in land speculations, and sank deeper and deeper into debt, for which, in 1808, he was imprisoned. In July, 1812, he was attacked by a mob while attempting to aid his friend, Alexander C. Hanson, in defending the press of the *Federal Republican,* at Baltimore, was taken to jail, and the next night was assaulted by a gang of hoodlums who had been admitted to the jail, sustaining injuries from which he never recovered, although he lingered on for nearly six years.

Washington died at Mount Vernon on December 14, 1799. Four days later, at the very time when his body was being consigned to the modest tomb which he had himself built to receive it, and which was to become one of the world's great shrines, the rumor of his death reached Philadelphia, where the Congress was in session, and John Marshall, a member of the House of Representatives, rose and asked permission to speak.

"Mr. Speaker," he began in "a voice that bespoke the anguish of his mind," [1] "information has just been received that our illustrious fellow citizen, the Commander-in-Chief of the American Army, and the late President of the United States, is no more!" and he thereupon moved that the House adjourn.

By the next day, Thursday, December 19, 1799, the news had been confirmed, and Marshall, rising again in the House, after a short eulogy of Washington, introduced and moved the adoption of the following resolutions:

[1] *Annals of Congress*, 6th Cong., 1st Sess., Col. 203.

1.—That this House will wait on the President of the United States, in condolence of this national calamity.

2.—That the Speaker's chair be shrouded with black, and that the members and officers of the House wear mourning during the session.

3.—That a joint committee of both Houses be appointed to report measures suitable to the occasion, and expressive of the profound sorrow with which Congress is penetrated on the loss of a citizen, first in war, first in peace, and first in the hearts of his countrymen.

There can be no doubt as to the wording of this resolution. It is so recorded in *The Debates and Proceedings in the Congress of the United States,* Sixth Congress, column 204, and also in the *Journal of the House of Representatives of the United States at the First Session of the Sixth Congress,* p. 45. The former publication usually referred to as the *Annals of Congress,* was not published until 1851, and while its title-page announces that it was "compiled from authentic materials," it might be subject to error; but the latter was printed in Philadelphia probably early in 1800—in any event, very soon after the adjournment of the session—and so was practically a contemporary publication.

It is not surprising that Marshall should have been universally supposed to be the author of the resolutions, which he had offered and moved without any indication that they were by another hand, and so when, a week later, on December 26, 1799, General Lee, at the request of the Congress, delivered a funeral oration [1] on the death of Washington, and used the already-famous phrase, he should have been suspected either of quoting Marshall or of stealing his thunder.

Marshall, however, refused to permit history to give him credit for something which belonged to another, and stated over and over again that Lee was the author of the resolutions, but since error always outstrips truth, he is sometimes quoted, even yet, as the originator of the phrase. Finally, in a letter to Charles W. Hannan, of Baltimore, Md., written March 29, 1832, he told the story in detail:

As the stage passed through Philadelphia, some passenger mentioned to a friend he saw in the street the death of General Washington. The report flew to the hall of Congress, and I was asked to move an adjournment. I did so.

General Lee was not at the time in the House. On receiving the intelligence, which he did on the first arrival of the stage, he retired to his room and prepared the resolutions which were adopted, with the intention of offering them himself. But the

---

[1] *A Funeral Oration, on the Death of General Washington.* Delivered in Philadelphia, at the Request of Congress. Philadelphia, 1800.

House of Representatives had voted on my motion, and it was expected by all that I on the next day would announce the lamentable event and propose resolutions adapted to the occasion.

General Lee immediately called on me and showed me his resolutions. He said that it had now become improper for him to offer them, and wished me to take them. As I had not written anything myself and was pleased with his resolutions, which I entirely approved, I told him I would offer them the next day when I should state to the House of Representatives the confirmation of the melancholy intelligence received the preceding day. I did so.

You will see the fact stated in a note to the preface of the *Life of Washington*, and again in a note to the 5th volume, p. 765.

And he added in a postscript:

Whenever the subject has been mentioned in my presence, I have invariably stated that the resolution was drawn by General Lee, and have referred to these notes in the *Life of Washington*.

But a curious mistake crept into Marshall's account of the proceedings, as related in his *Life of Washington*, which was published at Philadelphia in 1807. In volume five on page 765-6, there is the following:

The resolutions * after a preamble stating the death of General Washington, were in the following terms:

400

Notes on Familiar Quotations

[Then follow the first two resolutions, differing in a number of places from the version in the *Annals*: "mournful event" for "national calamity"; "black" for "mourning"; and finally the third resolution is given as follows:]

Resolved, that a committee, in conjunction with one from the Senate, be appointed to consider on the most suitable manner of paying honour to the memory of the MAN, first in war, first in peace, and first in the hearts of his fellow citizens.

At the foot of the page is a note indicated by the asterisk given above:

* These resolutions were prepared by General Lee, who happening not to be in his place when the melancholy intelligence was received and first mentioned in the House, placed them in the hands of the member who moved them.

It can only be supposed that Marshall, not having at hand the record of the proceedings in the House, relied for his version of the resolutions upon his memory, or perhaps upon some rough notes made at the time, and so led many writers into thinking that the resolutions, as adopted by the House, read "fellow citizens," and that "countrymen" was coined and first used by Lee in his oration a week later. They were so quoted by John Bartlett in his *Familiar Quotations* (p. 445, footnote), the note indicating that they were taken from Marshall—an error repeated by Mr. Carroll A. Wilson in his recently published *First Appearance in Print of Some Four Hundred Familiar Quotations* (p. 60). But the evidence is indisputable that Marshall erred and that "countrymen" is correct.

Henry Lee has, of course, another claim to remembrance in that he was the father of Robert E. Lee, who, in 1869, published a memoir of his life, in which he says (p. 52),

But there is a line, a single line, in the Works of Lee which would hand him over to immortality, though he had never written another: "First in war, first in peace, and first in the hearts of his countrymen" will last while language lasts.

And this is probably not an exaggeration!